# Praise for *Faithfull*

"Thank God we have this book."—*The Village Voice*

"A pungent, poignant, and highly irreverent autobiography. . . . Faithfull is an enthralling storyteller."—*The Chicago Tribune*

"From her tumultuous four-year relationship with Mick Jagger through her descent into junkydom to her 'comeback' in the late '70s as a punk-rock diva, Faithfull embodies rock culture at both its most glamorous and most destructive."—*Publishers Weekly*

"All the pop gods are here—Dylan, the Beatles, Hendrix, the Stones—captured like satyrs on Keats' Grecian urn."—*The Cleveland Free Times*

"With wit, candor, and a certain detachment, Faithfull evokes Swinging London at its most decadent."—*The Seattle Times*

"A searing autobiography by one of rock 'n' roll's most tragic and romantic figures."—*Kirkus Reviews*

"A harrowing and sometimes hilarious chronicle of a life that howls sex, drugs, and rock 'n' roll."—*The Portland Oregonian*

"Unlike some other celebrity drug confessionals, Faithfull's is mercifully free of self-pity and moral judgments."—*The Boston Herald*

# Faithfull

## AN AUTOBIOGRAPHY

MARIANNE FAITHFULL

with David Dalton

Cooper Square Press

First Cooper Square Press edition 2000

This Cooper Square Press paperback edition of *Faithfull* is an unabridged republication of the edition first published in Boston in 1994. It is reprinted by arrangement with the authors.

"Live with Me" by Mick Jagger and Keith Richards used by permission of ABKCO Publishing.

Designed by Barbara Werden

Published by Cooper Square Press,
An Imprint of Rowman & Littlefield Publishers, Inc.
150 Fifth Avenue, Suite 911
New York, New York 10011

Distributed by National Book Network

Library of Congress Cataloging-in-Publication Data

Faithfull, Marianne.
    Faithfull : an autobiography / Marianne Faithfull with David Dalton.
        p. cm.
    Originally published: Boston : Little, Brown, c1994.
    Includes index.
    ISBN 0-8154-1046-8 (pbk. : alk. paper)
        1. Faithfull, Marianne. 2. Rock musicians—England—Biography. I. Dalton, David. II. Title.

ML420.F218A3  2000
782.42164'092—dc21
[B]                                                                          00-029040

⊖™ The paper used in this publication meets the minimum requirements of
American National Standard for Information Sciences—Permanence of
Paper for Printed Library Materials, ANSI/NISO Z39.48–1992.
Manufactured in the United States of America.

*Dear Reader,*

Here is my book at last and I hope you like it. I do.

Never apologize, never explain — didn't we always say that? Well, I haven't and I don't.

*So, love,*

*For Nicholas*

# *Out of Her Shell*

FIRST met Marianne Faithfull when we were working on a production of Brecht and Weill's *Threepenny Opera*. For some months before this meeting I had been struggling to make singable lyrics from the wonderfully intricate webs of Brecht's German, because it had taken me ages to discover the best, the simplest solution to the problems posed—listen to Weill's music, again and again and again. That was how to crack the language. And if I'd met Marianne earlier, she would have told me that immediately, for if I had to sum her up in one statement, it would be that she is a woman who knows about music. It surrounds her life, it centers it, and it's saved it.

I didn't know what to expect when I first met her. I'd loved her voice from the first time I'd heard it. In the 1970s, when the rest of the world didn't want to know, Ireland embraced passionately her beautiful song "Dreaming My Dreams." This was released during the darkest days of our still dark, still continuing civil war. That acknowledgment of grief in the song, the belief in survival, the insistence on love, turned it into a subversive national anthem. In ways, this might explain why she's chosen to live here. This country owes her one. And so I went to meet her, in her house, Shell Cottage.

From the music and the history I expected that she would be an interesting woman, difficult and strange. Interesting, difficult, strange she was—she *is*. What I had not expected would be that she is such a bloody funny woman. *The Threepenny Opera* is a comedy. Brecht is at his most wicked, malicious, anarchic. Marianne was the first person to read my lyrics, her laughter was a relief, but the big test I'd set myself in working for her voice was "The Solomon Song," a beautiful litany of time past and passing. It was to be sung with practically no accompaniment. And in it I put the secret that all playwrights leave hidden for their actors to uncover. This secret was contained in the single line, "How sad the heart, when it has won." She read it through and said, "I can do this." She could.

Since the first meeting she's become a friend, a good one. She still lives in Shell Cottage. At first the house seems like a refuge, a sanctuary. All sanctuaries cost something for their upkeep though. This one is quiet, contained, lonely. In Gaelic the word for lonely, *usdigneach,* is nearly synonymous with haunted. I hope in Shell Cottage she's come to peace with what's gone before. I hope this book is part of that peace. I think it is, for I have never met any one with a more fierce determination to confront the future. I've no more idea than she does what the future will be, but I'm dying to hear about it, from her own lips.

Frank McGuinness

# Contents

Faithfull

# *Childhood Living*

MY earliest memory is a dream of my mother covered in armor, a coronet of snakes entwined around her head. I am three years old. I'm in my bed, in the little room with the blue curtains. In the dream it is daytime, and sunlight is streaming through the curtains. Everything is blue, the blue of Ahmed's hashish-and-jewelry shop in Tangier. Blue curtains blowing in the wind. And beyond them a garden. The green green green of an English lawn. I hear a voice calling me. It says, "Come, Marianne, come." I feel helpless. I have no choice.

"Marianne! Marianne!" the voice calls again, so piercingly this time that I get out of bed. I float to the windowsill the way Alice does, with her feet just off the ground. I open the curtains and fly down to the end of the garden, where my mother has planted an asparagus patch. I see a fantastic figure looming over me. It is my mother-as-goddess, wearing armlets, breastplates and greaves like the ancient warrior queen Boadicea. She is cooking, raking the coals with a pair of tongs. She lifts me in her arms and places me on the fire. The dream ends as I lie down and allow her to roast me on the grill.

This happens night after night; again and again she arranges me on those hot coals. The dream always stops at that point. There is no pain; not really a nightmare at all, but rather a ritual that I obscurely recognize. A very Middle European apparition—a proper, collective-consciousness dream about the mother, the goddess. Some form of training, perhaps. It certainly prepared me for later life!

My mother, Eva, was the Baroness Erisso. She came from a long line of Austro-Hungarian aristocrats, the von Sacher-Masochs. Her great-uncle was Leopold Baron von Sacher-Masoch, whose novel, *Venus in Furs,* had given rise to the term *masochism.* During the war, Eva and my grandparents, Flora and Artur, lived in the Hungarian Institute in Vienna, where they were more or less free from harassment by the Nazis. My grandmother was Jewish, and the family was in great danger throughout the war (and even greater danger after the Russians invaded Austria in 1945).

Eva had been raped by occupying Russian soldiers, got pregnant and had an abortion. She was worn out by the privations of the war, and then along came my father, Major Glynn Faithfull, who was working as a spy behind the lines with British Intelligence. He had a message from Eva's brother, Alexander, who was fighting with Tito's partisans in Yugoslavia. Alexander had given Glynn a letter and directed him to find his sister, mother and father and tell them he was alive and well. Well, Glynn arrived with the message and fell in love with the sister, Eva, at first sight. She was distant and proud and a bit strange. She was also very beautiful. Before the war she had been a dancer and an actress. She had just done a screen test for Hollywood as the war started, but by war's end she was not the same woman.

When she married my father Eva was under the illusion that she was marrying an English gentleman of the kind that you see in films of that period. The terrible black joke was that she married my father because he seemed so *normal.* He was polite and charming and made her laugh and he was so well fed. Peace and normality was what she needed after the tumult of the war and her high-strung family. Glynn does have a side to him of gentle well-being and sanity, but there is also a very nutty side to him—very nutty indeed. My poor mother in fact married a truly obsessed eccentric, with utopian schemes for humanity and avant-garde theories of reform. Two people so unalike that had they seen each other's true natures they would not have stayed together for *one day.*

Naturally, it didn't take long for all this to become apparent to my mother. The war was over by this point, but Glynn, still working for British Intelligence, was sent briefly to Cairo. She asked him to get her some shoes and stockings in Milan en route. You can get very nice shoes in Italy, as we all know. Instead of the exquisite shoes she'd imagined he would bring her, he came back with a pair of awful, cheap shoes and stockings. My father's thinking would have been — and he's right — that she was lucky to have shoes and stockings at all. But Eva was not a realist; her heart sank.

In the beginning we lived in Ormskirk, in Lancs, while my father was working on his doctorate at Liverpool University. We had a proper house and a normal life. Just what my mother wanted, really. But soon the more bizarre aspects of my father's preoccupations became apparent. He came from a very strange family himself. My grandfather, Theodore Faithfull, was a sexologist who had left my granny, Frances, and run off with a circus dancer. He had invented a contrivance called the Frigidity Machine, which he thought might be the cure for the ills of the world. It would unblock the primal libidinal energy, and a new golden age would be set free. He once tried to get my mother to use it. No chance, of course. Along with these proto–Orgone Box theories went all sorts of other harebrained notions. He never took baths, for instance. He would come to stay with my parents and Eva would try desperately to make him wash. And he wouldn't. Said he didn't *believe* in it. She claimed he was the most horrible dirty old man you could imagine.

What also drove her crazy, being from Vienna, the home of Freudian psychotherapy, was Glynn and his father's credulous embrace of all this psychosexual stuff. She deeply despised it and taught me to despise it, *tant pis* for me! She thought psychoanalysis was crude and gimmicky and medieval, basically. She loved to quote the Karl Krauss aphorism: "Psychoanalysis is the disease for which it claims to be the cure."

Glynn's crowd all thought that the answer to everything was good sex. My mother apparently didn't think that way *at all*. My poor father was obsessed, sexually, with my mother. It was not at all reciprocated; she had only married him to get out of Vienna! And have me, I guess. She didn't really like sex. Once she had a child, she wanted as little to do with him as possible. I don't know what Eva thought men were, but it didn't have much to do with reality.

Eva was quite out of her element in England. Her family had been the center of her life. It was a huge adjustment for her to marry a foreigner and go and live in England away from everything she knew and loved. She had been ravishingly beautiful and expected to be treated like a princess (which is, unfortunately, the way she brought me up, too!). Eva presumed she was going to be pampered and adored, the last thing my father wanted in a mate. He wanted a coconspirator with whom he could share his vision.

Glynn's eccentricities began to blossom when he hooked up with a certain Dr. Glaister, who shared his devotion to utopian causes. With Dr. Glaister's financing, they bought an eighteenth-century manor, Brazier's Park, and the surrounding land to set up their school for intensive social research in Oxfordshire. So when I was four, we moved south and I went to the little school in Ipscomb, the village near Brazier's Park. Brazier's Park was a big rambling house with lots of nooks and crannies and battlements to crawl around on. It had beautiful grounds, endless cornfields to run in and stands of old gnarled Arthur Rackham trees to climb. I had a lovely time. Mother hated it.

Brazier's Park was and still is a working community. Everyone pitched in. Mother cooked for the whole of the community. There was no room for a lady of the manor. Eva began to feel increasingly alienated. She was different. She was difficult. She was foreign. She liked to drink wine at lunch. And she was very spoilt. Only now am I beginning to see how spoilt she was. My father was ultra-careful with money, and that created other problems. Eva was extravagant and abundant and over-the-top and theatrical. Glynn was the diametric opposite.

They rowed incessantly, usually about me. One of their basic fights was over whether to leave my landing light on at night. My father didn't want to spend the money, my mother didn't want me to be afraid. Now, it's clear to me that this business with the light was just a metaphor for their other problems, but naturally I thought it was all my fault. Children often need a light on at night. I know I did, because of the nightmares. Terrible, strange dreams about frightening entities that I called Daddy Hats. There were lots of them and they were all just like my father. Funny little men with mustaches. They had long nails and they would tickle me and pour hot tea over me.

Every year we took deprived children on an annual camping holiday to the New Forest. One morning my mother wandered into a glade and came across a quasi-mystical ritual going on in the woods. The participants were wearing brightly colored costumes and chanting: "Hail to the North Wind! Hail to the South Wind! Hail to the West Wind! Hail to the East Wind! Swear your oaths, Woodcraft Folk! Hail, thou Ineffable Essence!"

Unbelievable! And then, on cue, they all made a sign — the "Blue Sky" salute — with single arms extended towards the sky. My mother spoke English but not *that* well, and observing what to her looked like Druidic rituals she was horrified. The paraphernalia and slogan chanting were all too familiar to her from the Weimar Back-to-Nature cults of the thirties. My father was more Iris Murdoch than Third Reich, but she found the incident quite unsettling.

I don't know over which incident they finally came to blows, but Eva used to tell a very funny story (in Eva's realm, for everything that occurred there was a good story). Which was: Things were getting worse and worse. Glynn began having affairs and Eva was miserable. And then one day she just decided she'd had enough. My grandfather by this time had died and my grandmother was alone in Vienna. Eva wanted to bring her over to England. And my father, for whatever reason, violently opposed this. For my mother, this was the last straw. But instead of just quietly packing her bags and leaving, like most demure exasperated English wives had always done, Eva went down to the great hall at Brazier's and rang the gong. People came running from all directions. Eva started shouting at the top of her voice and making a full-scale scene. All these English people were completely appalled. My father was horrified.

Eva was in mid-aria in the great hall, when Bonnie, who was Dr. Glaister's mistress, came running up to her, saying:

"Eva, Eva, stop this kerfuffle at once! In England ladies simply don't behave like this."

Eva drew herself up and said, in her funny accent, "My dear Bonnie, my ancestors were ladies when yours were still hanging by their tails from trees." And on this note, she swept out.

I loved that. She possessed a genuine talent for shocking people. Even as an old lady she loved and understood high drama. She altered everything — family chronicles, personal anecdotes, history itself — to make life conform to the way she wanted it to be. It always made me uncomfortable. As wonderful as her stories often were, it would have been far more helpful for me in most cases to know what actually happened. But that, she was never going to tell me. When I was first in recovery and went back to see my mother, I wanted to ask her about her childhood and what it had been like. I'd heard she'd had an incestuous relationship with her brother, for instance, and I wanted to know how that had affected her. And she just unflinchingly looked me in the eye and said:

"My childhood was perfect."

"That's not possible," I said. "Nobody has ever had a perfect childhood."

"Mine was."

"Well, *mine* wasn't," I said.

But she wouldn't budge an inch: "Well, that's your problem, isn't it?"

When I was about six, my parents separated. I went to live with my mother and grandmother in Alemead House, 12 Milman Road, the poor area of Reading. After that, my relationship with my father deteriorated rapidly. We were penniless. To keep body and soul together Eva worked at a lot of menial jobs. She worked in a shoe store, she worked in a coffee bar, she even worked for a while as a clippy on a bus, collecting fares. But she always put up a big front. My childhood was filled with embarrassing incidents born of delusions of grandeur on my mother's part.

One summer Glynn invited me to spend a week at Brazier's. He had a colleague from Italy staying with him who had a daughter my age, so Glynn thought this would be an ideal time for me to visit. Eva, in her mad way, dressed me as if I were going to spend the day at the court of Franz Josef. She sent me off on the bus got up in a long, beautifully embroidered dress with lace cuffs and a collar. This is how she sent me off to the *country*, like the little princess she wanted me to be. The girl I was to spend the week with was dressed in jeans and T-shirt and when I got off the bus looking like Little Bo Peep she giggled and asked: "Are we going to a costume party?"

It was obvious that Eva was sending a message to Glynn at my expense. He sent me back to my mother with a letter saying: "Have you completely lost your mind? How could you do this to your own child! Sending Marianne dressed in that ridiculous outfit. How could you humiliate a little girl this way in front of her friends?"

My mother showed me the letter. It was an unnecessarily mean thing to do, but I was her sole companion and confidante. She was forcing me to take sides. Everything for Mama was black and white. After that I never felt quite the same about my father. Looking back, I realize he was right, of course. He saw what she was trying to do, the ludicrousness and pretentiousness of it all, raising a princess in the back streets of Reading!

Eva had been brought up with a sense of great privilege. She was high-handed and ruthless. We were like creatures from another planet, really. She brought me up like one of her cats. My father now describes her autocratic behavior as if it were almost a medical condition. A condition she passed on to me. But in me such presumptuousness was an even odder trait, because there was nothing to back it up.

Their next major battle was over Catholicism, and in retrospect my father was right about this, too. My mother decided when I was seven to send me as a boarder to the local convent school, St. Joseph's. Mostly because we were poor and because my grandmother, now dying of cancer, needed constant attention.

Glynn begged her not to. I wasn't even a Catholic! I remember him saying, "This will give her a problem with sex for the rest of her life."

It wasn't as if my mother herself was a devout Catholic. It would be absurd to say my mother was even religious. She went occasionally to Mass, and she hobnobbed with an old priest named Canon Murphy (what they really were was drinking partners). I eventually converted to Catholicism while at the convent, but it was entirely a social decision. I wanted to fit in and so I deceived the nuns into thinking I had had a revelation. Only when I was thirteen or fourteen did I start to appreciate the rituals, and only then because of the music. I joined the choir because I had a good voice and I loved singing. The Catholic Mass is very beautiful and intrinsically theatrical with the incense shakers and the vestments and the Latin liturgy. My conversion was prompted more by a Walter Pater aestheticism than veneration for the pope.

I was a charity boarder at St. Joseph's, a situation about which I was constantly reminded. It was very humiliating. It's ironic, too, that

that's how I ended up during my years of heavy drug use — as a charity boarder throughout much of my early adult life.

Despite my conversion I never quite fit in at the convent. I spent all my time alone reading while the others played and chattered. I didn't want to play hockey or any of that. Everyone thought I was stuck up.

I had one great friend, Sally Oldfield (her brother is Mike Oldfield of *Tubular Bells*), with whom I got on well because her parents were as odd as mine. Sally and I used to get out of doing physical education by lying. I told Sister Delores that I had terrible asthma and I couldn't play hockey, so we spent the hour walking around and around the hockey pitch discussing life and death, especially death. I must have been deep into my doomed Romantic period. The outcast!

Odd as the Faithfull household might have seemed, we were hardly the only dysfunctional family in that section of Reading. There were, thank God, the Oldfields. Sally Oldfield's mother was the first person I ever knew who was into drugs. Her husband was a doctor, so all these pills were readily accessible to her. Mrs. Oldfield was always staggering about with a drink and a few yellow pills. I'd never come across this kind of behavior before. I could see what a strain it put on the family and in particular on Sally, because it was Sally who had to keep everything together. She had to come home from school and make supper for the little boys and for the father. Her mother was just not there.

My going to the convent freed my mother from having to look after me and she began teaching at Bylands, a school for maladjusted children. Bylands was run by a Miss Garrard, one of those wealthy middle-class people who want to save the world. Because it was Gerry's school, she could hire Eva without any qualifications. Eva taught dance, painting and, bizarrely, current affairs.

The children at the school came from deprived and unhappy homes. Most had been battered or sexually abused. My mother objected to subjecting these already tormented children to endless psychological evaluations. Rorschach tests, interrogations about their childhoods and families. To Eva, all this was irrelevant and only confirmed that psychiatry itself was complete fantasy. She believed in action, empathy and love.

\*   \*   \*

Once Eva had set her mind to do something, neither hell nor high water could stop her. The most spectacular example of this was when she presented me at the age of thirteen with an older brother. She must have noticed when I was about twelve that there was something lacking in my social life. She saw how isolated I was; my inability to participate in the normal group things that children do together. Games, clubs, sports. Whenever I was confronted with these situations I would find ways of getting out of them. So Eva began picking people up and bringing them back to the house. Children, parents — whoever she thought might be helpful in giving me a sense of family and togetherness. One of her worries was that there were no men in my life.

One day my best friend and I brought over a friend called Chris O'Dell. His mother was very ill with multiple sclerosis. His father was paralyzed and became violent when he drank. Shortly after we met him, his mother died and his aunt had to help nurse his father. Although it was obvious that Chris was desperately unhappy, who but Eva would have taken it upon herself to intervene? *Noblesse oblige!* My mother just went in there and took over.

She rang his aunt Eyepie, who loved him, and told her: "The father beats him. The situation is absolutely intolerable, wouldn't you agree, my dear Eyepie?"

"Yes, Eva, it's just wicked what that poor boy —"

"Exactly my point! And, you will be so glad to know I have the solution. I'm taking Chris home to live with us."

Under normal circumstances the poor woman might have objected: "Well, that is terribly kind of you, Eva, but he's *our* nephew, you see, he's my sister's son and rightfully we should be the ones to take him."

But Eva left no opening for the aunt whatsoever. Nobody ever could resist Eva when she had made up her mind. She was a force of nature. You did what she said. So the following week Chris came to live with us. It was simply presented to us as a *fait accompli*. We were now brother and sister, and that was that. Chris was sixteen, I was thirteen. I remember going on holiday together shortly after he moved in. Neither of us knew what was expected, but eventually we became friends.

Chris didn't come from one of the normal families that I saw all around me and envied. Like me, he was a misfit. I could never have become friends with someone from one of those imagined ideal families that I have always aspired to, families who had money and security and a normal mother and father.

Chris fitted in very well, but with an arrangement as odd as ours it was inevitable that not everybody would approve. When I was sixteen I had a boyfriend whose father was the headmaster of Leighton Park, the Quaker boys school near St. Joseph's. He must have thought my mother and I were very odd indeed, which I suppose we were. What this poor man couldn't handle was Chris's presence in my family. He once made the mistake of questioning my mother about it in that insufferably snotty way English people can:

"Well, quite. I do agree with you that Marianne and Chris are very fond of each other, Mrs. Faithfull, but do you think it is quite advisable from a sexual perspective?"

To which Eva responded with deliberate opaqueness: "And what perspective is *that* exactly?"

"Well I should have thought that, uh, having Marianne and a teenager to whom she is unrelated under the same roof might appear a bit unwholesome."

"What nonsense," Eva replied. "My uncle was a von Sacher-Masoch. And I come from Vienna, the home of Dr. Freud. Don't you think I know more about these things than you do?"

That ended the conversation. And my relationship.

However high-handed my mother's absconding with Chris had been, it worked out well for a few years. His being with us was very good for me. It gave me my first friendship with a man that was not sexual, and, as it turned out, my best relationships with men rarely have been. That I learned from being with Chris.

Eva was very good to Chris, even if he had had no say in the matter *whatsoever*. She gave him a home and a family of sorts. She helped him through university. And it turned out fine, I guess, in that Chris has done really well. But it was such an act of overwhelming hubris on her part that I don't know if Chris has ever been able to think about it clearly. I often wondered how he must have felt because, happy ending or not, he was used. We all were. He must have had some profound misgivings because he eventually distanced himself from her and didn't see us again for twenty years!

Before Chris came to live with us there was only me to talk to, and my mother talked to me *a lot*. She told me stories, and she was never one to let the truth intrude on a good story! She remade reality as she wanted it to be.

I loved the story of my ancestor, the Spanish Moor. My mother's eyes would shine as she told me the family history of the von Sacher-Masochs:

"In the time of the Holy Roman Emperor, Charlemagne, came the first Sacher. He was a Moor from Spain who became a Christian and marched with Charlemagne. He was Secher or Sachre or something. This was my grandfather's family. If you want you can look it up in the Imperial Archives in Vienna. One day we will go together. Anyway, an Arab name that was Austrianized and became Sacher. So this Sacher was given lands in Hungary. He was a knight, the servant of Charlemagne, and because of his service to the Holy Roman Emperor he was given vast lands.

"Well, a few hundred years later this other family, the Masoch family, were about to die out. To prevent a name from disappearing the Emperor would proclaim: 'This name now goes with that one.' At court, you see, only those who could trace their ancestors back twelve generations could dance before the Emperor. But the Sacher-Masochs weren't interested in the court, not them. These English with their Gladstones and their Disraelis think they invented reforming! But tell me, why is our crest a salt pick and a salt hammer crossed? Because the Sacher-Masochs owned salt mines in the Ural mountains, my dear, that's why. These mines had been worked for hundreds of years by slaves, and when they were given to the Sachers, the first Baron Sacher freed them. A thousand years ago! He freed them! While the English were still painting themselves blue and dancing around stones!"

And then, dozing off by the fire, odd lines connected to some other fantastic story would trickle out:

". . . men in golden armoring and with great furling banners were there to meet the ship that was coming all the way from the Aegean Sea with this one horse and some oranges and spices for the Emperor. They are pulling the beautiful white stallion down the gangplank. Oh, darling you should see them! Such a magnificent horse all decorated with seashells . . . *und Blümchen. Ach, so schön!*"

I already know this story well; I have heard it a thousand times. This particular one is the story of the names of her title: the Baroness Apollonia and Erisso. How it came from two islands in Greece by that name, and how, long, long ago, these islands had to send my ancestors a white horse every seven years. I would listen to these stories night after night in our little house in Reading, with no money, no nothing. Certainly no castle. People were sneering at me at school because we didn't even have a telephone. No car, no gramophone, no father! And yet I had this fantastic secret history involving white tribute horses from the Aegean and Charlemagne, and Moorish ancestors on vast estates liberating the slaves in the salt mines.

I know now what Eva was doing, she was trying to give me a sense of who I was and where I came from; to make me proud of my background and compensate for all the things we didn't have. A fairy tale in which the woodcutter's daughter is told how an evil prince snatched away the kingdom that was rightfully her mother's. And I remember it was at such a moment that I decided, quite quietly: "I will set this right. When I grow up, I will bring back her glittering world."

When people met me later on in my life they invariably assumed that I was quintessentially English and from a wealthy and protected background. Part of the rage toward me in the late sixties came, I'm sure, from this misconception that I was somehow the epitome of everything English. Whereas my mother was Austrian, my father of Welsh descent, and I was part Jewish and descended from a Moor turned Christian. The strength in me that people mistook for English autocratic values actually came from the bond between my mother and me.

When I was about thirteen I joined the Progress Theatre, an amateur repertory theater company in Reading. I wanted to belong because you could act and meet boys. Vanessa Redgrave came to speak. She'd just played Rosalind in *As You Like It*. She talked about the theater and her parents and her life. She seemed very grown up. She must've been all of twenty-two. We did a production of *Our Town*. I played a middle-aged gossipy lady. My friend Mary Allen played the ingenue lead. Our parents came. For most of the kids, acting was a passing phase like horseback riding or ballet lessons, but I knew in some way this would be my life. Eva always assumed I would be an artist of some kind.

I began doing a little bit of folksinging in coffee bars and folk clubs. There was a beatnik dive in Reading called the Shades Coffee Bar and another one called Café Au Lait. I sang a cappella. "House of the Rising Sun," "Blowing in the Wind." All those Joan Baez songs. "Babe I'm Gonna Leave You" and other silly things. There were quite a few Joan Baezes in Reading alone.

I had a little record player at home and I bought things like "Venus in Blue Jeans" and "Brown-eyed Handsome Man." Buddy Holly, the Everly Brothers, Chuck Berry. I remember hearing "Not Fade Away" in the coffee bar and wondering what sort of person had written that. One of the records I bought that made a terrific impression on me when I was about fifteen was Miles Davis's *Sketches of Spain*, but I had no similar experience with a Rolling Stones record. Rock 'n' roll in the early sixties, especially in England, didn't have the hip reputation it eventually acquired. Jazz was hip and blues were hip, but rock 'n' roll was thought to be very slick and commercial. Rock 'n' roll at that time meant Billy Fury and guys with bleached blond hair.

I went up to London a great deal in my early teens with my mother's friend Deborah and her son, Anthony. Anthony was a dancer. We went to the ballet or the opera. I remember seeing Maria Callas in *Tosca*. I once went to a trad jazz festival in Beaulieu with some friends from Leighton Park. It was great fun, lighthearted. The music was terribly silly, English trad jazz. The English have always been keen on moldy forms of American music. It was the height of the bebop era in the States and they're into this daft stuff. The names of Sartre, and Simone de Beauvoir, Céline, Camus and Kafka were in the air. I repeated their ineffable names like a catechism. I devoured papers for every scrap of hipness and outrage I could find. Articles about Brigitte Bardot and Juliette Greco. She was the big Existentialist icon. I tried my best to look like her. I used to wear white lipstick, but it didn't really work if you were blond.

I was just a typical child of my time, I guess—open to everything.

I was being a teenager: curious, rebellious, in quest of the forbidden. You heard about these hip clubs in London from a friend who had heard it from another friend who had actually been to one. The names alone took on a magical talismanic quality. The Marquee, Ronnie Scott's. I used to come up from school and go to clubs when I was about sixteen. I'd go to the Marquee and the Flamingo, jazz clubs. People like Zoot Money and John Mayall and Nina Simone played there. The audiences were pretty scruffy. Students and beatniks and a scattering of older jazz aficionados. I liked jazz, and I was dazzled by this scene, rudimentary as it was. Just a girl from the provinces, going up to the big city to see what gives. I didn't know anybody; I never spoke to anyone. It was all connected to hipness. I wanted to smoke Gauloises and drink black coffee and talk about absurdity and *maquillage* with wicked women and doomed young men. I tried to understand Sartre and Camus and Kafka, but I liked Céline and Simone de Beauvoir. (I had actually read *The Second Sex*.) I was putting together a persona out of a lot of diverse elements. It was all unfocused. The sixties hadn't happened yet. There were only very hazy intimations of what was coming. The clothes were still very dull. But I knew there was a bit more to it than shuffling around smoky jazz clubs and I was hell-bent on being there when it happened, whatever it was!

The distinctions were getting blurred between upper and lower, male and female, recreation and work, politics and life. The uniforms were disappearing, the idea that you were meant to look like who you were — doctors were meant to look like doctors, steamy call girls were meant to look like steamy call girls. In the sixties all these things blurred.

The fading memory of the war as much as anything set the whole thing rolling in England. All my life I was brought up in the shadow of the Second World War. I had felt it more intensely than my friends, because living through the war in England wasn't quite the same as being in Vienna with the Nazi *Anschluss* and Hitler marching in. I hadn't naturally experienced any of this myself but I had absorbed it through my mother. It was as if I too had crawled out from the rubble and, having survived the worst, I now wanted to have fun.

Somewhere in the back of my mind I had made a decision to get out of Reading. Eva never suspected this. I've always laid my plans very secretively and never let anyone in on them, which more often than not has turned out to be a mistake. I didn't know that it was possible to talk things over with people and not lose everything in the process. I thought the minute you confided anything it would disappear. This was definitely true of my mother. I learned very young to conceal my innermost thoughts from her.

In those days men for me were creatures from another planet. Before I slept with one of them, I'd never seen a specimen of the species up close. How they acted and why they behaved the way they did was a complete mystery to me. But I obscurely knew that men in some form or other would be my means of escape. And that's how it turned out to be. When I was seventeen I went to a Cambridge ball with a Leighton Park boy and there I met my first love, John Dunbar. He was to be my catalyst, my Virgil. A world opened up when I met John.

John was different from any boy I had ever met. He was certainly the hippest. He wasn't actually at the ball. Too cool for that. He would never have been caught dead at a bourgeois event such as that. But there was a party on the staircase at Churchill College, and as I was going up to the kitchen I passed one of the students' doors and on it was a poster of the famous Da Vinci drawing, "The Measure of Man." It was stunning and I remember turning to the person I was with and saying "*Who* lives there?" And at that moment John came through the door. When I saw John it was one of those things where everything else just pales around you.

John had a beautiful, sensitive face and he was the very model of hipness, circa 1963. He was wearing pressed jeans and a jacket and little horn-rimmed glasses. He wasn't quite twenty-one when I met him and in his first year at Cambridge. We were immediately attracted to each other. I ditched my date. He was intense and unusual and had a background very similar to my own. His mother, Tatiana (called Tania), is Russian. The Dunbars were filmmakers and — equally irresistible in my eyes — they were a *family*. This was the beginning of my long addiction to families. Wherever I find a family, I try to get into it.

I came up to London on the train. I was invited to stay with John's parents, Bob and Tania, and his twin sisters. They were my age, Jenny and Margaret, and they were ravishingly beautiful. John and I had our own rooms and John came to mine in the middle of the night and we made love and it was all very exciting, although not quite as earth-shattering as I'd imagined. I thought it was all a lot of fuss about nothing. John and I were like puppies. It wasn't a very sexual thing. I didn't know my way around at all.

His parents were very cosmopolitan and sophisticated. They took the *New Yorker*, which I remember impressed me terribly. They had it sent from New York every week. John reveled in all that. He'd been born in Mexico and lived as a child in Russia. His father had been posted there during the war. It was all awfully grand and exotic, I thought.

John was the epitome of the tormented youth of Romantic tales. He was very nihilistic and, like a Dostoyevskian hero, would talk breathtakingly about killing himself. All of which I found terribly attractive and a little frightening. I was to be his muse. I thought if he had *me* he couldn't possibly kill himself. John was into bebop jazz. Coltrane, Charlie Parker and Beethoven's late quartets and Mozart and black music and all that great stuff. He was my Pygmalion and I was more than ready for all that. I soaked it up like a sponge.

John introduced me to all his friends. He seemed to know everybody you would ever want to meet in London. After all, he was great friends with Peter Asher (of the pop group Peter and Gordon). They had just had a hit with "A World Without Love." Very shortly after I met John, Peter Asher put the money up for Indica, the art gallery and bookstore John ran together with Barry Miles. At the time, Paul McCartney was living with Peter's parents — in Dr. and Mrs. Asher's big house in Wimpole Street. A beautiful old Barretts of Wimpole Street house. Mrs. Asher had signs on all the doors reading "Jane's Room," "Peter's Room," "Paul's Room." I thought they were very odd; I'd never seen anything like it. Family life, you see.

Paul lived there for a long time. Paul was very young then, very friendly and open and very good-looking, very sure of himself, hip. The threads of a dozen little scenes were invisibly twining together.

All these people — gallery owners, photographers, pop stars, aristos and assorted talented layabouts — more or less invented the scene in London, so I guess I was present at the Creation. Sixties London actually has its own origin myth. The *ur*-myth was concocted, rather typically, in an espresso bar in Chelsea (just as we thought the Russian Revolution was plotted on a train in Zurich). Early in 1963 John and a man called Paolo Leone, a left-wing beatnik type, and Barry Miles, John's partner, put their heads together and hatched a plot. I was just a young girl watching these mad intellectuals all dressed in existential black charting the future of the globe. They had it all worked out.

"It's going to be the psychic bloody center of the world, man!" Paolo announced portentously. John and Miles thought that Paolo was a little mad but the idea was infectious (why not!) and it all had the imprimatur of none other than Carl Jung (sort of). Jung had a dream in which Liverpool was seen to be at the center of the world. There was a piazza in his dream called the Golden Square and of course there is a Golden Square in Liverpool. There's one in London, too, but who's counting? The place in the dream hadn't exactly been Liverpool, it was called "the Pool of Life." Jung had made the connection later, while in England giving a series of talks. Paolo found, he said, that he'd had to make a few adjustments to the great man's theory. Jung was Swiss, after all, and could hardly be expected to zero in on a Brit vibe like this with one hundred percent accuracy. Jung's dream geography, he figured, had to be a tad off. It wasn't Liverpool that was going to be the center of the world, it was *London*. There were a number of other pieces of evidence that went along with this that I can no longer remember, but it was all terribly convincing in a mad way and once we'd all convinced each other that this was a fact, we all got down to it with a vengeance. We decided, "Right, this is our mission," and at once began to build the walls of our New Jerusalem — somewhat along the lines of the defenses of Paris in *Gargantua* and *Pantagruel*. Free love, psychedelic drugs, fashion, Zen, Nietzsche, tribal trinkets, customized Existentialism, hedonism and rock 'n' roll. And lo and behold, before too long there was a definite buzz going on.

# *As Tears Go By*

ACCORDING to Pop Mythology, my life proper began at Adrienne Posta's "launching party" in March 1964, for it was there that I first met Mick Jagger. Mick fell in love with me on the spot (or so the story goes), decided I was fit to be his consort, and wrote "As Tears Go By." I, on the other hand, immediately began shooting heroin and having a lot of sex.

Andrienne Posta was a teenage singer whose single had been produced by the Rolling Stones' flamboyant manager, Andrew Loog Oldham. This was the party to promote the record, and John Dunbar and I had gone as guests of Peter Asher. Paul McCartney was there with Peter's sister, Jane, along with various members of the Rolling Stones (Mick, Keith and Brian). At this point the Stones were not much more than yobby schoolboys. They had none of the polish of John Lennon or Paul McCartney, and compared to my John they seemed very crass and boorish indeed.

As for *him,* I wouldn't even have known he was there if he hadn't had a flaming row with his girlfriend, Chrissie Shrimpton. She was crying and shouting at him, and in the heat of the argument her false eyelashes were peeling off.

I didn't give a damn about Mick or the Rolling Stones, but the urbane and exotic Andrew Loog Oldham was altogether a different kettle of fish. Him I liked instantly. He was staring at me from across the room whispering conspiratorial asides to his partner in crime, Tony Calder. Most of the women at the party were wearing loads of mascara and false eyelashes and were dressed in their fancy party frocks. I was wearing a pair of blue jeans that I'd borrowed from the twins, with one of John's shirts tucked into them. I'd love at this point to pretend that I don't know quite what it was Andrew saw in me, but actually I do know because — with his customary candor — he's said so on numerous occasions: "I saw an angel with big tits and signed her."

I was sitting on the heater next to John when I noticed this strange creature, all beaky and angular like some bird of prey, *lunge* toward me. He looked powerful and dangerous and very sure of himself. I was glad when, at the last minute, he spun around and with his back to me addressed John:

"Who *is* she? Can she *act?* What's 'er name?" — handing John, in the same breath, an oversized, flashily printed card. "Andrew Loog Oldham, darling." He called everyone darling. *Especially* men. It made them nervous and that gave Andrew an edge. Andrew was all edge. He exuded menace, shock razor-blade hipness.

John said: "She's called Marianne Faithfull, actually."

"Oh, do come on, darling. You'll have to do better than that."

"I couldn't believe it either when I first heard it," said John, "but it really is her name. I must be magnetically attracted to chicks with outrageous names. I once went out with a girl named Penelope Heaven. Or so she said!"

Everyone laughed at that and then Andrew asked, almost as an afterthought: "Can she *sing?*"

John: "I think she can, why the hell not? You can sing, can't you, Marianne?"

And that was that.

I'd never met anyone like Andrew before. He was genuinely weird. He radiated an intoxicating sense of folly. All manner of mad schemes from fashion to movies to Pop art bubbled out of him in garbled, lightning asides. He was wearing eye shadow (*very* outrageous for those days). He was slightly effeminate looking, but this only added to his fascination. He later told me that he had exaggerated the effete posturing for John's benefit. It was Andrew's way of hoodwinking the boyfriends of girls he was putting the make on. Once they saw the pan-cake makeup and the eyeliner, they were off their guard.

Andrew would say things you only hear in movies, like: "I can make you a star, and that's just for *starters,* baby!" Or: "You don't need to audition, I can see the charisma in your eyes, darling." I honestly thought he'd had too much to drink. Everyone had, actually. That was the point of going to things like this. You went to get as plastered as you could for free.

A week later I got a telegram from Andrew at my mother's house in Reading—we still didn't have a telephone. It said: BE AT OLYMPIC STUDIOS AT 2:00 O'CLOCK STOP ANDREW OLDHAM.

I came up from Reading to Paddington on the 10:06 train with Sally Oldfield. There were several meetings with Andrew and the song-writer Lionel Bart, who had a big hit with the musical *Oliver!* at the time, before we actually went in to record. Lionel Bart was there be-cause I was originally meant to do one of his songs. That's how Andrew had wangled the money for the session. Another of Andrew's artful dodges!

Andrew was a great fabricator of selves, and once in the studio he transformed utterly. An agitated and distracted Maestro Loog Oldham strode up and down like a manic Ludwig Van on a handful of leapers. He did what I would later recognize as his Phil Spector imitation: dark glasses, Wagnerian intensity, melodramatic moodiness. It was all a game, but before you knew this about Andrew it could be quite unnerving. Mick and Keith also came to the session, but they were quiet as mice. It was Andrew's show, and they said not a word.

The layout of the recording studio was exceedingly odd. The con-trol room was far above the studio; Mick, Keith, Andrew and his part-ner, Tony Calder, Lionel Bart and the engineer, Mike Leander, all sat up there like gods looking down on us. We were like the workers toil-ing in the factory while the fat cats directed operations from on high. There wasn't even that much to *do* in a control booth in those days. At most it was two track. It was done live with the orchestra. The orches-tra played and I sang. All in mono.

The Lionel Bart song was awful. It was called "I Don't Know How (To Tell You)," it was in galumphing 3/4 time (I *don't* know *how* to *tell* you) and had lines like:

*It seems that fate would have it
that somebody else could love me. No!*

It was one of those show-biz songs that needed the proper register. My voice was just plain wrong. We did take after agonizing take. The musicians were becoming restless, but I simply could not do it. In desperation Andrew got me to try the song that had originally been planned for the B side, a song that Mick and Keith had written called "As Tears Go By."

This was the first song Mick and Keith had written. Andrew had locked them in the kitchen and told them, "Write a song. I'll be back in two hours." Andrew gave them the sense and feel of the type of thing he wanted them to write — "I want a song with brick walls all around it, and high windows and no sex." They came up with a song called "As Time goes By." Andrew knew a lot about how songs were constructed. Although it was still in a very primitive state, he knew he could fix it. There was another problem: the title. It was the title of a very famous song, the one Dooley Wilson sings in *Casablanca,* so Andrew changed it to "As Tears Go By."

Andrew played me a demo of the tune with Mick singing and Big Jim Sullivan on acoustic guitar. He handed me a scrawled lyric sheet and I went back into the studio and did it. As soon as I heard the *cor anglais* playing the opening bars I knew it was going to work. After a couple of takes it was done. Andrew came down from Olympus and gave me a big hug.

"Congratulations, darling. You've got yourself a number six."

"Six or eight," Tony Calder amended.

"*Definitely* a six, man. If not, in fact, a *three.*"

That's they way they talked. Seriously!

They mixed it then and there, and that was it.

After the session Mick and Keith gave Sally and me a lift in their car to the station. Mick tried to get me to sit on his lap, but I got Sally to instead. I mean, it was on *that* level! What a cheeky little yob, I thought to myself. *So* immature. And Mick, I'm sure, thought I was just a silly little girl who liked Odetta and Joan Baez.

"As Tears Go By" was like a Françoise Hardy song, really. Maybe that's what Mick had picked up from me when we met. Slightly existential, but with a dash of San Remo Song Festival. The Europop you might hear on a French jukebox. Or rather it's what Andrew saw in me at the party and told Mick to write. Andrew's always been into that. "The Andrew Loog Oldham Orchestra Plays the Greatest Hits of the Rolling Stones" type-of-thing. Everybody did those albums. Keith even made one. It was by working on dopey projects like this that Keith learned to produce records.

Mike Leander was the person I worked with directly and with whom I actually made the record. I could get along with Mike. He was the musical director and the person I actually dealt with on earth. Leander was young and reasonably hip, but he was locked into Denmark Street, the pop music mill. Except for Gary Glitter in the early seventies, he never got on the beam again.

Maestro Andrew's only bit of direction to me was to sing very close to the mike. It was an invaluable piece of advice. When you sing that close to the microphone, it changes the spatial dimension. You project yourself into the song. In folk music the song is usually handled quite preciously, like an Appalachian artifact. I probably would have tried to sing it like Joan Baez. The version we ended up with is more electric and subjective. Pop According to Andrew is more like Method acting. There's no distance. It becomes breathy and intimate, as if you're inside my head and you're hearing the song from in there.

There was about a two-week delay in cutting the B side — now that we were no longer doing Lionel Bart's song, Andrew had to find someone else to pay for the sessions. The new B side was "Greensleeves" (now credited to Andrew Loog Oldham rather than to Henry VIII).

I was never that crazy about "As Tears Go By." God knows how Mick and Keith wrote it or where it came from. It's a great fusion of dissimilar ingredients: "The Lady of Shalott" to the tune of "These Foolish Things." The image that comes to mind for me is the Lady of Shalott looking into the mirror and watching life go by. It's an absolutely astonishing thing for a boy of twenty to have written. A song about a woman looking back nostalgically on her life. The uncanny thing is that Mick should have written those words so long before everything happened. It's almost as if our whole relationship was prefigured in that song. A lot of people felt that way!

"As Tears Go By" was a marketable portrait of me and as such is an extremely ingenious creation, a commercial fantasy that pushes all the right buttons. It did such a good job of imprinting that it was to become, alas, an indelible part of my media-conjured self for the next fifteen years.

I rerecorded it at the age of forty, and at that moment I was exactly the right age and in the right frame of mind to sing it. It was then that I truly experienced the lyrical melancholy of the song for the first time.

Shortly after "As Tears Go By" had got onto the charts Andrew called and said we had to go up to Newcastle for a promotional TV appearance. "We'll drive up in Lionel's new sports car. We'll have a wonderful time, darling. Pick you up around noon. Wear the white suit, but lose the boots. No hat, try a scarf. *Ciao*."

I was a little dubious. They came by to pick me up and guess what? It was a bloody Lamborghini, a two-seater. I sat in the back. You couldn't call it a seat. It was a sort of hat box thing where I perched for six or seven hours being bumped and jiggled around as Andrew and Lionel got more and more silly. So it was an incredible relief when after the show they passed out at the hotel and couldn't drive me back. I then found myself on a nice comfortable train with a first-class ticket sitting opposite this delightful old Etonian pop star, Jeremy Clyde, one half of Chad and Jeremy.

When we got to London we went back to his place and, without a great deal of emotion, we went to bed. It was great sex and in the morning I must have got up a bit dewy-eyed and wistful. I immediately discerned a look of distress on Jeremy's face. My experience in these matters was limited to John, so I naturally assumed that having sex with someone meant romance. Jeremy, I could see, was a bit concerned I was going to fall in love with him. It must have been obvious to him I didn't know the ropes.

Over toast and marmalade he tried to tell me the code of casual sex. Love and sex are two different things. Sometimes they happen together but then again they may not. My lesson concluded with: "Lovely being with you, Marianne, perhaps we'll run into one another again soon."

I've spent most of my life trying to grasp that particular bit of sexual etiquette and, let's face it, I still don't get it. When you're nasty they pursue you like crazy and when you're nice they run away screaming. Those courtly games are something I've never been very good at. I'm foolishly enthusiastic, whether it's therapy, Narcotics Anonymous or a man. It makes me feel very anachronistic. It's all very well to be bumptious and eager at seventeen, but by the time you're in your mid-forties you are meant to have got the hang of it at least a little.

It was around this time that I had my first lesbian affair with a beautiful Indian girl named Saida. It was all part of my great experiment. When I was seventeen she gave me a Tuinal and seduced me in my flat in Lennox Gardens. She was sixteen and absolutely gorgeous. Small, stark, short hair. Exquisite, like a little figurine in an Indian temple. And in the middle of making love my mother walked in on us. I had forgotten all about her! But Eva simply shut the door, and never mentioned it again.

Just before "As Tears Go By" came out, John had gone to Greece for the summer and while he was away the record broke, climbed the charts and I became a soi-disant pop music celebrity. It was something I was both pleased about and embarrassed by, and for some time I wondered how exactly I would explain this new state of affairs when he returned.

Shortly after he got back we had coffee in a little delicatessen near South Kensington tube station. I was casting around in my mind how to tell him what had happened to me. I was afraid of being mocked by John. There's a whole bunch of English people, my father is one of them, for whom even aspiring to success is, well, just not done. And I knew John would likely be appalled by this pop star business and look down on me from a great height. Anyway, I was sitting there sipping the most god-awful coffee I'd ever tasted with John across from me looking yearningly into my eyes. I practically choked when "As Tears Go By" came on the radio. We both sat and listened. Neither of us said a thing. After the record had played the deejay came on again: "That was Marianne Faithfull singing her new hit record 'As Tears Go By,' now number nine in the charts. She came out of nowhere with this wistful song written for her by Mick Jagger and Keith

Richard of the Rolling Stones." Poor John was speechless. *I* was speechless! But John was cool, and to his credit he was tolerant of my new "condition." He hardly ever put me down for becoming this pop creature!

It wasn't only John who was affected by my altered state. When "As Tears Go By" became a hit record, I left St. Joseph's in my last term and was gone, almost overnight, from my mother's life. She was utterly unprepared for this development. The dream child on whom she doted up and left without warning, never to come back.

I got out, all right, but the moment I left her things began to fall apart. I escaped into a kind of nightmare. I entered a terribly threatening life at a time when I was far too young and sheltered. From the nurturing house of my mother I was thrown into this freakish half-life. The tours were brutal and there seemed to be no end to them. The relentless hurdy-gurdy of one-night stands went on and on for over two years. It wasn't only the performing that was such a strain (although that was a nightly ordeal itself), it was all the other stupid things you had to do. Every day there were four or five interviews with the local papers and the same dopey questions over and over again ("Anyone special in your life, Marianne?"), radio shows ("Who's your favorite Beatle?"), photo sessions ("Look *pensive*"), community functions ("The mayor's daughter is quite the budding violinist, you know"), lip-synching TV shows (*Ready, Steady, Go! Top of the Pops*) and then slogging to the next hotel. The pace was hectic and without relief. Here's my schedule for November 1964:

November 15th    Concert at Winter Gardens, Bournemouth.
16th–19th    Recording Sessions.
20th    London Students Glad Rag Ball, Wembley Stadium.
21st    Gliderdome Ballroom, Boston, Lincolnshire.
22nd    Manor House Ballroom, Ipswich.
23rd    Barrow Assembly Hall, Aylesbury.
24th    Nottingham, also on *Scene* at 6:30, Granada TV.
25th    Twisted Wheel, Manchester.
26th    Majestic Ballroom, Newcastle-on-Tyne.
27th    Town Hall, Kidderminster.
28th    *Ready, Steady, Go!* & Lyton Baths.

29th    B.B.C. TV *Top of the Pops.*
30th    Day off.

I was absolutely terrified and there wasn't a soul to talk to other than my chaperone, Mary Allen. It would have helped had I been able to speak to my mother, but because we didn't have a telephone I couldn't even do that. What could she have told me anyway? As it was, she barely understood what it was I was doing.

I recently found a heart-wrenching letter from her on my first tour:

9th 10 1964

*My Dearest Marianne,*

I am a little sad that I have not heard from you or Mary at all. Not a line to tell me if you are alright. I *cannot* phone from strange people as it takes hours to get hold of you or not at all. And I am getting frantic. . . .

I think I would give everything for a phone so that you could ring me. But obviously you have quite forgotten my existence or I would have heard something.

My love to all and a big hug and kisses for you my faithless darling.

Eva Mamma

The loneliness of life on the road was awful. Now I can't imagine *not* touring. I've adjusted and I like it. I'm very good at being by myself; it's being with someone else that I find quite hard!

I went on my first tour at the end of 1964 with the Hollies, Freddy and the Dreamers, Gerry and the Pacemakers, the Four Pennies — tons of people all thrown together.

The tour went through Lancashire and what was so strange was that I was traveling through my own past. We passed through Ormstead, where I had lived as a little girl, and near Liverpool, where many of the others had grown up.

Tours in the early sixties were indiscriminate assemblages of groups and stars and unknowns. In a Chinese Imperial classification of types—folksingers, Beatle clones, country singers, dollies, lounge

acts, *Americans* (a category unto themselves) — we were thrown together higgledy-piggledy. The only thing we had in common was the
charts. Anyone who recently had a hit, and some who would never
have one.

We all got on the bus just behind Madame Tussaud's. It was a
group my convent school had not prepared me for. Rowdy northern
lads. Cramped together on the bus, I got an instant education in social
migration. It was like being packed off in a submarine with the Manchester United soccer team. It was bitter cold and if you didn't want to
freeze to death you had to get yourself a seat at the front next to the
driver. The old geezer would regale you with stories about the Green
Line route through East Kent he used to drive ("They switched the line
through Ashford, which I, for one, will never understand") or various
stars' autographs he'd collected (always for someone else, of course, his
nephew Percy, his sister in Grimstead). The seats in those days didn't tilt
back, so unless you were an experienced trouper and could sleep bolt
upright, sleeping on the bus was almost out of the question. If you did
manage to doze off, you'd be jerked wide awake soon enough as the
bus swung into one of the million roundabouts on English roads. Out
the window was the sullen landscape of the Midlands. Endless grimy
brick factories and row houses, rusting old bridges and canals filled
with debris.

The others on these tours laughed at me because I would lug piles
of books around: *The Merchant of Venice,* Jane Austen, *Paradise Lost,*
Wordsworth, Keats, Shelley. It was very odd. I spent the endless hours
on the bus poring over my reading list for English literature as if I were
going to go back to school. They couldn't believe it.

The guys I toured with mostly read comic books, traded soccer
statistics, told dirty jokes and sang loony words to current hits. I was a
curious combination of insecure and arrogant. What I was really trying
to do was hide my fear, but my snottiness drove people wild with fury.
It still does. I didn't know why I was doing it, but I realized I had to
come up with some reason for my behavior and I decided, okay: shy.
When asked by some prying journalist I say: "I'm not really aloof, you
know. I'm fantastically shy and introverted." Well, I'm certainly not shy
and never was. But I *admired* shy. Keith was shy.

The only ones not unnerved with my frosty front were Graham

Nash and Allan Clarke of the Hollies. They were friendly, sunny and approachable. Allan Clarke sat down next to me at once and started chatting in his sweet Mancunian accent.

"Whatcha readin', luv?"

"*Pride and Prejudice.*"

"That the one with 'Eathcliff?"

"No, actually. . . ."

Graham Nash was my favorite. He was much more articulate and interesting than anyone else on the tour (but even then I was smart enough not to have sex with him). I'd have lunch with Graham and spend the night with Allan. Allan was nice but married. Not that that bothered me. I was enjoying my new freedom, the way a man would in the same circumstances. The awkward bit came with the arrival of his wife. He then pretended not to know me. I don't know what I thought he should have done. Did I expect him to introduce me enthusiastically: "Darling, I want you to meet this lovely girl I've been fucking on the road. She's been a super stand-in for you." Nevertheless, my nose was put a bit out of joint and, for the first time in my life, I got dead drunk and had to be pushed onstage.

The nightly ordeal. Getting up on stage in front of hundreds of hostile teenagers who had come not to see me but Freddy and the Dreamers or the Mersey Beats and let you know they had. "Get 'er off!" "Where's bloody 'Erman!" "Silly bitch!" I was absolutely petrified. Still am. But I soon learned to make paralysis part of my performance.

The dolly girls all jiggled and jumped up and down and shook their moneymakers, doing little go-go steps in their thigh-length white boots. I didn't want to compete with that, so I decided to go as far as I could in the other direction. I simply stood there in front of the microphone, very still, my hands dangling by my side and sang from some place deep inside me and out came this clear, ethereal voice. It wasn't the least sexy or hip. It was about as far as you could get from sexy.

I was absurd. It must have been a hoot. I didn't make the slightest movement for the very good reason that I was quite unable to budge. I was glued to the spot by sheer terror. When in doubt, stay still. It turned out, by default, to be a very effective pose. I still use it. I move about a bit more now and I let my hands do their own reflexive semaphore. I realized that that's what you see from the audience: the hands and the face. That's why I wear black, so that's *all* you see. And the hands move by themselves involuntarily. When I'm doing a song that's hard for me, like "Times Square," my hands begin to do all sorts of funny things on their own.

I'm still as scared now as I was in 1964. That hasn't changed at all. The fear is exactly the same. I would have thought that after thirty years of this fucking game you'd get over that. But you don't. The whole trick of this thing, for me anyway, is to get out of your own light. And I can only do that by staying very still. Keeping my feet on the ground and my back straight, and just doing it.

After a while I began to realize nothing that terrible was going to happen to me; I was going to be okay. It wasn't going to consume me. And I discovered that after the initial terror I loved the exhibitionism of performing. The feeling of safety. No one can get near me. The world as I want it to be!

Anyway, the idea of my performing in front of large numbers of sullen, boorish teenagers was so dismaying that even the dauntless Andrew never came to see me. He stayed as far away as possible.

If performing was anguish, I had no trouble dealing with the press. I just said the first thing that came into my head:

"I don't give a fig whether I'm a success as a singer. In the pop business, talent doesn't count."

"Andrew's different. He's sincere. Well, he *says* he is, so let's pretend he is."

"I believe in living on several different planes at once. It's terribly important, don't you think?"

All very mystifying! My natural contrariness was provoked and I gained a reputation for not acting the way a pop star should. Whatever that was. We were writing the book in any case; there *were* no rules. You could do whatever you wanted. That's what Andrew always said. "Nobody knows what you're meant to do anyway."

The more outlandish I was with the press, the more Andrew loved it.

And I gave them not only the acerbic, aphoristic Marianne but the dotty daughter of the Baronessa as well.

After the interview in a ritzy club, Marianne dashed out into the street. She returned with a small gift, a volume of the two act light opera *Big Ben* by A. P. Herbert from a second hand book store. "You simply have to have it," she said. Her face partly obscured by the large horn rim glasses she was wearing, clutching a copy of Lawrence Durrell's *Bitter Lemons.*

What a scene! I hope I'm not quite as pretentious as that now. Please, tell me I'm not!

Journalists came to these interviews with an image of me that had been rather skillfully prepackaged by Andrew and Andrew's publicist, Andy Wickham. Andy Wickham had a fixation about blondes. (He finally found his Galatea in Goldie Hawn.) I didn't quite fit his specific obsession, but I was wrapped up with a bow nevertheless. It was with his press release for "As Tears Go By" that most of the misconceptions began:

> MARIANNE FAITHFULL is the little seventeen-year-old blonde . . . who still attends a convent in Reading. . . . daughter of the Baroness Erisso. . . .
>
> She is lissome and lovely with long blonde hair, a shy smile and a liking for people who are "long-haired and socially conscious."
>
> Marianne digs Marlon Brando, Woodbine cigarettes, poetry, going to the ballet, and wearing long evening dresses. She is shy, wistful, waif-like. . . .

All these half-truths strung together created a very misleading image. That press release (along with the *Village of the Damned* photo of me on the other side) projected an eerie fusion of haughty aristocrat and folky bohemian child-woman. It was a tantalizing ready-made fantasy. Unfortunately, it wasn't me.

The follow-up to "As Tears Go By" was "Blowing in the Wind." A *total* disaster. All I remember about that session was how dreary I sounded. I had just come off the road and I was exhausted. I was over-whelmed, too, by the very idea of doing a follow-up. When I did "As Tears Go By" I thought that I would do this one record and then go back to school. Here I was doing a *follow-up*, and a lousy one at that! For the flip side I did "House of the Rising Sun," and that was even drearier and soggier than "Blowing in the Wind."

At the time I did "As Tears Go By" I'd seen it as a way of getting out of my A-level exams, but now I had to face the possibility that this was not going to be just a break in my old life; it was something that was going to go on and on and on.

I did my best to blame Andrew and Decca for "Blowing in the Wind" but it was my own doing entirely. Poor Andrew, it wasn't his fault at all. Somebody must have said to him, "Why don't you just let Marianne do the sort of thing *she'd* like to do?" I can just see it. And, of course, I worshipped Bob Dylan. Andrew went against his better judgment and it was a fiasco.

Despite the fact that he was inevitably right about everything, I was having problems with Sir Andrew. It was the fog-and-amphetamine factor that bothered me. He was really *out there* at the time. I was intimidated by the cool, mystifying jivespeak of his that passed for chat. I had no idea what he was talking about most of the time. He was too hip for me, he was too fast for me and on top of everything else to have the Mad Hatter as your manager — it was all too much.

The most disturbing thing about Andrew was all the wild, purple-hearts-fueled *Clockwork Orange* stories that seemed to be confirmed by the unnerving, ever-present Reg, that criminal chauffeur of his. Andrew loved to put out stories about breaking people's fingers or hanging recalcitrant club owners out seventh-story windows by their ankles. It was all pretend, a boy's game of cops and robbers and old gangster movies, but I didn't know that. He scared me to death. I remember going white and shaking after a meeting at Andrew's and rushing over to the Dunbars' to pull myself together. I felt trapped. He was a Sven-gali, I thought, with too much control over me. But control is always reciprocal; it cuts both ways. It took me years to realize that he was just a sweet thing.

After "Blowing in the Wind" I jumped ship. I left Andrew for his partner, Tony Calder. Tony was not a bad guy. A bit sleazy in the nicest possible way. Tony split away from Andrew to take care of me and we made a couple of very good records. "Come and Stay with Me" and "This Little Bird" are my personal favorites from that period.

"Come and Stay with Me" was written by Jackie DeShannon. It was during my third tour and I was suffering from "nervous exhaustion." I was drained and I was homesick. In the room next to mine in the hotel were Jimmy Page and Jackie DeShannon having a very hot romance. Jimmy I knew because he'd played on the session for "As Tears Go By." He played on almost all my sessions in the sixties. He was very dull in those days. This was before he went away and got interesting. I guess what he was doing in that hotel room was *getting* interesting. (Having an affair with Jackie DeShannon is a good place to start.) She was *born* interesting. She was brassy and a bit tarty. Naturally very beautiful, but she had her hair all frizzed and she wore tons of makeup. You could see from the moment you met her that she had been distorted and thwarted by show biz, like a beautiful woman who'd been forced into a corset and twisted in some way.

Tony had said to them in his sharp way, "As soon as you two are finished fuckin' each other's brains out, why don'tcha write Marianne a song as well." And she did.

There's a part of me that always wants to fly off, to escape. That's what drew me to "This Little Bird." The words are from Tennessee Williams's *Orpheus Descending*. It's that famous speech about the bird who sleeps on the wind and touches the ground only when it dies. John D. Loudermilk took the words and put music to it. Interesting how far Tennessee Williams infiltrated the culture without anybody noticing it!

But in the end Tony had no more idea of what I should be doing than Andrew did. He just gave me more attention. Andrew was, after all, the Rolling Stones' manager and he had all these other people as well, Chris Farlowe and Herman's Hermits. I couldn't deal with that. Andrew was hurt, of course. He couldn't understand it. But I didn't want to be seen as just an adjunct to the Stones. I didn't like the fact that the press were already printing that I was their girlfriend or their this or their that. Whereas I'd barely spoken two words to any of them. I wanted to distance myself from Andrew's empire.

The next package tour I went on in spring 1965 was the typical collection of pop oddities currently on the charts: Gerry and the Pace-makers, the Kinks, Gene Pitney and the Mannish Boys, myself and my guitar player, Jon Mark. The lead singer of the Mannish Boys was David Jones, later David Bowie.

I wonder if in my pea brain I did that whole tour with Gene Pitney to somehow be closer to Andrew. Pitney, whom Andrew had be-friended, had hung around a few Stones sessions giving Mick and Keith the two-week Gene Pitney songwriting course. After I split from An-drew I had always felt badly about leaving him, and this was my rather bizarre way of dealing with it. Not realizing that Gene Pitney was going to be a complete asshole.

But oh what a good fuck he was! I had just discovered sex in earnest. Mary Allen, my chaperone, fell for a guy in the Four Pennies called Lionel. They sang a dopey song that went "Juuu-lee-ah." It was quite a tour for both of us!

The Kinks were very gothic. Creepy and silent. They never spoke. This was long before the drunk and rowdy Kinks. They were uptight and fearful of everyone. Terrified. Underneath which there was all this weird dysfunctional family stuff going on. They hated each other. They weren't good old northern lads, like the Hollies. It was a tense London vibe. And in the middle of all this angsty London set was this weird American guy. It was all very odd. It was one of the most mixed-up tours I ever did.

The only way I could handle being on tour with all these weird people was to treat it as a sociological study. Of all these savages Gene Pitney was the most interesting specimen. I'd never met anybody like him before. He was absolutely the most pompous, self-satisfied person you could ever imagine. No humor about himself whatsoever, not one drop of irony. And I thought this was absolutely fascinating and very American. Americans are much more literal about things than we are in Europe. Gene's attitudes seemed over the top to me, like the cheap fake emotion he stirred up onstage every night. My only other experience of Americans had been Andrew's strange friends Phil Spector and Jack Nitszche, but they were like creatures from outer space, with their dark glasses and their speed. Anyway, they never *spoke!*

My final encounter with Gene was a hoot. By now I had my own flat in Knightsbridge, which I shared with Mary Allen. One of the things I insisted on having, and people thought it very strange, was pure Irish linen sheets. In summer linen sheets are wonderfully cool but it was now the dead of winter in London and bitter cold in my flat. There was no central heating, but I was tough. I'd been brought up in Brazier's Park and didn't feel the cold.

It was the end of the tour. We got back to London from Birmingham on the bus at one or two in the morning. We got undressed and I'll never forget poor Gene Pitney, taking his clothes off, slipping quickly under the covers — those beautiful Irish linens were now like sheets of ice — and as soon as he touched them he leapt six feet in the air. He hopped about the room like a man on fire. It was hilarious! Probably better to have cotton sheets with a hot water bottle in the winter, but it would never have occurred to me. Hot water bottles, that was for old people. I knew Americans had things like electric blankets, but it wasn't *my* business to make sure Gene Pitney was comfortable in my bed!

After the tour Gene went back to Connecticut and I never saw him again. It was a tour a month in those days, so when he went back I didn't give it another thought. But not too long ago, when I opened a trunk from my mother's house, in it were many letters and urgent telegrams from Gene Pitney. In one of them he says "I know you're only seventeen and I'm twenty-four." So he was a child too. Reading his letters twenty-nine years later was an odd feeling — nostalgia mixed with relief. Most of these letters paint a very clear picture of me as an insecure child under the wing of her dragon lady mother. Stuff like: "I'm sure your mother won't give you these letters if they are proofread at home." Or, "I didn't call the other night to say goodbye because of the Baroness." As if Eva were some Gorgon coiled up guarding the door to my chamber. And perhaps she was; God knows I never saw those letters.

For one brief, blissful moment I thought I saw a way out of my pop nightmare. Anthony Page, an up-and-coming director, approached me to appear opposite Nicol Wiliamson in John Osborne's new play, *Inadmissible Evidence*. It was a prestigious part without being very demanding (for much of my time onstage I would have my back to the audience). I was ecstatic. "My God, I'm actually going to be able to do something I really want to do." But my chances were immediately dashed by Tony Calder, who told me I couldn't do it. Tony naturally wasn't interested in the prestige of being in a John Osborne play at the Royal Court. It was the eighteen pounds a week I'd be getting that disturbed him. All he cared about was the money he'd be losing by not having me out on the road six days a week. Tony was very good at making me think I had to do things. I played along with it for too long and eventually I burnt out.

I was devastated the night the people came from the Royal Court and I had to tell them I couldn't do it. It was an awful night. And after that I had to go to a stupid *Ready, Steady, Go!* party.

Mick Jagger was there very drunk. Drink never suited Mick; he could never handle it. He had been trying to get my attention, but I was very sad and withdrawn. I was doing my usual bit of ignoring him, pretending not to see all the little winks and long meaningful stares, so he walked over to me, flourishing a glass of champagne, and said in a mock campy tone reminiscent of Andrew: "It's been altogether too long, Marianne, *darling!*"

"Has it?" I said in my frostiest manner.

Which only provoked him to further impishness. I had on a frock with a low-cut front. Mick came up very close to me with his glass as if he were going to propose a toast and then tipped the entire thing down my dress. It was childish, but I suppose it was the only way he could think of to get my attention.

I was already depressed and Mick's pouring the champagne down my front was the last straw. I wandered into another studio to be alone and get away from all the nonsense and in this dark and quiet room there was Keith playing the piano. Very moody and intense and completely silent. He didn't speak at all in those days. I stood there for a long time in the shadows listening to him play.

After "This Little Bird," I dumped Tony Calder too. For Gerry Bron. Bron was a straight, boring, Jewish show-biz agent. By then I'd had enough of all these exotic people. I wanted a little old fat man, preferably bald and wearing glasses. An agent from Hollywood movies about Tin Pan Alley. What had unnerved me about Andrew and Tony and that whole crew was that they were *so young*. Andrew was barely

older than I was. I wanted someone more *adult*. I thought that if you
were older it meant that you had more sense. Was I wrong on that one!
Gerry Bron was a fool, and I ended up playing the lowest dives and the
stupidest places imaginable. Tin Pan Alley indeed!

For years I was in continual litigation with these people: Andrew,
Tony, Gerry Bron. Always getting out of these things. Most were of a
*truly* basic nature:

> The expression "wearing apparel and accessories" as used
> herein shall include all items of clothing as such term is ordi-
> narily used (but not underclothing) and shall extend to hats,
> gloves, shoes, handbags, scarves. . . .

That was the whole subtext to my life in pop music: grotesque
contracts, lying, cheating, crafty legalisms, mad and bungling managers
and barbaric schedules.

I did one last tour with Roy Orbison. At some godforsaken hotel
up north Roy appeared at my door. He stood in the doorway in his
cowboy boots and shades. Black shades, black leather vest, bolo tie. The
legendary Roy Orbison. He was large and strange and mournful looking, like a prodigal mole in Tony Lama cowboy boots. In spite of his
looming presence he was curiously removed, as if he'd left himself at
home and sent a cardboard cut-out on the road.

"Hiya, Roy!" I said. "How goes it this evening?"

"Ahm in room 602 [pause], *behbeh.*"

The "baby" was tacked on almost indifferently but I knew what it
meant. There were no preliminaries. This wasn't just Roy trying to pull
me. He was a real old southern gentleman. It was just good old road
tour tradition. He was top dog and any women on the tour were his by
*droit de seigneur.* It still goes on, but in those days it was *expected.*

On the Roy Orbison tour John came up to Wigan and, on Wigan
Pier, he proposed and I accepted. The affairs with Jeremy Clyde and
Allan Clarke and Gene Pitney unnerved me. I saw myself as a good girl
and suddenly I was being very promiscuous. The convent girl reappeared. I started to think, "I'm a bad woman. I am a whore and a slut. I
better get married and then I'll be good again."

The sixties and the to-hell-with-what-they-think attitude hadn't happened yet and the big thing that came out of the sixties, feminism, wouldn't happen to me for another fifteen years. And there was John whom I loved and wanted to marry. Things were happening so fast and we were changing with them. I had been this sweet little girl whom he loved but dismissed somewhat as being very silly (and I was). And then suddenly I seemed to be someone else entirely. John knew me very well and he knew that if he asked me to marry him I would just say yes. And I've always thought it was a very good match, an ideal relationship, really, because we were so alike. We could understand each other very well. With John I never felt that I was in a foreign country, speaking to people who didn't know my language. I know now that I did the right thing. I had a child with the right man and it was the best thing I ever did.

My engagement to John Dunbar caused a great flurry in the Lilliputian world of pop, where normally nothing happens of any consequence and anything can become a major story with all the usual malarkey. Reporters asking me utterly daft questions: "Can John Dunbar sing?" Help! To protest my engagement, the bass player in Roy Orbison's band, the Candymen, suddenly went berserk and smashed up the hotel. My first demented fan!

# What's a Sweetheart Like You Doing in a Place Like This?

I DISCOVERED I was pregnant in April of 1965. I had terrible yearnings for a child, so when I got pregnant with Nicholas I was thrilled. I was harboring the somewhat fanciful delusion that getting married and having a baby would help to ground me.... Things seemed to be spinning out of control. I had a premonition that this might be my last chance. On the horizon I saw turbulence, displacement, God knows what looming up. I was determined to settle down to blissful, humdrum domesticity.

I vowed to myself that I was going to be "good." Marry John, have my baby, stop going from man to man. I desperately wanted to escape this random life. But whatever arranges human destiny apparently cared little for my plans, because on April 26 God Himself checked into the Savoy Hotel. Bob Dylan came to town wearing Phil Spector shades and an aureole of hair and seething irony.

Dylan was, at that moment in time, nothing less than the hippest person on earth. The zeitgeist streamed through him like electricity. He was my Existential hero, the gangling Rimbaud of rock, and I wanted to meet him more than any other living being. I wasn't simply a fan; I worshipped him.

I was quite aware that the tribute traditionally laid at the feet of pop stars by their female fans was sex. I was incredibly ambivalent. I told myself that I was pregnant, for God's sake, and about to be married. . . . On the other hand, John was still at Cambridge and wouldn't be back for a while. And what he didn't know *might* not hurt him. . . . So I went to see the gypsy.

I'm not even sure how I got there. Perhaps unknown forces whisked me there against my will! In any event, I found myself at the Savoy Hotel staring at the door to his room. Like a dissolve in a movie, one minute I was walking down Oxford Street and the next I was knocking somewhat trepidatiously on a mysterious blue door. Of course, with Dylan you are drawn willy-nilly into his world of encoded messages. Doors are no longer doors; they take on Kafkaesque significance. There are answers behind them.

Behind the blue door there was a room full of hipsters, hustlers, pop stars, swallow-tailed waiters, folkers, Fleet Street hacks, managers, blondes and beatniks. Some of them I knew, like Mason Hoffenberg, a friend of John's, and Bobby Neuwirth, whom I'd met on a brief trip to New York the year before. Others were familiar from *Top of the Pops* or folk grottoes I habituated.

This was a movie, all right . . . with *subtitles*. There was even a film crew, for God's sake, and they were filming *everything*. A dozen heads tracked me in a silent pan as I walked through the room. I found a corner and tried to disappear.

We all sat on the floor of Bob's room talking and drinking and playing guitars while Bob pretended none of this was happening. He would walk in and out of the room, he would sit down and type, he would talk on the phone, he would even answer incredibly stupid questions, but only if he felt like pulling that particular thing into focus. Otherwise we might as well have been invisible.

I was amazed just to be there. Here I was actually hanging out with all these *engagés* and elite bohemians. Meanwhile, I was trying to read the room as fast as I could. And what were they talking about in the holy of holies? The weather! This was the table talk of the gods obviously.

They had just come down from the north. "And the rain came down for *two days straight.*" The way he said it made it sound almost biblical. Didn't someone once tell me rain meant memory in Dylan's songs? Dylan was so cryptic that everything seemed to take on at least one other meaning. When he asked for something with which to stir his coffee, people did a fast double-take. Did he mean *spoon?*

I was completely overwhelmed by this very cool guy on lots of methedrine, and I didn't want to be the first to make a foolish move. After all, he had a reputation for being incredibly nasty. My throat was dry, my mind seized up. I mean, what if I said something *really* stupid? The gates of Eden would be closed forever. I was, naturally, unable to speak. I just sat there trying to look beautiful. If I so much as opened my mouth in this rarefied atmosphere, I was bound to sound inane. They were all so hip, so devastatingly hip. (They were also all so fucking *high.*) Every five minutes or so someone would go into the bathroom and come out speaking in tongues. *Sparks* were flying off them. I was scared to death.

I knew very well what was going on in that bathroom, but I was never invited in. I remember making a vow to myself then and there that come hell or high water one day I was going to get into that bathroom. I found all this "boys only" stuff unbelievably irritating. I'd spent most of my life wanting to be one of the boys (and did manage to end up joining the most exclusive boys club in the world!).

The only person I could carry on a conversation with was Allen Ginsberg. I liked Allen immediately. Allen, God bless him, has never been very hip. He's really uncool; always has been. He was such a relief to be with in those days, mostly because he wasn't so high. With Allen, you could have a normal discussion — the way you would in, say, a faculty lounge. That particular day, he'd just come from Czechoslovakia where, he told me, he'd been made King of the May. Then, as if explaining the Acts of Succession from the Beats to Bob, he told me:

"First time I heard Dylan was when I came back from Asia in sixty-three; Charlie Clemel in Bolinas played me 'Masters of War.'

"'And I'll know my song well before I start singing. And I'll stand in the ocean where all souls can see it.' When I heard those lines I burst into tears, and I thought: another generation, what a relief! Somebody, a soul, had risen up out of America and carried the torch.

"I first met Bob at a party at the Eighth Street Book Shop, and he invited me to go on tour with him. I ended up not going, but, boy, if I'd known then what I know now, I'd have gone like a flash. He'd probably have put me onstage with him."

But in 1965 Bob wasn't sharing the stage with anyone. Not even with a certified Beat bard like Allen Ginsberg and certainly not with his onetime lover and chief proselytizer, Joan Baez, the Lady Madonna of Folk. Apparently she had just shown up on the tour, and Bob was very grouchy about it, just sitting in the back of the hotel room and making faces. Most of the time he was courteous to her; he just didn't *talk* to her a lot. But she wasn't getting the message that things had changed between them (not too hard to imagine, given the nature of the messenger). Their bone of contention was Dylan's refusal to invite Joan out onstage to sing with him. She was having a hard time of it. But as troubled as she was, she looked absolutely beautiful with her radiant tan and her penetrating eyes. Compared to the pale sepulchral complexions of the rest of Dylan's entourage, she was glowing with health.

Singing was her way of dealing with this touchy situation. A sort of keening. Occasionally her high vibrato would get on Dylan's nerves and he would say something sarcastic. She insisted on singing her piercing tremulous versions of "Here Comes the Night" and "Go Now." Dylan moaned as she sang. Her voice had become the banner for a genteel folksinging movement that he had, by this time, developed a loathing for. At one point he held up a bottle as she sang a high note, and drawled, "Break that!" She just laughed.

The main vibe in the room emanated from Bobby Neuwirth, Dylan's somewhat daunting doppelgänger and soi-disant road manager. The supreme hip courtier, Neuwirth had given me my first joint in New York the year before. He was affable but as forbidding, if not more so, than Dylan. Dylan had a reputation for demolishing people, but when people told these stories it was really Neuwirth they meant. Neuwirth and Dylan did such a swift verbal *pas de deux* that people tended to confuse them. But the most biting commentary and crushing put-downs came from Neuwirth. And when Neuwirth got drunk he could be deadly. I never saw Dylan's malicious side, nor the lethal wit that has often been ascribed to him. I never thought of him as amusingly cruel the way I thought of John Lennon. Dylan was simply the mercurial, bemused center of the storm, vulnerable and almost waiflike.

The only person other than Allen whom I recognized as coming from the same planet as myself was the filmmaker Donn Pennebaker (whom everybody called Penny). He was making *Don't Look Back,* the first of two documentaries that together would form Dylan's celluloid testament and consolidate the Legend According to Bob.

The room buzzed and crackled with high-voltage egos all playing off each other at the court of King Bob. Apart from Allen and Penny, nobody introduced anybody to anybody else. A state of absolute coolness prevailed. Like the scene in "Ballad of a Thin Man," I half expected someone to hand me a bone. At one point Baez, whom I worshipped, picked up a guitar and began to sing "As Tears Go By." I've never heard it sound better, even by whatsisname. It quite blew me away. *Very* unlike my version! "As Tears Go By" as a folk song (it sounded like one of her records). When sung like that, the meaning is flopped: instead of being a subjective thought, the words become beautiful artifacts. Which is what folk interpreters do as a rule.

And while Baez was singing, Penny — to make conversation — turned to me and said in his ingenuous midwestern way, "Gee, I know that song from somewhere." I was too daunted by the whole scene to even attempt irony so I said, "Oh, you know that's a song I did, actually." To which Penny came back: "My God, I didn't realize that." And then someone said, "Of course, you're Marianne Faithfull." To which I said, "I am?" and everybody laughed. It was about the only funny thing I said in two weeks of hanging out at the Savoy. It may have been the *only* thing I said.

The most remarkable thing about Dylan was his rap. Stream-of-consciousness thought fragments that you just filled in (or not) as best you could. It was all that amphetamine. I wasn't accustomed to this at all. The people I knew in London smoked hash and tended to implode. You would sit in their high-ceilinged Georgian rooms for hours in complete silence except for the record player like an absent god spinning round and round with a gnomic message. Dylan was always a sacred taxt at these soporific séances. What would you *need* to say after "Visions of Johanna" or "Ballad of a Thin Man"? But here the room was filled with fantastic images colliding into one another. The absurd and the comic teetered on the edge of the genuinely enigmatic and profound, and it all ran together into one big cosmic joke.

What people saw as abrasive in Dylan was really his elliptical approach to everything. He was nothing if not a slippery subject, and he did not suffer fools gladly. His testiness came into play (mostly) with the press. A master of the anti-interview, Dylan fairly bristled at direct questions. The put-on was merely his way of *not* becoming churlish. When asked if he considered himself a poet he said: "I still can't decide whether I want to be a Pagan or a musician. First I'm one and then, bang, I want to be the other. I'm just driven crazy by this."

Day after day while I was there Dylan was constantly going over to the typewriter and pounding away. For a while he had a roll of that waxy English toilet paper in the machine. It was just the right width for song lyrics, he said. A little bit of *un hommage à Kerouac*, too, of course. Bob hunched over at the big black Remington, cigarette drooping from the side of his mouth, the very picture of feverish artistic genius *in flagrante*. In the middle of a conversation he would tear himself away and toss off a song, a poem, a new chapter of his book, a one-act play. It was a wonder to behold. How does he do it?! This practice was used, judiciously, to flabbergast the groundlings granted brief audiences. The young Mozart dashing off a sonata right before your eyes! He also used it to tune out. The Out-tuning and Seduction Machine.

For days I had been told that Bob "was working on something." I asked what (I was *meant* to ask).

"It's a poem. An epic! About *you*." Why bless his heart, I thought, he's hung up too! But you don't ever quite know with Bob; he wears his heart very close to his vest. No one was ever such a seducer as Dylan.

Within a matter of days I had been elevated to Chief Prospective Consort. There seemed to be no other rivals at all. I was the chosen one, the sacrificial virgin. Bob's soon-to-be wife, Sara Lowndes, was off in Europe somewhere (and anyway he'd given me the impression that she was just "some girl I know from somewhere"). Another one of those women who followed Dylan around; women whose souls (I assumed) had been sucked dry by breaking the taboo and copulating with the god, and who were now condemned to wander in a ghostly procession through expensive hotel lobbies: Joan Baez, Suze Rotello. Zombies of the Mystic Bob. Imagining this poor girl, Sara Lowndes (as sketched by the randy Bob), I could only picture a bedraggled graduate student who'd written a monograph on "The Masters of War," met

him at some folk grotto and gone to bed with him, and as a consequence was now a sort of Adele H. of folk rock, so hopelessly damaged
that her parents were seriously considering having her committed to
Payne Whitney.

Finally one night, when the scene began to thin out in the very
early hours of the morning, I found myself alone with Him, something
I had tried to avoid chiefly because I thought I wouldn't be able to handle it. Dylan sat down in a big overstuffed chair and stared at me for so
long that I thought I was going to dissolve and evaporate into the
smoky air of the room.

"Woudja like to hear my new record?" he asked. *Bringing It All
Back Home*. I knew it, of course; I'd bought a copy when I was on tour.
I was somewhere weird — Scarborough or Blackpool, one of those dismal English seacoast places. I had a little record player and I played it in
my hotel room, and the first thing I played was "The Gates of Eden."
My guitar player, Jon Mark, and I would play it every night after the gig
as a sort of ceremony. I did one of my psychic set-ups. Compulsively
playing it and thinking about it. I had this feeling I was going to run
into Dylan sooner or later. Didn't we all? He showed me the cover,
which was a photograph of him and Sally Grossman (manager Albert
Grossman's wife). The two of them are lounging in Albert's living room
surrounded by piles of magazines and album sleeves loaded with symbolism.

"You look very sophisticated, Bob," I told him. He seemed to like
that, and proceeded to play me the record. All these amazing songs on a
little gramophone. After every track he would ask in his urban Appalachian twang:

"Didja unnerstan what I was gettin' at? Didja know what that was
all about?"

I got quite flustered. He would repeat lines from the songs, em-
phasizing certain words, italicizing them. As if this would convey their
meaning! I don't know if he even knew what he was doing. He would
repeat a line leaning heavily on one of the words.

I realized that this was the way he delivered his songs in concert.
Perhaps this was why he often did such perverse readings of his own
songs. He wanted people to hear them again! There wasn't a great deal
of humor about the whole business, being so young. Occasionally he

would say something as if in response to a question. He would say, "They're just snapshots of the inside of your brain." Or, "When you find the tone, there's more dimensions, like Cubism." The explanations were *at least* as enigmatic as the songs. But I wasn't there solely as an exegete. I knew there was more to this than me sitting at the foot of the master, absorbing the arcana of Bob.

I adored Dylan as a prince of poets, hoped he'd be nice to me and dig me (the only possible word, that year), and that was what — miraculously — seemed to be happening. I was in heaven. Or would have been if there hadn't been all that other *stuff* whirling around.

Until it all came down on me like a lion on the fold all I thought was "Here I am in the inner sanctum. A private audience with his Serene Hipness! Bob Dylan explaining his songs to me!" But I knew there was going to be a price for this. As oblique as all this methadrine-driven, word-whirling rap was, a pass was still, I suppose, what one did.

I hadn't been at all sure before I met him that I'd find him attractive, but in person he was devastating. Proto punk hair, black leather and the *talk!* I didn't know anybody in London like that. Everyone was smoking too much hash. All that cerebral jangling was a lot sexier than I'd imagined, so it's not that I didn't find him attractive. I did. I found him very attractive indeed. I've always loved his wiry, coiled type of energy. The impeccable motley tailoring, the Spanish boots, the Rimbaud coif, the druggy shades. All that I adored. I just found him so . . . *daunting.*

I had this awful fear of being exposed as the prissy, naïve little convent girl with a thin veneer of sophistication that I actually was. Somebody like Gene Pitney was a much easier proposition because it was just very basic. Like a man would have sex. *That* I was able to do! But somebody as awe-inspiring as Dylan was terrifying. As if some god had come down from Olympus and started to come on to me. It was, I imagine, what *Leda* must have felt.

The sexual side of life, especially in the presence of the *Shekinah,* has never been easy for me to handle. It's my Primal Anxiety. Being so overwhelmed by someone that I would lose my self. This awful fear of sex + genius + fame + hipness all building in a cumulative ritual. I was terrified that I might simply vaporize when all these things came together. I was suspended between blissful adoration and abject cowardice. Typically, I lunged at the abject cowardice with both hands.

And suddenly he was cross and rejected. How could you lead me along like this? *I? Lead along?* I didn't even know what the hell was *going* on, never mind *leading* someone on! I hadn't even specifically rejected him (that I knew of). But it seemed I had transgressed the bounds of the great man's hospitality. A pop divinity had extended himself and I had shunned him. I sat there petrified as he ranted on.

"How can you do this to me?"

"I'm not doing anything to you, Bob." In my leather jacket and blond hair I should never have said the truth: "I'm pregnant and about to get married next week." That did it.

Without warning he turned into Rumpelstiltskin. He went over to the typewriter, took a sheaf of papers and began ripping them up into smaller and smaller pieces, after which he let them fall into the wastepaper basket.

"Are you satisfied now?" he asked. I was witnessing a little tantrum of genius.

With that he stormed out in a rage. I sat there pinned to my chair. He returned a moment later with renewed fury and threw me out.

"Out!"

"Excuse me?"

"This is a private room! Disappear! Now!"

The saddest thing for me was that I never got to see that poem. Maybe he tore the pages up, I reasoned, but did he, you know, tear up the *thoughts?* Did these thoughts, perhaps, end up in *songs?*

His, of course, is the classic, naughty writer's come-on to little girls. Mick was forever going around saying, "Oh yeah, that one was about you, darlin'. It's your song, babe." What could be more flattering?

One of the funniest things in talking to Allen Ginsberg — and a cautionary lesson for us all — is that Allen thinks that nearly all Dylan's songs are about *him.* Well, I never say anything. I just hold my peace. "Yes, I'm sure that one is, Allen." It's very sweet, isn't it? And there is one that really is about Allen. "Just Like a Woman."

A week after I had left the hotel room in tears the not-so-ghostly Sara Lowndes, the future Mrs. Dylan, arrived. He was very pleased with himself. Do symbolist poet-stars *get* engaged? When Sara came from Paris I remember thinking, "Oh, this could all have been very different." But I wasn't one to be put off by this. I showed up again at the Savoy. I wasn't just going to disappear from the face of the earth, especially not if I was *asked* to! Anyway, I wanted to see what she was like. She was behaving like a wife and Dylan like "the victim of her passion." Far from being this infatuated pre-Raphaelite apparition, Sara was as solid as marble. Sara didn't say much; she didn't need to.

When Sara arrived the druggie-hipster scene chilled out a bit, but not that much. Dylan carried on basically pretty much the same whether Sara was there or not.

Dylan was intrigued with Donovan. At odd moments when he didn't think anybody was watching he'd put on Donovan's "To Catch the Wind." Dylan liked the lyrics, I think, and although everybody said the tune was lifted straight from Dylan's "Chimes of Freedom," Bob didn't care. One afternoon he decided to ask Donovan over.

"There's a poet folksinger," he was telling Ginsberg. "You've gotta hear him, man, Donovan."

"You really think he has something on the ball?" This is the way Allen talked, slightly old-fashioned expressions that had been hip in high school.

"Man, he's got Poetic Genius." Initial caps. "I wantja to meet him and tell me if he's a poet or Charlie Chaplin." Allen was to be the litmus test.

For days there'd been this tiresome thing with the press: "Is Donovan the English Dylan?" It got to be such a big joke. So the first night that Donovan came to visit, Dylan decided to play a prank on him.

They'd all been to some music business affair where everybody had been given masks. And Dylan said, "We gotta put 'em on. We gotta put 'em on when he gets here. Let's fake him out, man." So we all put on these little domino masks.

Neuwirth opened the door, and this little curly head peeps in and then three or four others, beards and long hair and sheepskin jackets; Donovan's entourage. A very earnest bunch. Donovan came in, glowing. He was just such a sweet little person, very elfin and jolly. Not a bit like Bob. Donovan tried to ignore the masks, pretended he didn't see them. He must have thought it a bit strange but he wasn't going to show any astonishment. He was at the court of King Cool and he wasn't going to blow it. Perhaps he thought this was one of Dylan's eccentricities. Maybe this was the way Dylan and his crowd behaved. After dinner they all put on masks. Of course! It was perfectly believable. Anything in those days could be imagined about Dylan.

Donovan sat on the floor like everybody else. Penny was itching to shoot this scene and reached for his camera. But Dylan waved him away:

"No, no, no, not now, man."

And then Bob said, "Well, Donovan, won't you do us a tune?"

Donovan unpacked his guitar and began to play. I'll never forget it. Oh, God, it was one of the most excruciatingly embarrassing and funny scenes I've ever sat through because what Donovan proceeded to play was "Tambourine Man." It was the tune to "Tambourine Man" exactly. But Donovan had made up *new words!* It went "Oh, my darling tangerine eyes . . ." That's almost all I remember of it. A song that's never, I'm sure, ever been heard since. After halfway through, Dylan got this very wry smile on his face. Neuwirth over in the corner was cracking up. Almost everybody in the room was trying to keep a straight face because, besides Donovan and Gypsy Dave, they all knew the song well. "Tambourine Man" was on *Bringing It All Back Home.*

Donovan kept playing away, "My darling tangerine eyes, girl, won't you ramble with me down my rainbow road . . ." It was so apparent what was happening that for a moment one might have thought Donovan was putting everybody on. But the possibility of this quickly evaporated. Donovan was incapable of putting anyone on.

The suspense was nerve-racking, and finally Dylan put an end to it.

"You don't have to sing anymore of that one," he said.

Donovan stopped playing, slightly bewildered.

"You know," said Dylan, with a perfect aphoristic pause, "I haven't always been accused of writing my own songs. But actually, *that's* one I did write."

Donovan was just stunned, dumbfounded. Oh, my God, such consternation. The poor fellow almost died. Penny said later: "There's a song that was just written right off that poor cat's book. He'll never sing it again in his whole life! It was kind of a nice little song that he had, too."

By way of explanation, Donovan said, "Well, I didn't know, man. Heard it, you know... somewhere, at some festival I think it was. And thought maybe it was an old folk song."

And Dylan said, "No, it's not an old folk song *yet*."

Then one of the little gnomes who had come in with Donovan must have heard the words "old folk song" and, as if fulfilling that request, picked up the guitar. He was an Irish folksinger of a very specific type. He sang songs about nights in the fields of wheat, the salty brine, the poetry of the peat and such. Traditional songs that I loved, but that had been played too often at folk festivals.

I think he must have thought Dylan was a folksinger or that he was *still* a folksinger. He wasn't aware that there was a new Bob. Aside from Joan Baez, nobody really sang folk songs around the hotel room. That was corny stuff. Country music was the latest rage with Dylan and Neuwirth. As Neuwirth so charmingly put it: "Country music's the last authentic goddamned shit left for us to rip off."

The folksinger droned on and on and Dylan got very bored. You could always gauge the level of boredom on Dylan. It had to do with how fast his left foot shook. When it was going really fast you knew he was interested, but when it slowed down you knew you were losing him and when it just dangled there, that meant his brain was falling asleep. He never slept openly. He would kind of turn off and go some-place else.

However hip he appeared to be, Dylan was young and still very naïve in many ways. He was well read but it was selective. There were certain poets that he was obsessed with. Rimbaud, Villon. Often obscure writers like Lautréamont that he'd got into. But then there were others, like Wallace Stevens, say, or Victor Hugo, that he'd just never heard of. History for Bob was a series of blinding shafts of light. The past was a condensed block, the layers tightly compressed on top of each other so people as diverse as Shakespeare and Thomas Hardy seemed like contemporaries.

His statements had a quirky, spiraling logic to them. The more I thought about one of his comments, like "if words rhyme, they mean the same thing," the more it made sense in an archaic and pre-literate way. It was his poetic reasoning about the archaeology of words. Much of what he said was quite off the top of his head. He was generally very good at winging it, but sometimes he would trip himself up. One afternoon he was trying to explain his novel, the as-yet unpublished *Tarantula,* to a journalist. He'd written it, he told her, using William Burroughs's and Brion Gysin's cut-up technique. The woman was initially intrigued:

"Oh, what's that?" she asked. "Is it a literary theory?"

She'd obviously never heard of it and so Dylan proceeded to explain it to her, using a copy of the *Daily Telegraph* and a pair of scissors. But as soon as he started trying to assemble the scraps of newspaper, you knew he'd never actually done it. He was trying to figure out how to do it as he went along.

To change the subject Dylan turned to me and asked, "So who is this guy you're marrying? What does he do?"

And I said, "He's a poet."

"Oh, he's a poet, does he have a license? What kind of a *poe-tree* does he write? Is he a poet like Smokey Robinson or like Jeremiah or Cassius Clay? Can he write poems about monkey wrenches and atomic alarm clocks and fat black mamas?"

"No, not exactly, he's more of a —"

"Well, now, he ain't a poet, he *cain't* be if he doesn't write about stuff like that, 'cause . . ."

He began a rant about poor old John. Meanwhile, John was standing outside the Savoy in the rain.

So I said: "Why don't you ask *him,* he's right down there."

Everybody went to the window to see whom it was I had turned down Bob Dylan for. There were a lot of conversations about John waiting outside, which amused everybody. There was some discussion about what to do about my John. They were all saying, "Well, why don't we drop a bottle on his head" and nonsense like that.

Eventually Dylan met John. Rory McEwan gave a party for Dylan. McEwan was a folk singer and a friend of John's. Rory had a beautiful house and it was a very beautiful party. John came down from Cambridge for it in his horn-rimmed glasses and his tweed jacket with a copy of the *Guardian* stuffed in his pocket. This was the moment Dylan had been waiting for. He said, "Hell, he ain't nothin' but a goddamned *student*. Whadja wanna marry a *student* for? I know this type, he's gonna be the eternal student." It was supposed to be an altruistic comment on his part.

"But actually, Bob, I do want to marry a student. I love him."

He started on another tack. "How can you take a guy who wears glasses seriously? Only undertakers and college professors and grandmas and people who can't even see what's in front of their noses wear glasses. He's an intellectual jerk, that's the worst kind of jerk there is."

With avuncular solemnity Dylan told me I was making a grave mistake in marrying John. He may have been sincere, but I assumed he just wanted to go to bed.

Finally came the night of the concert at Albert Hall. I had to have an escort because Sara had arrived, so Dylan set it up that I'd go with Allen Ginsberg. And Allen was very sweet about the whole thing, wondering aloud about how he deserved his good fortune: "Oh, boy. Here I am in the high life. A pretty blond date, a free ticket to the concert in merry London and a limousine to take us there."

Flash of pulling up to the Albert Hall's back entrance. We walked in and everybody parted. This is how I remember it. Sitting up in the balcony, first circle. I think this might have been the first time I saw Anita Pallenberg and Brian Jones together. They were wandering about the Albert Hall on acid, and in their sashes and silks and feathers they looked like transformed anima-into-mock-human characters who had stepped out of a Charles Perrault fairy tale.

Dylan has always been high-strung, and at that concert he was especially tightly wound. By the end of it his nerves were very close to the surface. When he came back the next year with the Band, he was a completely different person. He was so happy, just jumping up and down. What a drag it must have been, out there all by himself with an acoustic guitar, just moaning away. Especially in England, where all the musicians he was meeting were in *groups*. One of the reasons Dylan had even *come* to England was his fascination with the Brit rock scene. The Animals, Manfred Mann, the Bluesbreakers, the Pretty Things, the Beatles, the Stones. All that boys-club stuff that makes life fun.

After the concert we all went back to the hotel. We were milling around in Albert Grossman's suite, with Grossman holding court. There was no doubt now who was the crown prince of rock; it was Bob. The

Animals and the Stones had all come to visit, serious bad boys come to pay their respects and sit meekly on the couch as the mad dauphin came in and out talking of Apocalypse and Pensacola. And now, to bestow the confirming touch, the Beatles had come to pay him hommage.

Although I knew both John and Paul quite well by this time, meeting "the Beatles" as a group was always a bit of an ordeal. On top of their Olympian fame was their scouse badgering. They would always *run* things on you. On each other, too, but mostly on other people. Anybody new into the crowd had to be ready to go through a terrible gauntlet of verbal abuse and voodoo vibes. You were never sure whether you were being tested or totally ridiculed or perhaps not being spoken to at all.

Dylan went into the room where the Beatles were sitting all scrunched up on the couch, all of them fantastically nervous (for once). Lennon, Ringo, George and Paul and one or two roadies. Nobody said anything. They were waiting for the oracle to speak. But Dylan just sat down and looked at them as if they were all just total strangers at a railway station. It wasn't so much a matter of being cool; they were too young to be genuinely cool. Like teenagers, they were all afraid of what the others might think and simply froze in each other's company.

Neuwirth walked through the room balancing a balloon on his little finger. All heads turned as he passed, as if we were at Wimbledon. It was such a funny image, all these millionaires sitting around in a circle watching Neuwirth doing some silly thing with a balloon. Just watching *anything* like children at a circus. I thought, "Jesus, how could I ever have thought these scared little boys were gods?"

Then Allen Ginsberg came in. The silence deepened. Simply by walking into the room Allen was laying himself open to ridicule, but he didn't care. Instead of trying to protect his dignity, he deliberately made himself into a target. He went over to the chair Dylan was sitting in and plonked himself down on the armrest. No one at first reacted to this, but by now the room was bristling with hostility toward Allen. The tension built and built and then John Lennon broke the silence by snarling:

"Why don't you sit a bit closer, then, dearie."

The insinuation — that Allen had a crush on Dylan — was intended to demolish Allen, but since it wasn't far from the truth anyway, Allen took it very lightly. The joke was on them, really. He burst out laughing, fell off the arm and onto the lap of Lennon, who was on the couch with his wife, Cynthia. Allen looked up at him and said, "Have you ever read William Blake, young man?" And Lennon in his Liverpuddlian deadpan said, "Never heard of the man."

Cynthia, who wasn't going to let him get away with this even in jest, chided him: "Oh, John, stop lying."

That broke the ice.

"Lovely gig, man," Lennon offered as if he were just passing through.

Dylan just rocked back and forth hypnotically in his chair. Then he said: "They didn't dig 'It's All Right, Ma.'"

"Maybe they didn't get it," said John. "It's the price of being a head of your time, y'know."

To which Dylan said, "Maybe, but I'm only about twenty minutes ahead, so I won't get far."

Dylan didn't pay much attention to the Beatles at all actually, except for John. John he adored, so hanging out with John was always good. But Paul got a very cool reception. I saw Paul come in with an acetate of a track he'd been working on. It was very far out for its time with all kinds of distorted, electronic things on it and Paul was obviously proud of it. He put it on the turntable in his eager, earnest way and stood back in anticipation but Dylan just walked out of the room. It was unbelievable. The expression on Paul's face was priceless. And it was the same way with the Stones. They'd all sit on the couch with their topsy hair, like little teddy bears devouring the room, and he'd hardly look at them. Dylan was so funny about all of them. He simply carried on as if none of them was present.

I married John Dunbar in May of 1965 in Cambridge. I was eighteen and he was twenty-two. We walked through the fields around Cambridge picking wildflowers. I had started to cry because I'd forgotten to get a bouquet and John went out and picked a big bunch of light May blossoms and gave them to me. And they had great long black thorns on them. It was all so beautiful and enchanted. But as it turned out, it was the *wrong* kind of magic. It's very bad luck, you see. May blossom belongs to Pan and is one of those bewitched flowers. It was appropriate to dress my mother in her coffin in white May blossom. But it was not appropriate to be married wearing them. Still, the wildflowers were beautiful (if not propitious) and it was a glorious day. He was great, John, whatever Bob Dylan said about him. So there.

A little piece came out about us in the *Cambridge Evening News*. I remember it because it was so silly: "Marianne will keep singing, says John." Everything comes out sounding so daft in the papers but I bet he did say it. He'd got the goose that laid the golden egg and he knew it. Never have to work again. Well, it's the ambition of any self-respecting bohemian isn't it?

And then on November 10, 1965, the light of my life was born. I looked down at Nicholas and decided that maybe there was a God, after all. I wondered how something so pure could come into such a cruel, imperfect world. Nicholas gazed back at me with the eyes of a very old soul indeed. He had the answer, but he wasn't telling.

# Courtfield Road

AM on my way to Brian and Anita's flat in Courtfield Road, carried along the river of Sloane Street before catching a taxi to Earl's Court. Smoke a couple of joints at Anita's, then on to Robert Fraser's gallery. After which . . . *something,* but what? Oh, well, it'll come to me.

It's the summer of 1966, but for me it is Year One. I've been adopted by Brian and Anita, and their flat in Courtfield Road has become my second home. I'm trying to make a beeline there, but everywhere I look there's some insane distraction. Bengalis selling scarves with magic signs on them, two buskers in Elizabethan rags playing hurdy-gurdies and tiny drums, a couple of hustlers selling knock-offs of those big plastic Biba bracelets. God, will you look at David Bailey with that little tart on his arm! Harrods looming up like a great liner, and a little farther on, Walton Street with dozens of seductive boutiques. Shop windows filled with bright Smarty colors. Miniskirts, sequined gowns, slinky thigh-high boots, brass earrings, boas. Everything sparkling, modern, dazzling.

I am trying to suppress my natural urge to enter each and every one of these shops. Of course it's my talent for dropping several thousand pounds in forty-five minutes that chills John Dunbar to the depths of his being. He never *has* been able to grasp the beauty of wretched excess, the poor darling. It should be obvious enough by now, even to me, that the more appalling the tour, the more ghastly the people involved, the easier it becomes to blow every shilling I made *doing* the damn thing.

Hmm . . . bells ringing somewhere. Probably in my head. God, what time *is* it? Five-thirty already? No, no, it can't be. Missed Deborah at El Cubano. Jesus. I've really done it this time. Must be those two dopey interviews this morning. God, did I really tell the BBC that Tom Jones was a werewolf from Aberystwyth? Why don't I *think* before I blurt these things out? They're going to think I'm crackers. Oh, who gives a flying fuck?

Who's that waving from across the street? Gerry. My manager, Gerry Bron. "What, darling? I can't hear you." Christ, better just duck in here and try on that velvet-and-pearl outfit. *Ready, Steady, Go!* tomorrow. Can't exactly be seen in this frumpy thing. I'm *already* late, I tell myself, so what the hell. . . .


Courtfield Road, Brian Jones and Anita Pallenberg's apartment off Gloucester Road during the heady Paint-It-Black summer of 1966. It's almost thirty years since I last set foot in the place. A veritable witches' coven of decadent illuminati, rock princelings and hip aristos. In my mind's eye I open the door. Peeling paint, clothes, newspapers and magazines strewn everywhere. A grotesque little stuffed goat standing on an amp, two huge tulle sunflowers, a Moroccan tambourine, lamps draped with scarves, a pictographic painting of demons (Brian's?) and decorously draped over a tatty armchair, a legendary leg — Robert Fraser's, I should guess. There's Brian in his finest Plantagenet satins, fixing us with vacant, fishy eyes. On the battered couch an artfully reclining Keith is perfecting his gorgeous slouch. The hand gesturing in the manner of Veronese could only belong to the exquisite Christopher Gibbs, and hovering over the entire scene with single-lens-reflex eye, the invisibly ever-present photographer, Michael Cooper. At the center, like a phoenix on her nest of flames . . . the wicked Anita. I'm here somewhere, too, looking up with hashish-glazed eyes from the Moroccan rug.

A dissolute "Night Watch" of mid-sixties swinging London. Hipness, decadence, and exquisite tailoring such as England had not seen since the Restoration of Charles II. We were young, rich and beautiful, and the tide — we thought — was turning in our favor. We were going to change *everything,* of course, but mostly we were going to change the rules. Unlike our parents, we would never have to renounce our youthful hedonism in favor of the insane world of adulthood.

Now here was a climate to which I was ideally suited! I'd always had a hard time with adults. What exactly were they? Early on I made study of them, mistakenly assuming I would someday be one. From what I could observe of my mother, the most salient features of adulthood were smoking and drinking. I knew I could manage those with no trouble at all (I'd always been a quick study). It was the more arcane aspects of adulthood that eluded me: sex, money, social life, parenthood.

Consequently, at a time when my life as a grown-up should have begun, I was still very much a child. And everything that has happened to me, it's as if it happened to a child. All my attempts at growing up were really no more than a child's playing make-believe. Convent girl reading forbidden books in the loo, budding bohemian, pop star, wife, mother. Between the ages of seventeen and nineteen I shed any number of old lives and grew new ones overnight without any of them seeming quite real to me; I discarded them as cavalierly as a child who moves from one game to another. Pursued in earnest, any one of these might have led to a reasonably happy life. But then again, I wasn't interested in happiness. I was looking for the Holy Grail.

And so it was that in the summer of 1966 I set out in search of my next incarnation. I was alert for any sign. Anything that remotely resembled my ongoing fantasy life would qualify, and Courtfield Road was certainly that. Ever since my days at the convent my secret heroes had been decadents, aesthetes, doomed Romantics, mad bohemians and opium-eaters. I devoured books by De Quincey, Swinburne and Wilde. I cursed myself that I had been born too late while secretly believing one never is. I knew that out there somewhere (Chelsea was the most likely spot) there was a cabal of like-minded souls. And here, in the circle around Brian, I'd found the very thing.

Desultory intellectual chitchat, drugs, hip aristocrats, languid dilettantes and high naughtiness. I knew I was on my path! The antique dealer Christopher Gibbs was a Wildean aesthete come to life, plucked straight from *The Picture of Dorian Gray*. I guess they all were a bit like that: gallery owner Robert Fraser, young Sir Mark Palmer and Tara

Browne, the Guinness heir who "blew his mind out in a car." *Fin de siè-cle* Kings Road dandies with Smokey Robinson on the turntable. And Christopher and Robert, being gay, were even more extravagant.

It was at Courtfield Road that I got to know Anita Pallenberg. You can't begin to imagine what she was like in those days! She was the most incredible woman I'd met in my life. Dazzling, beautiful, hypnotic and unsettling. Her smile — those carnivorous teeth! — obliterated everything. Other women evaporated next to her. She spoke in a baffling dada hipsterese. An outlandish Italo-Germanic-Cockney slang that mangled her syntax into surreal fragments. After a couple of sentences you became hopelessly lost. God, did she just *say* that? She was either putting you on or this was the Delphic oracle. You were on your own. It was all part of her sinister appeal.

I was utterly in her thrall and would have done anything for her. When I told her some years ago how in love with her I was at the time, Anita nodded like some great old Cheshire cat being brought her tribute. Another rat tail to nail up on the barn door.

How Anita came to be with Brian is really the story of how the Stones became the Stones. She almost single-handedly engineered a cultural revolution in London by bringing together the Stones and the *jeunesse dorée*. Like many things in that era, it all began with a party. Through her boyfriend, the painter Mario Schifano, Anita had become friendly with Lord Harlech's children, Jane, Julian and Victoria Ormsby-Gore, and through them she had got to know a group of young aristocrats and wealthy dilettantes. In this circle were Robert Fraser, Sir Mark Palmer, Christopher Gibbs and Tara Browne. They were all infatuated with pop stars.

The *jeunesse dorée* were in awe of this pop kingdom where young girls threw themselves at the feet of yobbish dandies with guitars. Rock stars who were already parodying the decadent nobility of the past in their foppish clothing and manners were equally impressed by these young hip aristos. A union of the two later seemed inevitable. But no one had the foggiest idea how to go about it. Except for our Anita.

Anita happened to be in Germany working as a model when the Stones toured there in the autumn of 1965. She got backstage without much trouble and in no time at all had the whole group salivating over her. She immediately attached herself to Brian Jones. This was either love (it was) or a momentary lapse in Anita's otherwise impeccable social instincts. But it's not hard to see what happened. Brian was in the habit of telling people, far beyond the point when anyone who knew better would believe it, that he was "the leader of the group." Anita, being a foreigner and an outsider, took him at his word. She returned in triumph to London, introducing Brian to Robert Fraser and Christopher Gibbs and the rest of the circle as the "head of the Rolling Stones."

The Stones and these hip aristos were a perfect match for each other. The Stones came away with a patina of aristocratic decadence that served as a perfect counterfoil to the raw roots blues of their music. This *contetemps* suffuses their classic albums from *Beggars Banquet* to *Exile on Main Street*, and it transformed the Stones from pop stars into cultural icons.

I began going round to Courtfield Road a year after Nicholas was born. I had developed an irrepressible need to get out of the flat. I was bored, I felt trapped and I was exhausted. In the three years between Adrienne Posta's party where I met Andrew Oldham until I ran off with Mick Jagger, I made four singles and two albums, went on three tours, did six weeks in Paris at the Olympia, not to mention countless interviews, *Top of the Pops* and on and on.

Before I started working in pop music I was seventeen and having a good time, going to parties, hanging about in coffee bars, the usual seventeen-year-old stuff. And nice as it was to be "discovered" and become a pop star, I couldn't shake the feeling that I had missed something. My marriage to John had been a shotgun wedding, naturally. In 1964 if you got pregnant you got married. Our honeymoon, although spent in Paris, was anything but conventional. The only people we saw during our week in Paris were Allen Ginsberg, Lawrence Ferlinghetti, and Gregory Corso. Great slangy, mantra-slathering beatniks careening around our hotel room, throwing up, spilling cheap rosé all over the place and ranting on about the Rosenbergs, Rimbaud, Tangier and buggery. Gregory's idea of breakfast was to mix up a Brompton Cocktail — half morphine and half cocaine — and pass out on the floor of the Hotel Louisiana.

You might reasonably ask why we were sharing our honeymoon

suite with a bunch of drug-addled beatnik poets, but I didn't. Mostly we were doing it because it was what John wanted to do, and of course it *was* wonderful. But life back home at Lennox Gardens was more of the same. John's idea of a normal routine was to put liquid methedrine in his coffee in the morning before going off to work at Indica Bookstore with Miles. The bookstore was on the ground floor and John's gallery was in the basement.

My exquisitely decorated nest had turned into a crash pad for talented layabouts. American junkies, actually. This was when you could still get British pharmaceutical heroin legally, and that was the principal reason all these guys came to London. Mad types like Mason Hoffenberg would show up at our house and end up staying for months at a time. Mason had popped in to see John for a few days around Christmastime the previous year and the following May he was *still there,* draped about the house and conked out in various states of stupefaction. He was a wicked mimic with an undepletable store of salty anecdotes. An enormously funny man — he had written *Candy* with Terry Southern — and wonderfully good company. I might have found it all a lot more amusing if I had been allowed to join in, but that's not the way John liked it. Life was quietly becoming nightmarish.

I would get up in the morning, there'd be no heat, I'd have to step over several people crashed in the living room. I'd go into the kitchen to warm up a bottle for Nicholas and find the draining board strewn with bloody needles. One morning I went round the whole flat and collected all these jacks, these little heroin pills, hidden all over the place — there were hundreds of them — and I flushed them down the toilet. I just couldn't take it anymore. But I stuck it out for two years, trying to lead my normal middle-class life as best I could for as long as I could. In this bohemian/druggie household I had been badly miscast as mother-angel-girlfriend-wife and blessed Virgin Mary. An insufferable role that I finally began to hate with a passion. I was bored, I was lonely, I had begun to find John and his cerebral junkies tiresome. And all around me was the centrifugal whirl of the sixties. I wanted to see what all the fuss was about.

I've always liked going out on my own — you can maneuver better — and that's just what I started to do. I'd leave John at home with Nicholas and the nanny and his drugs and his friends, and I'd go off to *my* drugs and *my* friends. I loved getting dressed up and putting on my makeup with John quietly fuming. He knew he couldn't really stop me from going out, but that didn't stop him from trying. One night he threw all my jars of makeup against the wall. That was actually one of the main reasons I left him!

Jealousy played little part in all this. His main objection was my extravagance. Every time I left the house I would spend an absolute fortune. Sure, I kept the house going but everything else I made — and I made a lot of money — I spent on myself. I was mean and I was petty when it came to money. John was running an art gallery and when it went bust, I didn't lift a finger to help. I didn't behave like a human being at all. I was a shopping addict. My first really serious addiction.

My first stop of the evening was always Brian and Anita's. Keith Richards practically lived there, too; he and Brian were fast friends in those days. Every day Keith would walk all the way from his flat in St. John's Wood, about four miles, into Gloucester Road. After he broke up with Linda Keith, his girlfriend at the time, he took to spending even more time there. Supposedly he no longer had a place to stay, but I always suspected it was to get closer to Anita. Keith just exuded lonely bachelorhood, and naturally Brian and Anita always let him crash there.

The Courtfield Road flat itself was a grungy place. Mattress on the floor, sink piled high with dirty dishes, posters half falling down. But Christoper had insisted Anita buy it. "You simply *have* to get it, darling. With a little tarting up it could be absolutely ravishing." And of course it *could* have been. It was your classic artist's studio. Very high ceilings, skylights, huge windows and one very large room with a winding staircase up to a minstrels' gallery.

The place had definite possibilities, but we all knew that absolutely *nothing* was ever going to be done. During the entire time Brian and Anita lived there it remained exactly as it was the day they moved in, with the exception of a few sticks of furniture and a couple of bizarre, moth-eaten stuffed animals from a movie Anita had done in Germany.

Brian would sit on the floor, very high, and tell you what it was going to look like when he got it together. Anita and Brian were like two beautiful children who had inherited a decrepit palazzo. Every day they would dress up in their furs and satins and velvets and parade about and invite people over, and we would all sit on the floor and talk about the fantastic things we would do with the kingdom if only we could.

There were two secret rooms, which added to the flat's playhouse quality. A room below the kitchen that you got to through a hatch in the floor and an attic that you reached by means of a metal ladder you could pull down. This attic was a wonderful gothic-looking storage space where books and clothes and Brian's train magazines were stored.

A couple of times I dropped by Courtfield Road and found Brian there all by himself. He invited me in with a courtly flourish. Brian had lovely manners and a little whispery voice. He was so intelligent and would become very animated when the subject interested him. Trains, Ingmar Bergman movies, anything magical. Like a lot of people at the time, myself included, he was convinced there was a mystic link between Druidic monuments and flying saucers. Extraterrestrials were going to read these signs from their spaceship windows and get the message. It was the local credo: Glastonbury, ley lines and intelligent life in outer space. I've forgotten exactly *what* it was we believed, but we believed it fiercely! And if little green men were going to contact *anybody* on the planet it would have to be us, wouldn't it?

In the middle of one of these conversations, Brian began coming on to me out of the clear blue. I had the oddest feeling he was simply being polite. I was in his flat, I was a pretty girl . . . and he was a Rolling Stone, making it almost *de rigueur* that he make a pass at me. It was the new sexual politesse. And I for my part thought, "Oh, he's making a play for me. I really should let him." I figured that was what a flower child did. Hippie etiquette. You just sort of went along, didn't you?

I didn't really fancy Brian, and I was truly terrified of Anita. But Anita unfortunately was out of town and Brian and I, needless to say, were both very high. So after several large spliffs and what I gathered was courtship patter (involving the *Flying Scotsman,* Mary Wells, William Morris wallpaper and Tantric art) Brian led me up the little staircase to the minstrels' gallery. We lay down on a mattress and he unbuttoned my blouse. But after a bit of groping about, it just fizzled out. He was a wonderfully feeble guy, quite incapable of real sex. And of course he was doing a lot of Mandrax, which rendered him even more wobbly than he already was. Brian only had so much energy.

Every once in a while, Mick would drop in at Courtfield Road. Very fastidious always, with an absolute *horror* of bohemian living. The sink full of dirty dishes so appalled him he could never stay long. Mick's visits were of an almost proprietal nature. He'd come by sort of to inspect everything, see that all was going along well with the Firm, smoke a joint and split.

Mick and Brian were always far more interested in the power shifts in the group than Keith. But of course it was whoever allied himself with Keith who would have the power. The balance in the group was completely different from what it was later to become. The guitar players, Brian and Keith, were inseparable, with Mick and Andrew Oldham off in the other corner. They were all quite far from Their Satanic Majesties or whatever it is they are supposed to have become. Their personae were gradually forming out of a blend of blues mythology and Kings Road *noblesse oblige*. Like boys, playing in suits of armor shortly before a voice out of the clouds comes and tells them, "Thou shalt be Princes of Darkness."

One of the great attractions of Courtfield Road for me was getting high. I'd only recently started smoking hash but I couldn't smoke at home because John — an incredible piece of drug chauvinism, this — wouldn't permit me to. People shooting up all over the house and I wasn't allowed to roll a joint! I never actually went to John and said, "Let me try what you're doing, let me have a joint," because I knew damn well John would never go for it. It was a men's club that I couldn't join. I was the wife and the mother and the golden goose. I was doing three gigs a night in Manchester and coming back with thousands of pounds — in cash. John was not one to screw *that* up.

The entertaining at Courtfield Road was of the most basic kind. Joint-rolling, mainly. *Endless* joint-rolling. It was still quite a novelty and we would smoke until we were obliterated. Really fascinating stuff when you're eighteen. Every thought twined about itself so many times there was no way of articulating it, consequently very little was ever said.

At about ten o'clock at night everyone would be famished and we'd stagger out to Alvaro's for some wonderful pasta. But once we got there we'd be so stoned we could barely manage more than a mouthful. I'd stare at the exquisite china and watch the tiny dragons crawl over the fettuccine while Anita and Robert talked about shoes and art in Italian.

One of the best things about visiting Anita and Brian was watching them get ready to go out. What a scene! They were both dauntless shoppers and excessively vain. Hours and hours were spent putting on clothes and taking them off again. Heaps of scarves, hats, shirts and boots flew out of drawers and trunks. Unending trying on of outfits, primping and sashaying. They were beautiful, they were the spitting image of each other and not an ounce of modesty existed between the two of them. I would sit mesmerized for hours, watching then preening in the mirror, trying on each other's clothes. All roles and gender would evaporate in these narcissistic performances where Anita would turn Brian into the Sun King, Françoise Hardy or the mirror image of herself.

She loved him very much, but there was some ugly stuff going on between them. There were often bruises on her arms. No one ever said anything. What would there be to say? We all knew it was Brian. Anita is not the sort of feminine, confiding person who invites speculation into her private life. It would have been a point of honor on her part *not* to say anything. Anita wanted at all costs to be considered invincible. And she always seemed to know exactly what she was doing.

I think I knew very clearly how to detach even then. We were all doing so many drugs you had to be a bit careful what you focused on or you would become completely obsessed. It sounds a bit brutal, but as long as I wasn't the one being beaten up I didn't care. I was very, very self-involved, and I was walking a fucking tightrope myself.

When I first met Brian he was on one of his brief upswings, but even during this manic phase a doomed look began to set in his face. Inner demons had begun eating away at that Renaissance angel's head.

Whatever was wrong with Brian began a long time before; you have only to look at childhood pictures of Mick, Keith and Brian to see it. After looking at snapshots of a little cheerful Mick and a strong, very tough little Keith, to suddenly come upon Brian's baby picture is quite startling. A jowly, miserable child is looking up at you with exactly that expression of helpless victimization he gave off in the last year of his life.

Brian was a mess. Neurasthenic and hypersensitive. Twitchy. The slightest thing would set him off. He would let things gnaw at him and he would *brood*. This paranoiac condition worsened, naturally, on acid. Everybody would be laughing and looning about, and Brian would be over in the corner all crumpled up. It's Anita's belief that Brian never recovered from his first trip. But he *embraced* his horrors, as if on acid he was finally able to confront his afflictions in a palpable form.

Drowning voices in the pipes, traffic noises turning into sinister conversations. We've *all* heard these things on acid, God knows. Nevertheless, it's not too cool to announce that your appliances are plotting against you. For Brian these thoughts were so incessant that he couldn't help himself. Brian simply verbalized what everyone else was thinking. Things I, for one, was thinking! But these outbursts left him open to ridicule. And they *all* taunted him.

Keith would ask: "It's the snakes again, is it, Brian?" Then to us in a stage whisper: "The snakes in the wiring, they're talking to Brian." Gales of laughter.

Poor Brian was just somewhat uncool. He could summon coolness up, but fundamentally he wasn't cool at all. His was a false cool. Keith, on the other hand, really *was* cool, ice cool, always. And he hasn't changed at all. He's gotten more and more strange looking and developed this grand desperado carapace, but inside Keith is not unlike his twenty-two-year-old self. He has a wickedly twisted sense of humor that on acid could become quite diabolical. We'd be out on the balcony and he'd whisper to Anita: "Go on, darling, jump why don't you?" But she would turn with that wonderful smile of hers and tell him: "You little fucker, what are you trying to do?"

Keith was gorgeous in those days. When I think how he looked then, how beautiful he was — and pure. Long before I got to know him, I had a huge crush on him. For years. He was the epitome of my ideal of the tortured Byronic soul. It was quite clear even then that he was a genius. He isn't a bit shy now, but when I first met him he was agonizingly shy and painfully introverted. He didn't talk at all. I mean all that stuff that Mick did, like trying to make me sit on his lap, Keith would rather have died than do anything like that.

Mick and Keith both developed their tabloid personas while they were on the road. Mick became the grand seigneur and the great gentleman. And Keith developed this bravado. The pirate who sailed with Captain Kidd. Arrr!

\*　\*　\*

One of the things Brian liked to do when he was high was to make tapes. He'd record all night long and then in the morning erase everything.

Out of all the frenetic activity that went on, only one song, as far as I know, resulted during the entire time I was at Courtfield Road and that was "Ruby Tuesday." It was Brian's swan song. Jekyll and Hyde. At one point he began to paint a mural of a graveyard on the wall behind the bed. Just above the pillows was a large headstone. He never got around to writing his name on it, but you knew that the headstone was for him.

Today you would put anybody in Brian's shaky condition straight into a hospital. But I don't honestly think it crossed anybody's mind to "seek professional help." And he, of course, would never have accepted it. We saw ourselves as the vanguard of the new era. The admission that one of the elite was mentally unbalanced might have endangered the whole Children's Crusade before it had even got started. And the fact that Brian was a self-indulgent and brittle monster didn't help in eliciting sympathy when he began to unravel.

I remember one particularly harrowing scene. There was no bell at Courtfield Road, so in order to get into the flat you had to shout up. Brian or Anita would throw the keys down or go down and open the door. One day we were all at the flat, Keith, Brian, Anita, myself and one or two other people. We were all quite stoned and suddenly we heard people outside on the pavement calling up. But it wasn't the usual hippie growl, "Brian, open the fuckin' door, man!" It was two troubled-sounding voices, a man's and a woman's, calling up. We all went out on the balcony to see who it was.

There down below was Brian's old girlfriend with her two-year-old baby, Julian, and her father. She was raising the baby up in the air in a classic gesture of supplication, asking Brian for help, begging him. She wanted child support and the baby was very obviously Brian's. "It's your kid, Brian, you know it is. We're really in a bad way, we need some help. Please!" All with the father chiming in: "You bloody do the right thing by her, boy, y'hear!"

And Brian and Anita just peered down on them as if they were some inferior species. Foppish aristocrats in their finery jeering at the *sans culottes* below. Upstairs everyone was *laughing* about it. It was so appalling, like something out of a Mexican folktale. But Anita and Brian seemed to enjoy every minute of it.

# Colston Hall

THERE were lots of things I could have done at the age of nineteen that would have been more healthy than becoming Mick Jagger's inamorata. In the end it doesn't matter that hearts got broken and that we sweated blood. Maybe the most you can expect from a relationship that goes bad is to come out of it with a few good songs.

It all began quite inauspiciously with a casual invitation from Brian and Keith to see the Stones play at Colston Hall in Bristol. I drove down in my new Mustang, Mustang Sally (the Wilson Pickett song had just come out). Keith and Brian met me at the stage door and took me backstage. Ike and Tina Turner were on the same bill and in the hallway outside the Stones' dressing room Mick was getting lessons in the Sideways Pony from Tina Turner (much to the amusement of the Ikettes). Mick could dance, but compared to Tina he was, well, spastic. Black dance steps weren't something that came to him easily. Learning the Sideways Pony was for Mick like learning a *pas de deux*. He *is* English, after all.

"On the *two*, honey, on the *two*." Tina would demonstrate a few steps and Mick would try to follow along. "Let's try it again. One, *two*, three four five. . . . God! Mick, you're scaring me!"

Brian and Keith were standing in a corner giggling (and not exactly trying to hide it). They were bluesmen from England's mental delta, after all, and thought Mick was a jerk for getting so intense about this dance-step stuff — show-biz fluff that the real musos would despise. But it didn't rattle Mick at all. He was very good humored about the whole thing. When Tina rolled her eyeballs at Mick's flatfootedness, he put his hand to his head in mock desperation and said, "Does this mean I won't be black in the next life?" And Tina said, "Are you sure you *want* to be?"

After Ike and Tina went on, I stood backstage . . . watching Mick watching Tina. Then I decided to go catch the rest of the show from the front. Such a blast of energy! That flawless mix of precision and funk erupting like a tropical heat wave in this dreary port. The audience got into Ike and Tina okay; they felt the heat, they moved, they wiggled and jiggled. But in an odd way it didn't touch them personally; it was a novelty thing.

When the Stones came on, it was another story altogether. The audience caught fire. I had seen a lot of groups drive a lot of audiences crazy — but this was something I'd never seen. It was on another level entirely. Darker, more fanatical. And vaguely menacing.

Almost from the first notes of "I'm a King Bee" an unearthly howl went up from thousands of possessed teenagers. Girls began pulling their hair out, standing on the back of their seats, pupils dilating, shaking uncontrollably. It was as if they were on some strange drug that propelled and synchronized them. Snake-handling frenzy buzzed through the hall. Cases of clinical Dionysian mass hysteria were breaking out everywhere. Mick effortlessly reached inside them and snapped that twig. He knew exactly how to locate the North Africa of the teenage cranium. I was an infidel at a ceremony that only those of the true faith could fathom. I had lost all my bearings. I was on a beach in Tunisia surrounded by cannibalistic urchins, I was in the *Village of the Damned* unable to think of a brick wall. But I felt in no danger since I was, of course, quite invisible. It was not *I* they wished to tear limb from limb, it was Mick. Mick was their Dionysus. He was the dancing god.

While the other Stones stood rooted monolithically to the ground like Easter Island statues, Mick whirled about the stage. A slinky mod Frankenstein monster — lurching, jerking, writhing, convulsing — like a marionette being zapped every few seconds by a jolt of electricity.

Through these contortions he flawlessly telegraphed the whole Stones posture — swaggering, sullen, arrogant, androgynous. And you got it entirely from Mick's *dancing*, since the band was made all but inaudible by the ululating teenage girls.

After the concert my roadie went off in the Mustang and I stayed on at the Ship Hotel. I didn't book a room, I just went up to Mick's with Brian and Keith. Michael Cooper was working for Roman Polanski at the time and he'd brought down a print of *Repulsion*, the film Polanski had just finished editing. This was Michael's great talent, making all the connections — Polanski, the Stones, the hip aristos, Pop artists. It was at just that point before the Stones became the be-all and end-all. It was all still so hip that only Michael and Robert and Christopher really *knew*.

We all sat around and watched *Repulsion*. I smoked many joints and became extremely stoned. I was speechless and unable to move. Everybody was quite high, actually, and the film was so strange that we all watched it in a reverent silence.

There were a lot of girls in the room and there was a rather obvious business going on of who was going to sleep with whom. People began pairing off. One by one they all left to go to bed or hooked with someone or got bored and wandered out, and then there was just myself and this one other girl left in the room with Mick. She was one of the Ikettes and she really sat it out. I was still sitting there, I think, because I couldn't move. And anyway I didn't have anywhere to go: my car had gone off, I told myself, I hadn't booked a room, you know, that type of thing. Eventually the Ikette got up and left. I was left with Mick and that, as they say, was that.

We started chatting about Roman Polanski. I heard myself saying that I thought Polanski was a "magus." The words just hung in the air, the way they do when you're very stoned.

After a long pause Mick said: "It's one of the things I'm quite interested in right now."

"Excuse me?"

"Oh, y'know, *disturbed states of mind*, that kind of thing."

"Hmmm . . . what do you mean, exactly?" This was something I'd learned from John: If you don't understand something you insist they define their terms.

"Oh, y'know, the *pressures of modern life,* people going off the deep end."

"Like Bob Dylan. . . ."

"Yeah, but that's 'is *specialty,* innit, Desolation Row? We're just *strolling* past Bedlam, we don't actually live there yet!"

It was already dawn. We'd been circling each other that long, but I still didn't know what I really wanted to do. I found that moment where you're about to have sex so difficult, always have. It's just excruciating for me. So to put it off a bit, I said, "Let's go for a walk. . . ." And we went out and walked about in a park that was near the hotel.

I didn't know Mick *at all,* and my way of ascertaining whether he was all right or just a jerk was to ask him a lot of questions about King Arthur.

"Do you remember the name of Arthur's sword?"

"Come forth from the stone, Excalibur! I practiced that bit quite a lot actually in me backyard in Dartford using a wooden sword and a cardboard box."

"Have you ever been to Stonehenge?"

"Yeah, went with me mum and dad when I was little. All I remember is a lot of grown-ups standing around saying how in the world did they get *that* up *there?*"

"Yes, but how did they do it, do you think?"

"Druidic Department of Works. Merlin, wasn't it? They say the crafty old bloke transported the stones all the way from Wales by magic, but it probably just looked like magic, you know, some sort of prehistoric engineering. Maybe he liked saying 'Oh, I did it with a *wand.*' Sounds much better than saying 'The point of leverage of an object suspended above the angle of momentum. . . .' "

I remember asking Mick if he happened to know anything about the Holy Grail, and I have to admit he ran with the ball.

"The Holy Grail . . . let's see . . . Joseph of Arimathea. Isn't he the one that lost the damn thing? Supposed to be still somewhere in England."

"What was the name of that knight that Guinevere deserted King Arthur for?"

He paused and looked at me and grinned, "Sir Lancelot du Lac, was it? Am I going to pass my A-levels, Marianne? What do you think?"

It *was* quite ludicrous but that's how we were then. You would ask your date, "Do you know Genet? Have you read À *rebours?*" and if he said yes, you fucked him.

It was sunrise and my feet had got wet in the dew. Then when we got back to the room I remember he unlaced my boots and put them to dry by the heat. He was really sweet that night. I was completely moved by his kindness. And then we made love. And then I left. But, of course, I was beginning to think, "This guy is pretty *amazing!*"

A few days later I took off for Positano. I'd rented a villa so Nicholas and I could spend a few weeks in the sun with our nanny, Diana. Pat, my roadie, came too, of course. Just a couple of days before we left I ran into a black model, Kelly, in a boutique off Oxford Circus and we had a long chat. We liked each other immensely and quite on a whim I invited her to come with us. She paused for a few seconds and then went home and packed.

On my way to Positano I stopped for a few days in Paris. Awaiting me was a heartrending letter from John saying how wrong he'd been, begging me to come back. So uncharacteristic of him. The only way he could say these things he never said the entire time we were married was to write it. Wonderful letter. I threw it out the window.

After we'd been there a few days Kelly asked if she could invite her boyfriend, who was in Paris. He was a model, too, also American, and she thought I'd really get on with him. Of course. The boyfriend came and he *was* gorgeous and I did get on fabulously with him. The first night he was there we made love on the terrace under the stars. To this day Kelly has never spoken to me again. I don't really blame her, I suppose, but it was Positano, there was a full moon, he was beautiful. In those days that was my idea of extenuating circumstances.

Upon arriving in Positano I had been quite flattered to find there was a stack of messages from Mick, and after Kelly had left I had a lot of time on my hands to think about him. Something had been set in motion, but I wasn't quite sure what it was. Although I loved being unattached, I was very frightened of it. My career was beginning to pall on me. "Counting" was the record I had out at the time and I was thoroughly sick of it. I was going through one of those periods where I was seriously fed up with the whole business. This pop music thing had become a horrible millstone. It was just grinding on and on. One of the things I'm not very proud of (but I know is true): I was looking for a way out of my life, and Mick presented me with it.

Here I was with little Nicholas, married to an unworldly man who never made a penny. I was supporting us all by myself — something I never much cared for. And here was Mick being very attentive to me and romantic and courtly.

I remembered him coming round with Andrew when I was living at Lennox Gardens one winter. They dropped in for a cup of coffee. It was winter and I had no central heating and it was *freezing* cold; there was one little electric fire in the house. I hardly knew Mick at this point and I could see he was incredibly shocked and actually *touched* by my living conditions. And being the great romantic he is and really *was* then . . . I could see he was the kind of man that could *feel* that stuff, could empathize with me. *How terrible! This lovely girl with a baby.* I remember being amazed at how considerate he was, and that he would *show* it. John was never like that. He was much too cool and hip and arrogant to show his feelings.

But it was all incredibly odd, really, ending up with Mick. It was so out of character, I now realize, for him to choose me — given what I believed in and the way I was. Especially in comparison with what kind of woman he *thought* he was getting! Mick was young and very naïve. He may have been under the illusion that I actually *was* the slightly ditzy, aristocratic, virginal child-troubadour that Andrew Oldham and Andy Wickham had cooked up.

I heard somewhere that Mick had really wanted Julie Christie and when he couldn't get her, he settled for me. Who knows where that came from! Yet somehow it sounds quite real to me. It has to do with Mick's Dolly Fixation and goes back, no doubt, to the image of me that Andrew had invented. I remember being surprised that Mick didn't see through it.

Mick could be wonderfully nice when he wanted to be and I really thought I wanted to be with someone who would pamper me for a change. Living with John had been very trying because of, well, the way he was. He was incredibly selfish. Coming directly from this scene, I thought Mick was a genuine haven. Mick was affectionate, interesting, funny and very attentive. He called me *constantly*. He wasn't fucked up like Brian. You could actually lead a life with Mick, and let's face it, there was no way I could've gotten off my treadmill if I hadn't gotten involved with Mick. Once I became Mick's girlfriend I no longer had to work, not for the money anyway. I could do *Three Sisters* for just eighteen pounds a week and not give a damn.

I had brought one of their records with me to Italy. It was *High Tide and Green Grass*. I played that a lot. And I wonder if I didn't almost talk myself into Mick, the way you can, you know, with love. Invent it and then put it into practice. And every time I put on *High Tide and Green Grass* Mick would call. It was uncanny. Perhaps it really was fate, I began to tell myself. I didn't have the wit to really think things through. I couldn't imagine asking myself, "Well, what could be the *dis*advantages of this?" I never gave it a thought. And why should I? Did anybody?

Still . . . from the very beginning one part of me knew that I was involving myself in a somewhat curious situation. I had no idea what was going on, it was just an inkling I got of a very strong sexual under-current. Obviously I knew Mick had *that* side to him. Because of Andrew, really. He and Andrew were birds of a feather. Mick was always borrowing bits of business from Andrew. And somehow, I can't remember how, it sort of just filtered through that Andrew wasn't entirely heterosexual. In those days the concept of bisexuality wasn't all that familiar (especially to me). I knew Andrew wasn't homosexual, but on the other hand, he was obviously blurring the lines. Flamboyantly so. He was camp and he wore makeup at a time when this was still very unusual. It threw me for a loop.

So I think I knew in some part of my mind that Mick was bisexual, as well. But what I somehow thought that *meant* was that he would be nicer to me. "Real men" scared me, but Andrew and Mick felt safe and easy to be around.

I flew back from Positano and left Diana and Pat and Nicholas to drive the Mustang back across the Alps. I'd been away for a couple of months and on my first night back in London I checked into the Mayfair Hotel. This was a night out. I was free.

I went up to my room and called Brian's flat. Anita was away. Brian and Keith and Tara were there. They were delighted to hear from me; they would be over to get me in a matter of minutes. I may have been just a little bit naïve about all this, but I thought they all wanted to be with me because I was such fun and one of them. Of course, they were all wondering when and if they were going to have sex with me. That's the way things go. So they came over, picked me up and we all went back to Brian's flat where we promptly took acid. It was very good acid, Brian had got it from Robert who had got it from the CIA.

Keith, Brian and Tara lay around on sofas in exquisite clothes from various raids on Hung On You, Granny Takes A Trip and the Chelsea Antique Market. Giggling euphoria took over as the acid came on. How astonishing they all look, I barely managed to think, just before truly drastic alterations began to take place. Every thought I had took on a physical dimension. Molecules breaking up. One rarely gets to see one's friends in such *detail*. Subatomically. Great! It's something I've always hoped I'd be granted: second sight. Nothing was hidden from me. They were becoming transparent, as if I'd put on X-ray specs. Their true natures were being bared, their spirit selves. And, along with this — almost simultaneously — I saw enactments of their past lives. Tiny, mercurial operas. They, Keith, Brian, Tara — I was not surprised to learn — had existed throughout history.

In these soul genealogies Brian appeared as Pan, an urbane satyr in crushed velvet. Horned, goat-legged. A voluptuous, overripe god gone to seed. Not Pan himself, exactly, more a foppish noble *playing* a faun at the court of Versailles. Blowing on his reed pipe, silhouetted against a painted wild mountain backdrop. A debauched aristocrat pursuing a flock of diaphanously clothed peasant girls dressed as nymphs. . . . But Pan is out of breath, and reaches for his inhaler.

Now Keith as Byron: the injured, tormented, doomed Romantic hero, with wild hair and gaunt visage. Not Byron the *hooray*, the upper-class dilettante, musing on a crepuscular sky at Sunium. Darker, more alive, an eruptive, restless presence violently bursting through. Byron as punk. A fusion of decadence and surging yobby energy. Rock raunch, hipster cool and I-don't-give-a-fuck defiance deftly grafted on the languid world-weary pose of Romantic agony.

Where Brian was soft, malleable, vague and unstable, everything about Keith was angular, flinty, compact, hard, distinct. The hatchet face, chiseled, rock-hard features, Indian scout's eyes that bore through everything. The mysterious rider appearing out of nowhere. Hypnotic, sinister, disturbing. A cursed-by-fate intensity, set off against gorgeous clothes, self-mocking humor and a sardonic turn of phrase.

Tara Browne was pure courtier. He had none of Keith's incredible life force pulsing through him. I'd known Tara for a long time. He'd just split up with his wife, Nikki, who had spent most of their marriage having affairs with hunky Spanish guys in Marbella. Tara was very unhappy at the time and he was looking for someone. He liked me and since he was a Guinness heir I also knew that he must be very, very rich! But there was no strength there, no direct current. The Stones were the true aristocracy here and Tara faded in comparison.

Through the acid haze I soon became aware that the atmosphere was very sexually charged . . . and that I was the only woman in the room. It just buzzed in the air for a while, a sort of static electricity. And then Brian, being the most insecure and out of it, came over to claim me. I was even less attracted to him this time than I had been before, but I was unable in those days to say no to anybody. Luckily, people were so scared of me that very few passes were made at all. I imagined he was Pan in sheepskins and I was the moon-goddess, Selene. We went up to the minstrels' gallery. One didn't worry about the others because I knew they were tripping off into some other space. In a way our tryst was like a scene from an Elizabethan play where the lovers retire to a bower represented by a painted cloth. Brian and I diddled about a bit, but it was ridiculous (even on a mythological level). Leaning over me . . . a weary, asthmatic god.

At some point I felt uncomfortable and *de trop*. Perhaps it was Brian's weirdness, perhaps I was just exhausted, but I began to feel very strange. I knew that I'd be happier on my own. I wanted to experience my trip as intensely as possible. Obviously there was much more to LSD than letting Brian Jones touch my breasts. That was the dull bit! I wanted to be in the seclusion of my own house and see visions and commune with the cosmos and dissolve into bright little molecules and travel through space. I knew I could do this much better at home. By this point the Mayfair Hotel had begun to seem dauntingly adult. I crept out and made my way back to Lennox Gardens.

Sleep was out of the question. I lay down on the bed, but found that when I shut my eyes I could see right through my eyelids. My tastefully decorated bedroom was showing signs of mental unbalance. Even the stolid Sanderson wallpaper became animated. The cabbage roses on the trellis did a little dance. I was surprised I'd never noticed that each of those roses had a distinct personality. Fat little ballerinas doing a lumbering *pas de deux* across my wall. It was obvious to me that the designer must have had this in mind when he created the pattern. He was sending out a message, obviously, that only a few — *very few!* — would ever get. Like an inscription found in a pharaoh's tomb that would unlock the secrets of the universe. Hidden in the *wallpaper,* how perfect!

A breeze blew in through the window. The wallpaper ballet gave way to a more spectacular performance as the heavy purple curtains billowed in the wind. They were wool and the light shone through them. In an instant, a huge Cocteau line drawing of Orpheus the height and breadth of the window flashed through the room. It began to tremble like the threads of a cobweb and then another Cocteau drawing traced itself over that one and another and another until the room was filled with swooping black lines, arabesques looping and spinning into the room.

I was lying there being borne along on the incessant tide of fantastic images, losing myself in the surrealistic scribbling rolling before my eyes. When the phone rang I answered it in the spirit of "whatever it is, I can handle it." Always a mistake on acid. It was Keith.

"Where did you go, Marianne? We looked everywhere for you," he said urgently, like someone adrift on a raft.

"Oh darling, I was feeling a bit out of it and I —"

"But you can't just *abandon ship* like that! You don't know what your leaving did to the . . . uh. . . ." I had apparently done something to the mystic bond.

"Oh, how awful of me!" I said.

"We mustn't disconnect," Keith insisted. "Everything depends on it. The group has to stay together." Keith must've been bored or something. And those funny feelings you get when someone goes off on their own in the middle of a trip. Although it wasn't as if we had all been doing things together while I *was* there. Oh well, evidently the sacred vibrations had been perturbed, and I had been well trained by John Dunbar not to upset the vibe. People tripping were to be treated as gingerly as vials of nitroglycerine.

"Oh right, darling, I'll be right over."

I told Keith I didn't have a farthing to my name and he said he'd meet the cab downstairs and pay the driver. But when I got to Court-field Road we didn't stay; Keith got into the cab with me.

"Brian passed out and Tara's gone home. Let's go back to your hotel."

That was the night I ended up with Keith. It was a wonderful night of sex. My night with Keith was the best night I've ever had in my life, as a matter of fact. And although I did, of course, know Keith a great deal better than I knew Mick I still had to ask him that all-important question.

"Darling . . ."

"Yes?"

"What do you think ever happened to the Holy Grail?"

"*Whaaat?* The Holy bloody Grail? Christ, Marianne, you still tripping?"

As dawn came up over London I put on *The Four Seasons*. It was sublime. I was in heaven. I had always been a little in love with Keith, but very shyly. Now I was totally bowled over.

Next day I was fluttering around in a state of absolute rapture.

"Oh, darling," I say to Keith, "that was *such* a divine night!"

Keith is pulling on his boots and out of the blue, he pauses, cocks his head and says: "Y'know who really has it bad for you, don't you?"

"Oh, no, darling, who's that?"

"Mick! Didn't ya know?"

"Well . . . I . . . he does call me now and then."

"Oh, he's smitten all right, Marianne."

"Is he, really?"

"Go on, love, give him a jingle, he'll fall off his chair. He's not that bad when you get to know him, y'know."

I was speechless. Again. He was telling me that I shouldn't bother with him. I should pursue Mick, instead. It was so awful. I was crushed. He set me up and I simply accepted it as a fait accompli: "Oh, all right. I see, Mick and Marianne. I think that's what I'll do then." I'd been given my role. Incredible, isn't it? It's all these funny things you do when you're very young (and on acid!). I thought Keith was perfection, but I didn't think I was exceptional or glamorous enough for him.

And then . . . off he went! He never said a word to anybody about our night together and neither did I. It just stayed there, this perfect night.

I wish now I'd had the strength to say, "Fuck Mick, man. I like you." It's something I could summon up now, but in those days it was totally beyond my range. Not that it would have helped. I was being given the brush-off.

And I knew Mick would be kind to me. Keith was a much more dangerous entity, really. Much more mysterious. Maybe it was all for the best.

Anita was still with Brian when I spent the night with Keith. Keith and I were on our own. But I knew in my heart of hearts that Keith was already in love with Anita. And I could just feel that whatever he wanted, I wasn't it. I was too English and too conventional for him. The signals I was picking up were accurate; he was already a man obsessed.


It's really very odd, the whole business. Keith and Anita, Mick and I. The magic, the alchemy of the alliances was very powerful and had an impact far beyond our little romances. I don't, obviously, know why. I've always been extremely wary of Kenneth Anger and the Tower and all the dark stuff. But there was definitely something very powerful psychically about my alliance with Mick. And it enhanced us both in a way that, in the end, almost destroyed me.

# Harley House

THAT same morning Mick called me. You're back! Great! Come out and let's do something. He wanted to go *shopping,* bless his heart. It was always great fun going shopping with Mick. Not like most men, whom you have to drag around. It was almost like being with another girl. We would hop in a cab and off we'd go to Bond Street. Needless to say, it endeared him to me immediately.

I did notice he could be tight with money. He certainly thought about it more than anyone else I knew. I remember one moment when we were in Tangier and I wanted to buy a big white rug. It was nothing special. It wasn't even very nice, really, but I wanted it. Mick just dug in his heels and refused to buy it. It was too expensive, he said. I was appalled by that and we had a big argument about it. He was probably right — it was too much. But this was *so* beside the point! I wanted it and we could afford it, so I figured why not?

It was then that I realized I would have to use a few wiles. I couldn't just expect him to give me everything I wanted. I had to somehow engage him in the process, which I proceeded to do. I enchanted him with the house we would have and what we would have in it. Little by little I wore him down, and by the time we moved into Cheyne Walk, he was prepared to go all the way. My desire to spend money was very like my mother's and, unlike my father, Mick was prepared to spend a small fortune once I had convinced him we had a duty to live up to his position.

I was awfully good at thinking up great things to do with Mick's money. My attitude was: Wow, here's all this money. How can we have the most possible fun with it?

We went Christmas shopping. It was Christmas 1966. Mick bought a tricycle for Nicholas at Harrods and we had a late lunch at Lorenzo's. It was a glorious day. We were both radiant, the way one is in the first phase of a love affair when you are suddenly immersed in the life of a complete stranger. I remember getting a flash of how Mick and I looked together as we were walking through one of those arcades off Bond Street. Ambling along in the other direction came David Courts and his wife, Lotte. David Courts was a great friend of Keith's; he's the one who made those death's-head rings for Keith. I knew them fairly well because I'd seen him and Lotte often at Robert's and Brian and Anita's. When they caught sight of us they stopped in their tracks as if taking in some astonishing scene. The moment froze and this image of Mick and me reflected back, floating in the air between us for a fraction of a second, and then vanished. It was the first time I had seen that curious and perilous apparition; Mick and me as the Couple.


Things got off to a slow start with Mick. For one thing he hadn't yet got around to breaking up with Chrissie Shrimpton. Mick is somebody who, if he can, will sweep things under the carpet. Any straight, uncomplicated action regarding emotional life is almost impossible for him to manage.

It was in Italy that our affair really began. I was in San Remo for the Song Festival. I had gone there with my guitarist Jon Marks to perform some of my songs in Italian. The Stones had had a minor hit in Italy with "As Tears Go By" and I thought I might have some luck with mine.

Mick had been calling me for weeks, but I still hadn't made up my mind what I wanted to do. I wasn't quite sure I was ready to get involved again. Besides, I was having a good time.

One day I had a sudden desire to see him. I called up and said I was bored and lonely and would he come out and see me? He got on a plane the next day. He was only too happy at this point to put some distance between himself and Chrissie.

I met him at Cannes airport. The press were on us almost immediately and we had to devise some sort of escape plan. Mick had the brilliant idea of hiring a boat and simply taking off. We rented a dodgy little boat along with a captain and one mate, and Mick and I and Nicholas and the nanny set out to sea. We lived on the boat for a week, sleeping on board and during the day putting into Villefranche and Nice and tiny ports along the coast. I remember one day as we were sailing along the Riviera we saw a beautiful house on the cliffs with mimosa hanging off the balcony and we said to each other that one day we would live there. While the weather was fine it was quite lovely, but one day a huge storm blew up and the sea became extremely rough. It was very dramatic. The boat began creaking, waves crashed over the hull, the baby was crying. I was very frightened; I thought we were all going to die. Mick was wonderful. We all got into the same bunk, Mick and Nicholas and I, and held each other. I think that is where I really fell in love with him. After that I was never away from him for a second except when he was working.

When we got to San Remo the press began to hound us again and so we did what you do in those situations. You give them one little item to shut them up. The tacit agreement being that after that they would leave us alone. Which they did.

We did a joint interview with Don Short from the *Daily Mirror*. Dezo Hoffman shot some pictures of us against the San Remo skyline to go with the story. This was the first time we had admitted we were together, so when the picture came out it was official. That mental picture I saw in David and Lotte's eyes was now minted and sent out into the world where it was to have a life of its own. The press, of course, loves these ready-mades of Pop Princes and Princesses: Bob Dylan and Joan Baez, Charles and Di. We love to endow them with superhuman attributes and then at a later date tear them apart. This image would come back to haunt us in rather spectacular fashion a few months later.

Another fateful event occurred the following night at a local nightclub. I'd smoked a lot of hash and was almost catatonic. I decided I needed something to help me stay awake, so I bought some very mild uppers from the deejay. They were called Stenamina tablets — seasickness pills, as it turned out. Mick took one. I, of course, took several, and that was that. It wasn't a big deal. These little pills were of such little consequence that I put them in my pocket and promptly forgot about them.

Mick and I spent a few days alone together at the house I'd rented in Positano. There was a strange cast over the place; the boy I had rented the house from had been killed.

Positano is built on a hill. It's a bit like being on a stage set for *Romeo and Juliet,* with its arches and fountains and tiny piazzas, squares and steps leading up and down from one to the other.

We took acid and looked across at the old town and watched the steps cascading down from the hillside turn into music. We made love a lot and talked endlessly, which I love to do. Of all the people we knew — Keith, Brian, Bob, Christopher — the only one I could talk to properly was Mick.

I was trying to show Mick my life. I wanted him to know I *had* a life! I could feel I was going to be swept away. Some things about my life, however, I did not show Mick. Like my friend Valli. Valli was a strange woman who lived in a cave in the mountains overlooking Positano. She had a pet fox and did wonderful paintings. Valli used to talk to her fox, and the fox talked back. You can't get much closer to a real witch than that. She had tattoos that were like mustaches curling all around her cheeks, mouth, eyes. Just wild. One of those women who have always been an important part of my life — gay women dedicated to worshipping the Goddess!

When we got back to England, Mick wanted me to come and live with him at his flat in Harley House on the Marylebone Road, but it seemed almost indecent to move in lock, stock, and barrel right away. It had been Mick and Chrissie's place, and although Chrissie had moved out, all her stuff was there. Rummaging through her belongings I found some charming things. A rocking horse, a Victorian bird cage with a brass bird in it that sang, hoop earrings. I remember she used Givenchy perfume.

Shortly after Mick and I got involved, Chrissie had a nervous breakdown and was put in hospital. She had made a suicide attempt. I can't pretend that I was too sympathetic with her plight. On the contrary. I was feeling pleased with myself and thought myself quite secure.

I believed everything was going to be fine. Unlike Chrissie, I would have no trouble handling whatever came along. Here was a nice man whom I loved and who loved me. He would take care of me and we'd live happily ever after.

I *did* take the precaution of hanging on to my flat in Lennox Gardens! Diana and Nicholas stayed there and I went to live with Mick at Harley House.

Chrissie and Mick seemed to have been fighting nonstop ever since the day I met them at Adrienne Posta's party, three years earlier. In some way he thrived on these conflicts with Chrissie. I was always amazed at how vicious their relationship was. You can hear that ferocity all over the Stones' early records, all those scathing put-downs. Chrissie had the upper hand in the beginning; she was at least as strong as he was. But in the end he had completely worn her down. She was under his thumb, like the infamous song he wrote for her.

Chrissie was from the old scene, the Swinging London of dollies and pop stars. It was a very put-together look. The wig, false eyelashes and thick makeup. It took her simply ages to get ready. She could never spend the night anywhere because she might fall apart. Like Cinderella. The times were changing and Chrissie wasn't.

Chrissie had charge accounts in Mick's name at Harrods, at Fortnum and Mason. All over the place. That was Mick's way of controlling her. Women get used to all these trappings and suddenly find they can't live without them. I saw what a devastating effect this had on Chrissie.

The turning point in their relationship had come at Tara Browne's twenty-first birthday party in 1966, which was held at Luggala, a picturesque estate in Ireland. It was there that Mick and Chrissie took acid together for the first time. The result was apparently disastrous. You can glimpse the nerve-jangling fracture in Mick's pitiless recital of her crack-up: "Nineteenth Nervous Breakdown." A whole relationship gone haywire is ruthlessly appropriated in that song. He would later do the same to me, by the way!

It never occurred to me that whatever happened to Chrissie would eventually, *mutatis mutandis,* happen to me. Mick and I had a very different relationship, of course, but certain things would inevitably repeat themselves. Sometime during my four years with Mick I began to fall short. And I forgot the first two cardinal rules of relationships: they are never accidental and they always follow a pattern.

What Chrissie and I shared was the most curious and lamentable fate of the pop star's girlfriend. On the one hand you are elevated to the enviable role of Idol's Consort. On the other hand your life becomes fair game for the press, the public and the star himself to do with what he wishes.

It would only be a matter of time before my experience became material for songs in the same way as Chrissie's had. Chrissie was cast (quite unfairly) as the vapid, boutique- and disco-haunting bitch who gets her due. I was to become the tormented specimen, the butterfly writhing on the pin. When your personal pain becomes material for songs and the songs become hit singles, the process is strangely unnerving, however flattering it may at first seem. But then again, what else could the poor bastard have done?

There is quite a perverse side to Mick and it's no accident that his anguished relationships produced some great songs. Mick is so grounded as a person he never loses his footing. He can be right there next to the person falling off the edge but not slip himself. For a songwriter, this is a very useful talent. He is able to observe the car crash at the moment of impact and escape unscathed — a quality that is extremely exasperating for the victims. I always envied Keith and Anita because they looked into the jaws of death together. It was never like that with Mick and me.

I think in the beginning he knew to be quite careful with me because he realized I was not yet his. I had my own place and my own life and until much later my own money. Early on at Harley House we had a fight about it. I felt the silken cord tightening and I bolted. I ran off down the stairs with five pounds and a bit of hash. "I can go any time I damn well please. I've got cab fare and my hash and that's all I need." Mick thought it hysterically funny. He ran after me and teased me and I came back. He was good at that.

One night, coming home late from a rehearsal, I found Mick and Chrissie in the house, both looking rather sheepish. I had obviously walked in on some odd vibe. Mick was almost hyperventilating he was so anxious, but Chrissie, as if totally devoid of any volition, stayed glued to the spot. They must've smoked a joint together and had one last go.

She'd been crying. Her wig was on one side, her eyelashes had peeled off, mascara was running down her face. I knew perfectly well what was going on. One last fuck before you go. I wouldn't hold that against anyone, but once you've finished, dear, go!

From the very start I'd learnt that the first and most crucial thing about recording sessions was that they could be stunningly boring. I was nevertheless flattered when Mick invited me to come down to Olympic to watch them record. Stones sessions were less tiresome than most because they were social events as well, with lots of people hanging out. The studio was the Stones' court. Robert Fraser and Michael Cooper would be there, maybe Tara Browne, Anita, of course, and any odd musicians who were in town or whom Mick and Keith happened to run into that day.

The longueurs of the studio would frequently drive me into the street. I'd go round to David Courts', take a Mandrax and, if available, some LSD and then go back to the session. I'd sit in a corner and quietly vibrate.

They were finishing up *Between the Buttons* at the end of 1966. They had been on tour almost continuously that year and had spent little time in the studio. It would be the last of their catchall albums for a long while. From this point on, new albums would be undertaken with a sense of purpose, however vague. It was their last album as pop stars (before entering their mythic phase) and their last album with Andrew. Andrew had always wanted the Stones to make the kind of records he wanted to listen to himself, and this had served everybody very well for the early years. Andrew had impeccable taste, but he was losing track of Mick and Keith. *Between the Buttons* was for the most part an extension of the manic-paced acerbic social criticism of "Mother's Little Helper" and "Have You Seen Your Mother, Baby." Songs about bitchy models, bored housewives and derailed heiresses. The kind of vituperative and misogynistic songs that Andrew favored!

The sessions went on for ages. Most of their energy went into two new songs, "Ruby Tuesday" and "Let's Spend the Night Together." These were love anthems from the album, and they both became hit singles. Although Keith and Mick usually collaborated, there are some

Stones songs that are distinctly Keith's and others that are Mick's. "Let's Spend the Night Together" was Mick's. It came out of that night we spent in the motel in Bristol. "Ruby Tuesday" was Keith's.

"Ruby Tuesday" took forever to get down. It began, as I recall, with a bluesy Elizabethan fragment that Brian was fiddling with in the studio. Brian was obsessed by his notion of a hybrid of Elizabethan lute music and Delta blues and would hold forth on the essential similarities between Elizabethan ballads and Robert Johnson to anyone who would listen — a bemused Mike Bloomfield or an incredulous Jimi Hendrix, for instance.

Sitting on a stool in his great white hat with scarves tied around the brim, Brian in his sheepish way very softly played a folkish, nursery-rhyme melody on the recorder. It was nothing more than a wispy tune, but it caught Keith's attention. He cocked his head.

"Wha's that?"

"Sorry, man, I think I've got some matches upstairs."

"The thing you just *played,* man. On the recorder! Can ya do it again?"

Brian came back into focus and played the quavery, lilting tune again on the recorder. Perfectly. Beyond perfect!

"Yeah, nice, man," said Keith and went over to the piano to bang it out. Brian was beaming.

"It's a cross between Thomas Dowland's 'Air on the Late Lord Essex' and a Skip James blues, actually."

Keith was not interested in Lord Essex or Skip James for that matter. He had heard a riff and went at it like a dog with a bone.

For ages "Ruby Tuesday" had no lyrics, just this beautiful melody. It was very simple and that's when Brian loved it most. Brian's recorder dominates that song. It's a second vocal, a plaintive gull hovering over the song. It was Brian and Keith's song.

Mick, who'd collaborated with Keith on all the Stones originals for the last four years, had had little to do with "Ruby Tuesday." He just came in at the end and put on the vocals.

I'd seen during the sessions for "Ruby Tuesday" that this song had taken on an almost desperate significance for Brian. This collaboration was to be their last, and perhaps Brian could sense that. He knew it was one of the best things he'd ever done. He wanted everyone to say,

"That's great, Brian, wonderful! Good work!" But, of course, nobody did.

Every now and again a sullen pall would settle over the sessions. If one didn't like something the other was doing, he just wouldn't participate. And despite all the roguish posturing, they were very English. No one would ever say anything directly.

One of Andrew's principal functions was to act as a buffer, a medium between Mick and Keith. As long as Andrew was there, Mick and Keith could go to him and whisper in his ear. I have always maintained that *this* is why the Stones need two guitarists. Not for the *sound* so much as the need to have a go-between. Ron Wood is perfect for this, Mick Taylor was less useful, and it's a role no one should ever have entrusted to Brian Jones.

When the tension became unbearable, Mick and I would go up to the top of Olympic, where there were all these empty rooms and attics piled with old papers and crates and smoke a joint and make love.

Mick and Keith were extremely happy in those days. Keith was *so* full of life. They knew they were involved in something truly extraordinary. Brian, on the other hand, was fading in front of our eyes. His inner demons tormented him so that he could no longer bear any joy in his life. Why did he beat Anita, whom he adored? It was all so peculiar. On the cover of *Between the Buttons,* you see him as he was pretty much most of the time, hunched down, smirking, great dark bags under his eyes. Unable even to smile properly. Brian's decline in the midst of the Stones' dazzling trajectory was maddening and inexplicable. Nobody cared what the reasons were. If you couldn't get your shit together, you didn't deserve to be there.

In December Tara Browne was killed in a car accident. This was very shortly after we'd all taken the acid trip together. He was on acid that night and drove his Lotus Elan through a red light. This is the incident so eerily described in John Lennon's song "A Day in the Life." It wasn't just the drugs that killed him, though. After all, everyone we *knew* at that time was driving around London on acid. It could just as easily have been Brian or Keith. With Tara, you got the feeling his time was up.

Brian and Tara were very close, and his death affected Brian badly. It was shocking, almost obscene. We were young and most of us had never known anyone of our age who died. Tara had just met Suki Poitier — who looked just like Anita — and I remember feeling pleased that he'd found someone he liked. She was in the car with him and survived. After Anita had left him, Brian and Suki got together. They were a very haunted couple, she with her survivor's karma and he with his sense of doom.

During our first few months in Harley House, Mick and I spent a lot of time alone. It's where we got to know each other. Mick played me records — the Miracles, Slim Harpo, Robert Johnson — and I introduced him to books. It was one of the best bits of our life. But even at Harley House it wasn't easy to be alone with Mick because he was so magnetic and everybody wanted to be around him. After Harley House our privacy was hard to hold on to. As we moved, to the house in Chester Square and later to Cheyne Walk, there was a constant parade of visitors, people dropping by at all hours of the day and night, dinner parties.

Our drugs in those early days consisted mostly of grass, acid and the occasional "leaper." There were no hard drugs around. That was one of the nice things about Mick: he really wasn't into drugs. He was very straight, always. A little acid, a little grass. I'd probably be dead by now if I'd been involved with somebody like me. Mick just liked a bit of smoke and the occasional drink (he was a terrible drunk). We did acid — mostly because I was always egging him on: "We have to do some of this stuff, Mick. C'mon, let's get Keith and Brian and Anita to come over and all drop acid." Mick and I hadn't been in Harley House very long before we decided to take a trip together. And so one afternoon, as one did things in those days, we made preparations. We got out the Ravi Shankar records, *Blonde on Blonde*, Otis Redding, all the sonic spirits that would accompany us. We took the phone off the hook and dressed for the occasion.

Just as the acid was coming on, I remember Mick going over to the gramophone carrying one of those green transparent plastic records that the Indian ragas came on. He sat down very ceremoniously in the middle of the floor. It was Ali Akbar Khan, flute and tabla, and as the flute began to quaver Mick rose up, his whole body twisting in a corkscrew like a cobra coming out its basket. And then he started to dance. It was a specific sort of dance, an Indian dance, the dance brightly painted men and women do in Bengali movies, very different from the lascivious dance he does in *Performance*. This was pure beauty and exaltation, a great dance and dancer, another being.

And as Mick danced, an extraordinary change came over him. It was as if he were unwinding himself like a mummy shedding layers of wrapping, revealing at the core of this suburban English boy's body a many-armed, blue-headed dancing god. The macrocosmic Mick. I was seeing Mick, the brainbell *jongleur*, the *real* Mick, if there is such a thing.

The dance was very, very fast, practically on one spot. He was starting to vibrate so quickly that his body was breaking up into molecules. Shimmering phosphorescent particles. I was completely transfixed, hardly breathing. As he moved his hands in stroboscopic flutters, they multiplied and fanned out, overlapping each other. The formality was incredible. He had become Shiva. I hadn't realized until then that I was living with somebody who at odd moments could turn into a god.

It was a blissful, ecstatic moment suspended in time. We could have gone on all night. We hadn't even got to the part where we were going to make love. And fuck me if the bell doesn't ring and in walk all the Small Faces with their gear, amps and guitars and mike stands. At the high point of our trip they'd "dropped by to jam, man." That daft boys' game of all we want to do is rock 'n' roll. God! And we were too polite (and high) to kick them out. It was one of those awful moments of polarization, the mundane world bursting in, the gentleman from Porlock.

One of the strangest nights I've ever spent was at Harley House. It cast such an eerie light on the Unholy Trinity. Mick and I were in bed reading and talking, something we did a lot in the early days together before I got too fucked up. Obviously, once I started taking ten Mandrax a night, that was out of the question.

My bedside reading at this point tended toward the occult and the scandalous. I was dipping into magic, Eliphas Levi and Aleister Crowley. I was very fascinated by all this stuff. Forbidden books, forbidden pleasures. At the convent my friend Sally Oldfield and I would look in the Index of Banned Books and then go and get them, wrap them in brown paper covers and write *The Imitation of Christ* on the outside. I had always fantasized about delicious depravities. Like a heroine in a gothic novel, I wanted to be seized by terrible and voluptuous emotions. I wanted to know why it was forbidden.

Keith was in bed in the next room. He'd been staying with us for a few days for the same reason he'd been camping out for months at Courtfield Road (he was lonely and still had no place to stay). Perhaps things were getting too complicated at Brian and Anita's. Keith did have a home by this time, he had already bought Redlands, but since it was a two-hour drive from London and Keith still had no license he often ended up staying in town with Brian or Mick. In any case, it was an arrangement they all liked. By now I recognized it as being a pattern with them. They preferred hanging out together in each other's flats; it was a bit of the boys' camaraderie. Being in the same place made it easier for them to work together, but they also liked the physical proximity.

We turned out the lights. Mick began caressing my hair, whispering in my ear. And then in the midst of our lovemaking, Mick began saying in another kind of voice, "Do you know what I'd really like to do?" I thought, "Oh it's going to be one of those things where you whisper your deepest, inmost, filthiest fantasies into the other person's ear." The old male erotic turn-on, the fantasy of "what depraved thing I'd love to do to you, my darling."

We'd never played this one before so I was curious as to where it would lead. Would it be the garter belt and lace panties? Or something more on the kinky side, with handcuffs and mild bondage? Would we play roles? The merciless lustful Turk and the virgin in the seraglio? And so, knowing my cue, the helpless maiden about to be ravished (I rather liked that one) I said in my most wispy voice, "No, darling, do tell me what you'd like to do?" From the mercurial Mick I was ready for anything, or so I thought.

"If Keith were right here now," he trilled, "God, I'd like to lick him all over and then . . . why then I'd suck his cock!" And on and on, all said loud enough for Keith to hear through the wall.

It took my breath away but only because I didn't even appear in this erotic fantasy. It was all about *Keith*. And, of course, unbeknownst to Mick, I, too, was in love with Keith. For an instant I wondered if somehow Mick knew about my night with Keith. Perhaps this was some sort of ventriloquist mischief on Mick's part! This, obviously, would have been the moment to tell Mick the truth. That would have *really* turned him on! He probably would have liked me better for it. Maybe I was meant to say, "Well, why don't we get Keith in here," but watching the two of them going at it wasn't exactly my idea of fun. That would rather have eliminated me, wouldn't it?

It didn't exactly fit in with my idealized version of what love is, but he knew that I didn't judge him at all. Never have. I've never judged anybody for their sexual tastes. I was very permissive and I'm sure that was one of my charms for Mick. I was very curious about all this stuff, but I wasn't experienced enough to really know how to handle it. So I simply did what I usually do, I just put it away.

Nothing like this ever happened again while I was with Mick, but it obviously wasn't unique in the story of the Stones. Both Andrew and Anita told me similar stories. For Andrew it would have been a turn-on that Keith was in the next room hearing all this. At the time I thought, "How awful for Keith." It didn't occur to me that it was awful for me.

For Mick this homoerotic yearning for Keith may not have been something he ever intended to act upon. Better for it to remain an unfulfilled desire. *That* was what gave off the alternating current that drove the Stones!

It's curious that Keith lived through all this convoluted sexual stuff with these people and stuck around. He knew perfectly well what was going on. It perpetuated itself in the incestuous relationship between me and Mick and Keith and Anita. And at some level he must have found all this profoundly troubling. In the end he really couldn't bear it. Nor could I. Which is probably one reason he eventually ended up doing so much smack. To block it out.


I wasn't worldly at all when I met these people. I caught up very fast, though. It was shortly after this scene that I thought I had better go out and get some books and do a little investigation into decadent sex. I read everything I could get my hands on. I got hold of the Marquis de

Sade's *Bedroom Philosophers* and read it from cover to cover. That really did me in. Your basic *guide noire* to decadent sex. When I think about what happens in *The Bedroom Philosophers,* I have to say that it could have been a lot worse.

It wasn't until quite recently that I discovered that this strange sexual constellation between Mick and Keith and Anita and Brian and myself had a name. It's called troilism and comes up in Brenda Maddox's biography of Nora Joyce. Apparently James Joyce experienced a number of similarly disturbing episodes of transposed eroticism. He was very ambivalent about his sexuality and at various times in his life felt a very strong pull toward homosexual, scatological and sadomasochistic urges that he knew would have hopelessly entangled him. He used to say in later life that he was saved from God knows what by marriage to Nora, who had been able to accommodate his entire fantasy life. Like Joyce, Mick possessed the kind of sensual, erotic personality that puts disorienting impulses into art. Otherwise, they might both have destroyed themselves. So glad we were able to be of service, Nora and I. It's always reassuring to know one has been of help in the creation of a masterpiece.

# Redlands

B Y the beginning of 1967 there were highly placed people in Her Majesty's government who actually saw us as enemies of the state. It was wild! I envision the wizened gents of Whitehall — old Etonians dressed in frock coats, with umbrellas and exceedingly polished shoes. The cranky, ancient custodians of a crumbling empire, they had been breathing the dust of the Industrial Revolution for close to a hundred years, and they were used to having things their way. And so, improbable as it may seem, when these little men in Whitehall felt that the Rolling Stones were a threat to the safety and security of the United Kingdom and its dependencies, they decided to actually *do* something about it. Neville Chamberlain diplomats shuffling papers in a dusty, ancient office, plotting the downfall of the Rolling Stones!

This whole nonsense — from the bust on through Mick and Keith's trial — proved if nothing else that the Little Gray Men were perverse aficionados of the Rolling Stones, in the same way the censors at the Vatican are forced to become connoisseurs of pornography and blasphemy. I imagine them playing "Have You Seen Your Mother, Baby, Standing in the Shadows?" over and over with a cryptomaniac's delusionary paranoia — what the devil does *that* mean? Perhaps it is they who first came up with the idea of playing songs backwards!

Putting myself in their place I imagine Britain must have seemed suddenly overrun by frivolity and lunacy. Flashy clothes, miniskirts, promiscuity and drugs. The gents in Whitehall saw this as a challenge to their authority. Someone was, without their permission, bending reality! The battle was for the New Englishman. Was he to be the degenerate, effeminate Mick Jagger and his crew or, say, the archetypal graduate of Sandhurst?

They were also voyeurs, and like most voyeurs imagined far more lurid things going on than actually were. The idea that the Rolling Stones were about to undermine Western civilization with drugs, rock and polymorphous sexuality was completely farcical. But having established that the fate of the nation was at stake, this revolution must needs be led by a particularly dissolute and perverted bunch.

"We really have to stop these swine in their tracks. We have to make an example of them."

"Add Faithfull to that list, m'lord."

"Faithfull? Who the devil is Faithfull?"

"Marianne Faithfull, Jagger's new wench. Here's the file on the woman, sir."

"Let's see, daughter of Glynn Faithfull, well-known crank, runs a cauldron of obscurantist foment called Brazier's Park. Mother, the Baroness von Sacher-Masoch. . . . Good God!"

"I thought you might be interested in hearing this tape, sir, of an interview she gave to the BBC just last week."

"The BBC?"

"Yes, sir. Interview with Michael Barrett. Shall I play it for you?"

"Oh, well, yes, let's hear it."

Here's some of what I said:

"I remember as a little girl watching the coronation on the telly. It was so silly, we just sat there and *laughed*. I was five at the time. . . . We're getting nearer now. This studio, for instance, is *fantastic!* Light, communism and electricity! Electricity is the answer! We live in light — *light* — *fiat lux!* Do you see?

"Marijuana's perfectly safe, you know. It's an old scene, man. And drugs really *are* the doors of perception. That's just what drugs are. *Doors!* You don't go anywhere, you just see a crack like I'm looking at you now. Something like LSD is as important as Christianity. *More* important.

"My father taught me about the Group Mind. Are we going to let them control us or are we going to force our thought on to *them?* You know, like in Africa if thousands of people believe in voodoo, voodoo works. But we must *control* it! [I think I got this idea of control from Mick.] The people in Whitehall, they're *living in the past.* We are society, not them.

"Do you feel them closing in on you? I do. It could be Harold Wilson or MI-5 or *little men in offices.* They'll probably put me in prison, but in the meantime I'll mess *them* up. I'd like to see the whole structure of our society collapse. Wouldn't it be lovely! . . . We're taking orders from a bunch of *dead* men! It's insane, it's . . ."

(The above, believe it or not, is an accurate redaction from BBC Transcription Services.)

"That'll be quite enough of that, thank you, Soames."

"Damnable bolshy little trollop!"

"And what do you recommend we do about it?"

"Oh, you know, defamation of character, assassination by the gutter press. Supplemented, of course, by police action!"


Mick obviously holds me responsible for a lot of what subsequently happened. He used to say that I talked too much and the things I said were dangerous. Sure it was wild stuff, but you can see how silly it all was. Hardly a serious threat to the fabric of society.

While the Stones did in one sense represent anarchy in a much more concrete way than the Sex Pistols ten years later, the whole thrust of their rebellion was far too disorganized (true anarchy!) to have been any real threat to anybody.

But what is a revolution, even a revolution in style, as ours was, without stepping a few feet over the line? It was the symptoms of something beyond their control that bothered the little men in frock coats. Blatant hedonism, promiscuous sexuality, drugs, mysticism, radical politics, bizarre clothes and, above all, kids with too much money! It was all trundling in its own feckless way toward destruction of the status quo without even actually intending it, and the standard bearers of this Children's Crusade were the Rolling Stones.

Whatever it was that set them off, the little men made some deal with the *News of the World* and the police force. They busted us and slandered our names all over the gutter press. Especially mine. Somebody was out to compromise me, and did it very well.

I remember the morning Mick read the piece that set the whole thing off. It was Sunday morning in early February of 1967 and we were in bed with coffee and croissants when the papers came. Mick is a newspaper junkie, he reads everything from the *Observer* to the *Sun*. We were very happily going through the papers and suddenly Mick came upon the article in the *News of the World*. He completely flipped out.

"Fuckin' 'ell!" he raved, leaping out of bed.

"What is it, darling?"

"Listen to this: 'Jagger told us: "I don't go much on it (LSD) now the cats (fans) have taken it up. It'll just get a dirty name. I remember the first time I took it. It was on tour with Bo Diddley and Little Richard." During the time we were at the Blases Club in Kensington, London, Jagger took about six benzedrine tablets. "I just would not keep awake in places like this if I didn't have them." . . . Later at Blases, Jagger showed a companion and two girls a small piece of hash (marijuana) and invited them to his flat for "a smoke."' "

I began to laugh. "It's Brian. They've confused you with Brian! He's always going around telling everyone he's the leader of the Rolling Stones."

But I knew it wasn't an honest mistake. It was a cynical tactic to sell more papers. Brian Jones just didn't mean as much as Mick Jagger. Nevertheless, the article brought up a lot of bad feelings that were already out there about Brian. It was the beginning of the end for Brian; a stupid, meaningless incident that brought on six months of horror, almost wrecked the group and landed Mick and Keith in jail. This little "night out" of Brian's turned out to be the last straw.

The next day Mick got on to his solicitor, and had him slap a writ on the *News of the World*. We didn't see what was coming *at all*, although I did have a twinge of fear when Mick called his lawyer. Taking on the powers that be and all that. . . .

Of course nobody *knew* about this writ. The only people who knew were those at the *News of the World*. It wasn't released to the press. And it's this fact that makes everything else that happened highly suspicious. The *News of the World* obviously called the little men in MI-5 and said: "Look, these people need to be taken down. Will you help us?"

And the little men said, "Of course, we'd be only too pleased."

The snare was going to be drugs, of course. They would set it all up with the West Sussex police and that would be that. Their master stroke was to bring David Schneiderman (alias David Britton alias David Henry) over from California with loads of LSD to set us up.

They must have flown him in for this bust. He appeared very fast; right after the writ had been issued he showed up at Robert Fraser's flat.

Robert called up and said: "We've got this guy here, David Schneiderman, a Yank, just got in from California and he's brought this great acid with him from the States. It's called White Lightning or something fabulous like that and he wants to lay some on us, man."

So I said, "How fucking great! Wait, Robert, I've got a fantastic idea, why don't we all go down to Redlands for the weekend. I'll call Keith right now and set it up. What's this guy's name, again?"

"Schneiderman, David Schneiderman, the Acid King. Flew in this morning."

"Well, don't let him get away!"

Bang! Like that. That's the way it came about, this "most famous house party of the twentieth century." It was all very organized, like it was when you took acid in those days. We got hold of a van, mapped out an itinerary. You wanted to go and see marvels. The White Horse on the Downs, the Devil's Footprint, Glastonbury. Stonehenge and Avebury were favorite ones. Forests, follies, ancient ruins.


February 11, 1967. On Saturday night, after Mick and Keith had finished their recording session at Olympic studios, we went down to Redlands, Keith's house in Sussex. The party consisted of Christopher Gibbs, Michael Cooper, Robert Fraser and Robert's Moroccan servant, Mohammed, and Nicky Kramer, a friend of Keith's. Nicky Kramer was just a nice loon; a sort of Kings Road loon who happened along. There was Mick, Keith and myself. And, of course, David Schneiderman. *Very* West Coast; very pompous and opinionated. Getting high came with a little moral, its own California *koan.*

"This is the tao of lysergic diethylamide, man. Let it speak to you, let it tell you how to navigate the cosmos." It was all a bit too reverent and pretentious for our taste, but he *did* have the goods.

The next morning we woke up to a cup of tea and a tab of acid. David Schneiderman came round at nine o'clock in the morning with the "sacrament." We took it and the first bit was a sort of waiting-for-the-acid-to-come-on time. I remember getting quite sick and I think Mick did, too. It was very strong acid, stronger than anything I've ever had since.

This was an outward going-out-and-looking-at-things trip, there wasn't too much internal stuff at all. We were expecting to have a great time and treating it very lightly. Underlying that was a sense of excitement and possible danger, the slight *frisson* of going into another dimension. We all knew each other very well, and there were no terrible hidden tensions floating around. Also no Brian and no Anita. It was all pretty straightforward.

Mick is great on acid. Very calm, cool and steadying. Keith and Mick are very similar in that way. You can see how profoundly connected they are. What I remember more than anything about tripping with Mick is that a lot of his grown-upness fell away. He shed his facade and became much more open, younger in spirit. He was terribly young as it was, but in his day-to-day way of being he had a lot of defenses and mannerisms that kept everyone just slightly removed. On acid, a much purer form of him came through. Less artifice. He didn't have anything like the level of artifice he has now, but he always had more front than the rest of us.

Keith really doesn't have that. With Keith there was no question of things falling off him. He was already way out there. On acid Keith goes deeper into himself, but his basic personality doesn't change all that much. He acts the same, whether he is tripping or not!

Nobody talked a lot that day. The usual conscious babble subsided. It was very strong acid and the experience was so overwhelming that there wasn't much you could put into words.

Except for Michael Cooper, that is. He talked *all* the time. Very dazzling and spacy. I think Michael's unconscious was already pretty close to the surface anyway, so it just bubbled right out, an incessant stream of hilarious commentary:

"'Ere we all are together on this *great* adventure, innit brilliant?

Innit too *much?* Innit, uh . . . wot *was* that? Not another bloody
Mekon!" Michael's spirit was crucial to the whole vibe.

Robert Fraser became a wee bit more sparkly on acid but he retained pretty much his usual caterpillar cool. None of us at the time
could have guessed, if our lives depended on it, *why* he was so laid back
in the presence of the overwhelming zing. We discovered later that it
was because he was also on smack. We didn't even know what that
*meant.* But the effect was that he would be a lot more reserved than the
rest of us. The apocalypse as viewed through a rather thick pane of
glass.

Christopher was wonderful. Christopher and Mick are both Leos,
and you can see that Leo quality very clearly on acid. Quite grand and
slightly haughty in manner, but great fun and very playful.

It was this trip (not to mention its aftermath) that really bonded
Mick and Keith. They tuned into each other's wavelengths and began
to see each other in a much more sympathetic light. For years after this,
they became that inseparable entity, the Glimmer Twins. This was essential if the Stones were to move into a new phase. The constellation
of the group could no longer remain on the petty level it had been. It
had been one of Andrew's adages that a group has to reinvent itself
every five years. What Mick and Keith saw during this trip and many
subsequent ones were Jumping Jack Flash, the Midnight Rambler,
Brown Sugar. . . . The new personae that would populate their albums
for the next five years.

The idea was to go and see Edward James's house, a surrealist folly
from the thirties. Edward James was a millionaire, a great patron of the
surrealists and a spoiled little boy, but he had a very marvelous odd
house with — among other things — sculptured laundry hanging out
of the windows and wild surrealist carpets.

With great expectations we set off for this wonderful house, but
when we got there it was locked and we couldn't get in. We ended up
spending almost the whole day in a van, just driving around. Any time
we were outside it was wonderful. But van life was, uh, not so great. It
was just one of those Plans That Go Awry on Acid. You set out to do
something dazzling, and reality intervenes. (And *that* becomes the cosmic lesson!) So you're wavering for millennia between how amazing
and, well, interesting it is spending the day in a *van,* for God's sake, to

feeling like you could, with very little encouragement, freak totally *out!*

It was a tremendous relief when we finally got to the beach and raved around and looked at things and under things and through things. Gulls and seashells and waves and crabs and sand patterns. Whew! How beautiful (*and* benign). We were like a load of kids on a trip to the ocean. I've always had a knack for play in any case. Playing quietly or noisily, whichever is required. This was definitely a boy's trip, and I aspired to being one of the boys. I've always prided myself on losing my sexuality when I want to! I'm sure this has something to do with my father and my upbringing in the commune at Brazier's. Because of my father's insights into the Group Mind, I learned early on how to merge with other people without there being great thorns in the way.

Then there was getting back to Redlands after being outside all day, muddy and tired and sweaty from being in the van *and* on acid. I remember how well the transition was managed within this group. There was no wandering off and imploding or getting into subjective dramas. On acid there's often that bit where you go back to the house after being out all day and people can get into their own little trips, get paranoid, uptight and depressed, but nobody did that. What they all did was calmly and matter-of-factly change into other fabulous costumes.

My clothes were all covered with sand, dirt, twigs in my hair, the normal sort of wear and tear of being on a trip outside. It was such an intense trip that I was quite relieved when we started to come down. That's when I went and took my bath. I was the only one who hadn't brought a change of clothes and I dealt with it by wearing this beautiful fur rug. It was very large, six by nine feet or something. It would have covered a small room.

We were all in a very good mood by then. We were coming down very gently from the intense part of the trip. It was evening. I think it must have been six or seven o'clock; it was dark outside by then. Actually there had been a real absence of psychodrama all day, considering the circumstances. Until the cops walked in. Then all of a sudden we found ourselves in a full-blown *melodrama*. At first we all thought we'd *imagined* these weird creatures prowling around outside, conjured them up, perhaps, out of our sick minds!

I remember having this absurd idea of telling everyone to be still. "If we don't make any noise, if we're all *really* quiet, they'll go away." A typical Marianne response if ever there was one! Make *yourself* very small and *it* will disappear. This time, I'm afraid, it didn't work.

Once we'd let them in, the first thing they did was to divide everyone up into two class groups or three class groups, actually. There was Christopher Gibbs and Robert Fraser, the old Etonians, whom they treated with the utmost reverence; there were the Rolling Stones and Michael Cooper and Nicky Kramer and the servants, whom they treated to a man with characteristic contempt; and then there was *the woman*. I was the lowest of the low because I was in a room full of men, naked under a fur rug. The slut. Miss X.

And because I was the only woman there they immediately began fabricating this absurd "SCANTILY CLAD WOMAN AT DRUG PARTY" nonsense. That's one of the things they made such a big thing about at the trial. The rug was introduced as *evidence!* But of course the trip had nothing to do with sex. I was there really in my role as one-of-the-boys. And until that moment when the cops arrived I'm sure nobody even *noticed* that I had no clothes on *or* that I was wearing a fur rug. It's the *last* thing they were thinking about. Apart from the fact that both Robert and Christopher were, of course, gay (and maybe Nicky Kramer too), my sexuality was not exactly uppermost in anyone's mind. But this would have been, I'm sure, incomprehensible to Them. . . .

What was most shocking about the cops' barging in was that we were in the midst of this most unusual and utterly overwhelming sensation of warmth and safety. It was a diabolical thing to happen at the end of a beautiful trip. And the awful thing (for Them, especially) was that we just couldn't take it seriously, which didn't exactly help us with the cops. They're not used to being laughed at and they didn't much care for it, not at all.

They went around searching everyone and taking pieces of evidence; doggedly collecting sticks of incense and miniature bars of hotel soap. Then they came to the green velvet jacket with the four pills of speed in it. When they asked who the pills belonged to, Mick very gallantly said that they were his.

The most suspect person there wasn't even searched. David Schneiderman had an aluminum case stuffed with drugs. And let me tell you, inside were the most suspicious-looking contents you have ever seen: incredibly lumpy packages of various sizes all wrapped in tinfoil. Almost the classic dealer's suitcase you'd see on any cop show, and they didn't examine one thing in it! Schneiderman's ostensible reason for not opening the packages was that they contained exposed film that would be destroyed if they opened up the tinfoil.

In retrospect it was obvious to all of us that Schneiderman had set us up. At the time this conspiracy theory business sounded like your typical drugged-out, paranoid hippie ravings, but if you read the recent revelations of what MI-5 was up to around this time, it doesn't seem quite so farfetched. And right after all this, Schneiderman vanished into thin air. (Whisked out of the country, I should think.)

He's still around. I saw him about five years ago in Los Angeles. He's become quite harebrained. I think the Redlands business derailed him. When somebody comes apart after something like this, it's usually because they've done something they can't live with. He was obviously used by the little men in the frock coats and their pals in Washington. I firmly believe they were all in cahoots.

The worst thing that happened during the raid was that they found heroin on Robert. He had twenty-four jacks of British pharmaceutical heroin on him in a beautiful little box. The police were searching us all, but because he was upper class and a gentleman they were incredibly deferential to him. Robert was doing his best to cow them in his best guardsman's manner: "Now, come on. You can't really do this sort of thing." And, of course, the cop, a respectful and working-class bloke, said, "Oh, well, sir. Yeah. I'm sure it's all right. I'm really sorry." Robert told the cop that these pills were for his diabetes and he had almost got away with it when the cop very apologetically asked him if he could let him take "just one tablet, sir, as a formality, you understand."

And then came the farcical scene on the stairs where the lady constable wanted to search me. I dropped the fur rug just for a second. It wasn't one bit lascivious, just a quick flounce done very gracefully, almost like a curtsy, so they could see I had no clothes on and that's all. I thought it was so hysterically funny. This woman wanted to take me upstairs to search me when I had nothing on but the fur rug. It was a great moment. I was on the stairs, surrounded by all my best friends, Christoper, Robert, Mick, Keith, all these people that I adored, and twelve cops and a policewoman. I must have thought I'd make a dramatic moment of it. I couldn't help myself. I always have been an incorrigible exhibitionist. Subsequently I learned how to channel my exhibitionist fix by getting up onstage, but in those days I hadn't worked that out yet. It was the gulf between us on acid and them with their note pads that made it seem so hilarious at the time. It didn't seem quite so funny later. I certainly got paid back in spades.

It was nearly all over and the tension was building to such a degree that it felt as if all the oxygen had been sucked out of the room. We couldn't have stood the excruciating suspense of the situation if Keith hadn't put on Dylan's "Rainy Day Women #12 and 35" ("Everybody must get stoned"), at which we all burst out laughing. It cleared the air. It made the cops absolutely enraged, but it made *our* predicament momentarily bearable.

Keith was rolling on the carpet laughing. We treated the cops with grandeur and disdain. It was a case of mutual contempt. There's no one on this earth more self-righteous than a cop. I've had that every time I've been busted since. More contempt than I would have believed possible. We were meant to be contrite and repentant. We had done wrong and now we had to learn our lesson. I *still* haven't learned anything, actually! Not in the way they meant me to, anyway.

The cops took various odd objects as evidence. As they left they said something to Keith like, "Well if any of this is found contraband, you're gonna be responsible." And he said, "I see. They pin it all on me." But aside from that there wasn't much talking at all. We were extremely stunned and amused, it was all so off-the-wall for us.

We were still high, and they looked very odd to us. Strange, alien life forms with their big boots and their bluster. They were awfully big and fat and rosy cheeked, and we were all so small and thin and *different*. They were one genus and we were another, like the two races in H. G. Wells's *Time Machine,* the ones who live under the ground and the ones who live above.

And they felt that too. They definitely saw us as not being part of the human race. I do think that's one of the reasons it happened, all the way from the little men in Whitehall to the West Sussex constabulary. They thought of us as mutants. And they were right.

# Aftermath

MICK and I had been like two children, gradually getting to know each other, when this ferocious, full-blown storm emerged out of nowhere, engulfed us and swept us away. It went on for well over a year. The fact that these pills were still in Mick's pocket is an indication of how early on it all happened. I'd gotten them in Italy on the first trip Mick and I took together. We may have had two months of innocence and joy before the Redlands bust.

After the bust, things were quiet for a while. The *News of the World,* in their characteristically understated way, came out with a generic story — no names were mentioned — entitled "Drug Squad Raids Popstars Party." But apart from that there was little indication of what was to come until charges were brought.

Finally charges were brought against Mick, Keith and Robert Fraser. At the hearing on May 10, all three were remanded to trial at the West Sussex Quarter Sessions in June. They were released on a hundred pounds bail.

At this point, I was still cheerful and reckless and "fuck 'em!" It wasn't until the first meeting we had with our barrister, Michael Havers, Q. C., that it began to dawn on me what had happened. Mick wanted to leave me out of it. He didn't want me to have to get up on the witness stand, but more than that he didn't want me *saying* anything. Mick always felt that I spoke my mind too much.

The only person who seemed to know what was going to happen to me was Michael Havers. I remember jumping up in the discussions and saying: "But they're *my* pills! Why don't I get up on the stand and just say they're mine? I'll go. I'll take the blame."

But Mick and Havers just looked appalled. Havers was horrified. He wouldn't hear of it. "No, no, no. Out of the question! I could never expose you to that. You couldn't go through that. You just couldn't. They'd *destroy* you."

Well, they did anyway. And what's worse, I somehow ended up as this passive sacrifice. I was cross about being excluded from the trial because I felt that I could have carried it off. In any case, I wish I had tried. At least I could have defended myself. (As it was, *no one* defended me.) Whatever the outcome, I would have felt better if I'd had a part in it. I would have given them hell.

And that, of course, is precisely why they didn't want me. I wasn't even allowed to *testify,* for chrissakes! Never mind taking the blame. The Woman, you see, is not meant to say anything. Of course, I might have gone to jail, but I wouldn't have come out of the whole thing with this *paint* on my name. Instead of doing my Joan of Arc bit I was stuck for years with this ridiculous rock-star-moll image. Or worse, the helpless little victim of the big bad rock stars!

Beyond the obvious objections to my testifying, Havers thought I would not, at this point, have been believed. They would have thought it was a cover-up, and, anyway, the process of demonizing Mick had gone too far. In the stereotyped cock-and-bull story that had been cooked up about us, Mick was a filthy, depraved maniac and I was the Dickensian innocent caught in the monster's clutches. This is as absurd a concoction as can be imagined, but these images proved incredibly adhesive.


Michael Havers decided to have Mick's and Keith's cases tried separately from Robert Fraser's. He felt that if Robert were to be tried with them it would reflect adversely on Mick and Keith. Robert had been busted for heroin, serious narcotics, whereas Mick's pills were legal (although, admittedly, in *Italy*). They were over-the-counter airsickness pills with the teeniest bit of speed in them.

The trials took place from June 27 to June 29. Robert and Mick were tried and convicted on the first day — Robert for possession of heroin pills, Mick for the four pills containing amphetamine — and both were sent to Lewes jail to await sentencing. The following two days were taken up with Keith's trial.

I wasn't at the first day of the trial. I was with Nicholas, staying at Steve Marriott's house with my girlfriend Saida. I really wanted to disappear while the trials were going on. The whole thing scared me. I also felt left out. Nobody had asked me how I felt. They were busy! They were in jail! They were going on trial! Now I am a person who, rather than sit around and wait by a phone, will do *anything*. So I called up Saida and told her what I felt and she said: "Oh, to hell with it. Come on, let's go out to Richmond and take LSD and stay with Steve Marriott for the weekend." Which is what we did. And then I would go back to my lonely station, high in Harley House, and await events.

I went down to Steve Marriott's house to hide. There was no question of anything going on between Steve Marriott and me. It would be much too silly. Besides I was there with my beautiful Indian girlfriend. No one would have dared come near us. Saida was very tough.

We took acid with the lads. Steve Marriott, Ronnie Land, Ian McLagan. They were always like that. They were always together, those guys. I don't think they even had girlfriends yet. We were tripping and there was a lot of insane stuff going on — people changing into frogs in the bathroom and then coming out and telling you about it in *epic* detail. The worst thing was that I knew Mick was in court twisting in the wind. I just couldn't handle it, so I tried to disappear.

But, of course, what must have happened is that in the middle of the weekend Mick must have said "Where's Marianne? Why isn't she at her post weeping outside the jail?" And Tom Keylock was dispatched to find me. I must say my heart went out to Tom that day, because when I want to go missing it's almost impossible to catch up with me. Somehow he tracked me down and yanked me out. I didn't have any time to get a costume together. So, still tripping, braless and wearing high-heeled sandals, jeans and one of Mick's shirts, I kissed Saida good-bye and off I went down to West Wittering.

All the way down to Redlands Tom kept saying: "Ow'd you 'spect me ta find yer? 'Ad to bloody *drag* it owtta Saida's girlfriend. She was cryin' 'n' tremblin' somethin' awful abowt givin' up your whereabouts but I tole 'er it's a matter of gravest importance, national security et cetera." It was a potent whiff of British petit bourgeois prudery. Tom had been privy to countless bawdy episodes with Brian, Mick and Keith but he was absolutely *scandalized* at my behavior.

Tom dropped me off at Redlands. Keith was there with Michael Cooper. Keith was a trouper. His attitude was whatever happens, happens. He liked the romance of it all. Bit of the old Billy the Kid rush. Of course he wasn't in prison yet. Only Mick and Robert were in jail at this point. I wasn't quite sure what my role was meant to be. Michael Cooper knew what he wanted — he wanted that great picture of Mick and Robert handcuffed together, and he got it.

The images of this whole period come to me as still photographs; it doesn't flow as a continuous story. There were the visits to Mick and Robert. I see Keith walking around the house not talking much.

The night I arrived at Redlands Michael and I ended up going to bed together. Just like two dogs on a cold night. It was really out of lone-liness and lostness, reaching out to somebody in this hellish situation.

Michael Cooper was a wonderful friend. We were very close. It was strange. I was in a daze through the whole thing. Whatever it was, I knew I needed someone to lean on. "Oh well, it was just water off a duck's back to her."

At Redlands we were all trying to keep our spirits up. Which I did mainly by continually dropping acid. We were all taking everything as lightly as possible. That's when Michael did that picture of me pointing to the front-page headlines of the *News of the World* with a big smile on my face. It just hadn't sunk in yet. And actually we thought all this legal hocus-pocus was just a lot of aggravation. Until we heard the verdict we thought it was a lot of nonsense. What kind of insanity was this? A blanket punishment, I think, for *everything* — for being different, for having fun, for being young even.

Mick was in prison and Robert was in prison. It's hard now to conjure up what it really was like because in the end Mick's conviction was overturned. But there was a long, terrible moment where it looked as if they were going to be destroyed. And for nothing, for taking LSD and seeing God, for Christ's sake.

Keith drove me over to the jail where Mick was in a holding tank with Robert. Robert was grim and accepting of his fate, but Mick was not. Mick was more upset than I'd ever seen him, quite desperate in fact. Never in his wildest dreams did he think that anything like this would ever happen to him. It was a grisly coming down to earth. He couldn't believe it and he couldn't adjust to it.

Mick was sitting there in his cell whimpering and wringing his hands saying, "What am I gonna do? What in *hell* am I gonna do?"

He began crying uncontrollably. At that moment I snapped. I simply couldn't handle an overwhelming display of emotion. Mick's helplessness rankled me and I must say, to my undying shame, I wasn't very compassionate about it.

"God, Mick, pull yourself together!" I bullied him. "What are these cops going to think of you when they see you falling apart like this? You're just confirming their worst images about you. They're going to think you're just a spineless, pampered pop star."

At that he almost flinched, but he stopped crying immediately. I don't think he knew that side of my character. A very tough streak. But it was entirely the wrong thing to do. I should have been touched that he felt he could let down his guard with me. It was actually quite a wonderful thing for him to have done, a real moment of vulnerability. And needless to say he never, *ever* showed that side of himself again. I've always regretted my behavior beyond words. A flash of real emotional honesty, and all I could say was "Straighten up and fly right!"

It might have been good advice coming from another man. Perhaps. But coming from me it was definitely not a Good Thing. I don't know the code of these things exactly, but I do know that it's a great put-down for a woman to behave in this way to you. It's like becoming his mother. *Definitely* against the rules.

Part of my reaction came from my own sense of helplessness. It hurt me terribly to see Mick in prison, and there was absolutely nothing I could do about it. I said to him what I say to anybody who ever cracks up in that kind of way. In the sweetest possible way I said: "Why don't you use the experience, darling."

"*Use* it? Whaddya mean, *use* it?"

"Use it to write a song, dear."

"What do you expect, the bloody 'Ballad of Reading Gaol'?"

"Well, think of all those blues singers you love so much, dear. You can write your own blues."

"Fuckin' hell, Marianne! I can't think about that now. My mind is completely spinning. I can't think of anything but being in this fucking hole and wanting to get out and forget the whole nightmare."

Where Keith reveled in the romance of being an outlaw, Mick was utterly heartbroken. He had no illusion about the glamour of it all.

But he did write those songs. Dark, gothic, spacey blues. They're all over *Satanic Majesties*.

One of the few pleasant things about the whole scaly business was that we got to see Mick and Keith wearing such beautiful clothes. If it hadn't been for the court case, Keith would never have gotten into a suit. His day-to-day getup was jeans and a leather jacket. And of course, he looked absolutely fucking great. He was so beautiful. Keith wore black and gray suits and Mick wore colors.

The press was obsessed with the minutiae of Mick's behavior. What meal he had ordered to be sent over to the courthouse from a nearby restaurant, what books and magazines I'd brought him (books on Tibet and modern art). The brand of cigarettes he smoked. As if he were the Duke of Windsor. There were endless itemizations of clothing, all slightly at odds with each other. For example, the color of a jacket varied from duck egg blue to jade green and every shade in between. Every day of the trial we got a full fashion report in the press of what the two dandies in the dock were wearing.

"Mr. Richards appeared in court today wearing a black silk suit with a white cravat. Mr. Jagger was in a green velvet suit with a pink shirt and frilly placets." That was the way all the press reports would start.

As frivolous as all this seems, I think their dandyish clothes actually helped turn public opinion in their favor. So exquisitely dressed, they seemed more like fragile aristocrats being bullied by beefy cops than the sinister types the prosecution were trying to foist on the court. The effect was to make them into romantic figures. There's always been great affection in England for that sort of foppish gallantry: Sir Walter Raleigh at the block, Francis Drake playing bowls before going off to fight the Spanish Armada.

All those fabulous clothes served as wonderful armor for Mick and Keith, and I should definitely have followed their example. Looking back, I can see that it would have behooved me to pull myself together a bit before heading into the fray. If I'd been using my head — if I'd been *straight* — I'd have gone back to Harley House, had a hot bath, put my hair up, put a very smart suit on, high heels, stockings, the whole bit and gone down to Redlands like that instead of in the casual hippie clothes I was wearing. My unassuming appearance was interpreted by the press and by the court as a slight. If unintentional, that was even *more* infuriating to them.

In my haste it didn't occur to me how I might be *perceived*. You can see how unpremeditated this was in the pictures of me at the time. There's no weight to them. Just this little creature with long blond hair, very thin and looking rather forlorn.


Before Redlands, Keith had been overshadowed by Mick and Brian, but his defiance on the stand made him a major folk hero. This was the beginning of Keith's legend. A symbol of dissipation and the demonic. And the amazing thing is that subsequently he actually *became* that. Satan's righthand man with the skull rings and the demonic imagery. He turned it all to his advantage.

The trial was stupefyingly boring and utterly terrifying at the same time. It was horrifying to see the tedious and inexorable power of the state, like a great granite wheel bearing down on them, crushing them very slowly.

Endless recitations of scenes from the corniest soap opera you've ever seen in your life, an awful sort of "Ironsides Goes to the Hippie Club" version of our lives. We were expected to subscribe to this nonsense.

Detective Constable Rosemary Slade: "The woman was in a merry mood and one of vague unconcern."

Malcolm Morris (the prosecutor): "She was unperturbed and apparently enjoying the situation."

Their story went like this: a group of dissolute rock stars lured an innocent girl to a remote cottage where, having plied her with drugs, they had their way with her, including various sexual acts involving a Mars Bar.

The first time I heard about the Mars Bar was from Mick shortly after the trial. Mick said, "You know what they're saying about us in Wormwood Scrubs, they're saying that when the cops arrived they caught me eatin' a Mars Bar out of your pussy."

I laughed it off, but my amusement began to wane when the damn story established itself as a set piece of British folklore.

The Mars Bar was a very effective piece of demonizing. *Way* out there. It was so overdone, with such malicious twisting of the facts. Mick retrieving a Mars Bar from my vagina, indeed! It was far too jaded for any of us even to have conceived of. It's a dirty old man's fantasy — some old fart who goes to a dominatrix every Thursday afternoon to get spanked. A *cop's* idea of what people do on acid!

It was as if I were watching a pornographic movie based on my life! I became very detached. I was in shock. I can see that in photographs taken of me at the time. I have a perpetually stunned look on my face. As if to say: I can't believe this is happening!

There was one shining moment at Keith's trial when a wonderful series of exchanges took place between Keith and the prosecutor, a prissy Mr. Morris.

Mr. Morris: "Would you agree that in the ordinary course of events you would expect a young woman to be embarrassed if she had nothing on in front of several men?"

Keith: "Not at all. We are not old men and we are not worried about petty morals. . . . She had been up stairs and bathed."

Mr. Morris: "Did it come as a great surprise to you that she was prepared to go back downstairs still only wearing a rug in front of ten police officers?"

Keith: "I thought the rug was big enough to cover three women."

Mr. Morris: "I wasn't talking about impropriety, but embarrassment."

Keith: "She doesn't embarrass easily. Nor do I."

The jury took five minutes to find Keith guilty (a minute less than it took them to convict Mick). At the sentencing on June 29, Mick was given three months. Keith was convicted under a diabolical statute for allowing drugs to be consumed on his premises and got a year's sentence. Robert got a very severe sentence, six months in the Scrubs, along with some unnecessarily offensive remarks from the judge and a vicious attack by the press.

By the time the trials got under way we knew Robert would get it. Twenty-four jacks of heroin was serious stuff. And, honestly, he was never the same after he came out of prison. He got very, very disillusioned by the whole thing. He came out with a black vengeance in his heart, but he turned it all against himself. He lost his gallery while he was in jail, and then, fifteen years later, he died of AIDS, one of the first cases in the UK. Not that the game is simply to stay alive. But I do think it's important not to let them make you bitter. When that happens you've let them win. Poor Robert, I miss him terribly.

It was only when Brian got busted that it finally dawned on me that this was actually some sort of conspiracy. I mean the day that they arrested Brian was the *same day* that Mick and Keith got out of jail, the day after the trial ended. Give me a break, they weren't even trying to be subtle about it anymore. The whole thing was carefully planned. Obviously. Quite clearly an attempt to make Mick and Keith appear guilty by association. *Another* Rolling Stone caught with drugs! Well, what do you expect from degenerates like that?

Brian's bust was the work of the infamous Detective Sergeant Norman Pilcher (the "semolina pilcher" in John Lennon's "I Am the Walrus"). He was a bent cop trying to make a name for himself. He busted Mick and me several times after that, and later on got John Lennon. He was a bit of a groupie, I suppose! I admit I experienced a great deal of satisfaction when, in the early seventies, he was brought up on charges of corruption. Just the sort of person they *would* send out to get us: evidence fixers. Good at it, too!

That night we all went to the Hilton Hotel to do some serious unwinding. Mick and Keith were there of course. Also Allen Klein and his nephew, Ronnie Schneider. While the four of them were talking I was fiddling with the latch of a beautifully inlaid jewel box. Now this pretty little obi had a false bottom. Suddenly the latch sprang open (these things always happen to me). A trap door came out and with it a lump of hash. My stash. . . .

Allen stopped talking and peered over at this round, nubby, brown object. He had no idea what it was.

"What is that?" he asked somewhat disgustedly.

"It's not what you think, Allen. It's hash."

"Hash, as in *hashish?*" Allen was instantly enraged. "What can you be *thinking* of, Marianne? We've just sprung Mick and Keith from jail, Brian's just gotten busted, and you are going about smoking hashish?"

"How can you throw it out, it's good stuff?" I said, equally vexed.

In a fury he took the hash and flushed it down the toilet, and then he took my gorgeous little box and flung it from the balcony of his hotel room which was on the forty-first floor. He turned back to us and, without missing a beat, picked up the conversation at the point where he'd left it. I was in shock.

It was a case of persecution pure and simple, and Andrew Oldham was shrewd enough to see it for what it was. They wanted Andrew too, of course, and he was petrified. He basically stayed out of the country until it was all over, which is one of the things that caused the irreparable rift between Andrew and the Stones. Mick and Keith felt he'd abandoned them.

Every one of us was freaked. A mysterious and menacing enemy pursued us at every turn. Like the pervading darkness of *Satanic Majesties,* we felt ourselves under a malign bewitchment.

And then just at the darkest hour, a *Times* editorial by Rees-Mogg appeared titled "Who Breaks a Butterfly on a Wheel?" Suddenly the public began to see the Stones as victims.

Rees's editorial essentially said that Mick and Keith were being persecuted and that the case against them was so flimsy as to call into question the British judicial system. This protest from the heart of the establishment press changed everything. Overnight the Stones came to be seen as scapegoats. But until that moment the powers that be were really gonna do it to them.

The weekend after Mick got out of jail at the end of June, I took Mick and Michael Cooper and Michael's son, Adam, to my father's college, Brazier's. I couldn't think of anywhere else we could go and not be hounded. We needed some privacy. Somewhere out of the fray where the press couldn't get at us.

We had a wonderful time. It was very odd, naturally. My father is wildly eccentric, the food was awful (and Mick is very fussy about his food). Brazier's was catnip to eccentrics. There were little groups of people sitting around a table and someone asking "And what did you *appreciate* today, Nigel?" And Nigel would be saying something like "I saw a tractor!" My stepbrothers, from Glynn's second marriage, the twins, were there completing each others sentences like characters out of a Tom Stoppard play.

I took Mick and Michael around the attics and the parapets where I used to play as a child. I wanted Mick to see where I had come from.

Brazier's is a fantastic place, just beautiful. You can just rave around. And we did; we took full advantage!

Mick was bemused by the prevailing nuttiness at Brazier's, all these strange people just wandering around. And nobody took the slightest notice of Mick; they wouldn't even have known who he *was*. These people were in another world. They had come to Brazier's to get *away* from it all. My father, I think, was giving one of his wonderful courses on Pope. Nobody gave a shit about Mick Jagger!

Michael Cooper took all those beautiful pictures of us, but what *I* see is Michael, taking those pictures, floating along in the moment, an almost invisible presence, hovering like a hummingbird.

Michael was from London. A Jewish Cockney boy, I think. He had the most beautiful face with a nose as big as Nelson's column. And wonderful big saucer eyes that shone with life. He was one of those people from the sixties that drugs had made wide open. Lay saints who do what they love and are brilliant at it. They have that charge in their face, in the eyes particularly. He was full of ideas and, unlike so many sixties projects, he actually *did* them! His covers for *Sgt. Pepper* and *Satanic Majesties* were mini-operas, complete with fantastic sets and impossible juxtapositions. He was one of the central spirits of sixties London.

Always had a camera, always taking pictures. He wasn't shooting Mick and Keith because they were the Rolling Stones but because they were the nub of energy. And he was always at the center of things, like a force that held everything together. I was shocked that death could ever overtake someone like that. I miss him a lot.

We'd all had a great time at Brazier's and as we were leaving — we were all in Mick's Bentley going up the drive — Mick saw something odd in the rearview mirror. "Your father is running after us," he said. "He is signaling frantically." And there I saw my father running after us, waving something. Mick pulled the car over and my father came puffing up the drive. It's a long drive. And when he caught up with us he presented Mick with the bill. Full price for the weekend for me, Mick and Michael and half price for Adam. We were speechless.

"You stayed the weekend and it's nine pounds each." There was nothing to do but pay up! At the time I was so terribly embarrassed, but my respect for my father shot up immensely.

Once outside the gates of Brazier's we were back in the madness again. In July, the Court of Appeals gave Mick a suspended sentence. He had taken the blame for me; a noble thing to do. Maybe that's why he got off. Maybe justice finds its own way. Keith's conviction was quashed, and the whole nightmare evaporated as suddenly as it had begun. Mick and Keith came out of it fine. It only added to the myth and the legend. Like salamanders they emerged from the fire not only unscathed but with bright new iridescent scales.

The powers that be thought rock 'n' roll records could get the youth of the country to throw off their chains! As if a bunch of London R&B groups could actually launch a Mao Tse-tung–style cultural revolution, anyway. That was the depth of their paranoia, and, in our wildest moments, we also began to believe it was possible. The Little Men had convinced us!

Even though it was a victory for all of us, we all came out of it feeling demoralized about England. In the sixties we were rebelling because we still had hope.

The powers that be shot themselves in the foot. Now, nobody in England gives a flying fuck about the Royal Family, the government, ethics, bobbies. The establishment blames it on the decline of moral standards, but that decline began with them. Sure we were baiting the establishment, sending it up, testing the rules, but never for a moment did we doubt the essential *decency* of the system.

The two casualties within the Stones camp were Brian and Andrew. Brian was in very bad shape. Because of Brian's ongoing legal problems, the Stones couldn't get visas for the States. Mick and Keith

bitterly resented this. The level of animosity toward Brian was ferocious. It wasn't as bad as it was going to get later, but it was intense even
then. At that time Mick and Keith's way of dealing with it was to make
fun of him. If anybody had really let their feelings go, they would probably have killed him. But for somebody as paranoid as Brian, this was
just about the worst thing you could do.

Another casualty of Redlands was my mother. It was after all the
scandal that things began to fall apart for her. She started drinking heavily. She stopped showing up for work. She rarely went out of the house.
She was ashamed about the Mars Bar gossip and the girl in the fur rug
stories in the papers. When the Redlands business happened, Eva had
been attending a teachers training college. She was going to get her degree and become a proper teacher with references and credentials and
better pay. But after the scandals she stopped going; she couldn't deal
with the shame. I didn't know any of this at the time. After she died, I
found all these letters from the training school saying "Dear Mrs. Faithfull: This is the third week that you haven't appeared. And we are very
worried about you. Please come in and talk to the principal if you're
having any problems." She never went back.

In the end, the assault on the Stones backfired because it hugely
empowered the Stones. The Rolling Stones and Her Majesty's government became powers of equal magnitude. No promoter (including the
fiendishly ingenious Andrew Oldham) could have done more to
mythologize the Stones.

Before Redlands, the Stones weren't perceived all that differently
from a number of other groups — the Who, the Yardbirds, the Kinks
— but subsequently they were on another level entirely. The only other
group in that category was the Beatles.

The truly devastating impact didn't get to me until much later on
— three, four years later — because I felt protected while I was with
Mick.

I was anorexic, I was doing drugs. The energy that you need to
oppose an assault like this is phenomenal. You need a huge amount of
psychic stamina just to withstand a pressure as unyielding as that, never
mind *combatting* it.

Last year when the *News of the World* was about to run an excerpt
from Spanish Tony's book, *Up and Down with the Rolling Stones,* I put an

My mother, Eva von
Sacher-Masoch, 1935

With my father

Sarah, my Dalmatian, and
me, 1965

This picture originally
appeared with the caption
"Beauty and the Beat . . ."

On tour with the great
Roy Orbison, 1965

Bailey picture for *Vogue*,
on Primrose Hill, 1964

Me and Nicholas
(newborn), 1965

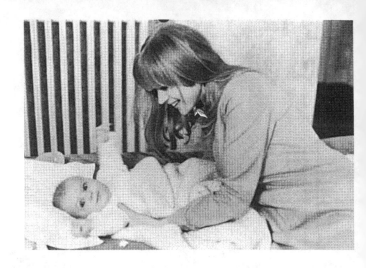

At John and my wedding party in the Lennox Gardens flat in London, three weeks after our marriage in Cambridge. From left to right: best man Peter Asher, my father, John, my mother Eva, and me

Me, by Terry O'Neill,
trying on a new image,
1966

With Mick Jagger, San
Remo, 1966. First photo-
graph together

Opposite: Girl in a Fur
Rug collage

Savoy Hotel, Decca Party
February 1967

During the trial, February
1967

NAKED GIRL AT
STONES PARTY

# STONES: 'A STRONG, SWEET SMELL OF INCENSE'

## Story of girl in a fur-skin rug

BY A SPECIAL CORRESPONDENT

The agony of seeing your idols jailed ...

REDLANDS, THE HOUSE IN WHICH POLICE SAID THEY FOUND DRUGS

Proper course

ROLLING STONE Mick Jagger

### Rolling Stone Brian remanded

Incense found

### Art man's sentence to stand

The Swinging City

"... all she wore"

No alcohol

Black suit

WHITE TABLETS

SPECIAL JASMINE

Pop idol Mick Jagger of the Rolling Stones went to court today in a lime green jacket, dark green trousers, a green and black tie and a floral pattern white shirt to answer drug accusations.

'TABLETS WERE FOUND IN A GREEN JACKET'

In pipe

GREEN JACKET CHANGE OVER

Green capsules BROWN SUBSTANCE

MICK JAGGER, lead singer in the Rolling Stones pop group, arrested at a court yesterday in a blue jacket, was left last night in a grey suit-bound with silver-must-be remanded to spend a night at Lewes Jail, Sussex.

JAGGER APPEAL

NEWS SUMMARY

### Jones (of the Stones) on drug charge

2 Stones for trial

## Stones: switch on way to court

SWINGEING LONDON 1967

WOODEN PIPE

Plastic Phial

### Meat in a cell for Mick Jagger

Mick, Adam Cooper and me recovering from the trial at Brazier's, 1967

Going to Nureyev's *Paradise Lost,* 1967 (just after the trial)

injunction on them. They backed down, and I realized this was the first
time I'd had the *energy* to fight the status quo, never mind the laws of
inertia. I didn't have it after Redlands. While I was with Keith and
Michael I was buoyed up, untouched by the day-to-day pounding. It
was only later when I got back home in London and I started to get the
hate mail, and even later, when I got clean and I started to really think
about it, that I faced the horror of it.

Every day a pile of letters would arrive in the mail that were pure
poison: "And the sooner you leave this island with your long blond hair
floating in the sea, it will be a cleaner place."

A curse is a very real thing. Like the Lady of Shalott I got into a
boat, painted my name on it and drifted downstream. I've always been
very suggestible. It's one of the reasons I have to keep so self-contained
now. I don't live with anybody. I don't want people to influence me too
much anymore. But then I was young and impressionable. I must have
believed those hate letters I got. And what they said about me came to
be. Somehow the grotesque folktale of the Mars Bar stuck to me and it
probably always will. I should have taken a cue from Mick. Mick
spewed it out, recovered and went on with his life. Forget what the
cops think. If you want to cry, then cry, cry, baby!

# Chez Satanic

AFTER the trial was over, Mick didn't miss a beat. He just kept going. I used to think, "How amazing that he came out of prison and we just went right on." We weren't going to let a little national scandal stop us. After all, we hadn't finished. We went right on with our quest.

I went out a lot on my own at that time; every night I'd go to a club. It was a habit I had acquired to escape married life; I think Mick rather liked it. Chrissie had always stayed home and made him dinner in the oven.

On one of my sorties I saw Jimi Hendrix at a little club called the Seven and a Half. I'd gone because Mick told me about him. He said he'd seen Hendrix in New York and that it had taken his breath away. "'E's gonna tear the world *apart!*" Mick didn't say things like that too often, so I thought I'd better check it out.

When I got to the Seven and a Half there were perhaps a dozen people there, including a couple of roadies. I sat in this tiny basement club for hours and watched him play. A Tantric vision in crushed velvet pants and a ruffled shirt. He was very fashionably dressed. Chas Chandler had obviously taken him to the Kings Road.

He was very awkward. He sang with his back to the stage or into his guitar and mumbled so badly that you couldn't understand one word. There were long unexplained gaps while he discussed what he was going to play next with Mitch Mitchell and Noel Redding or fiddled with his amps. He hadn't got his persona together — he wasn't yet the voodoo chile — and you could see he was *painfully* shy. But once he began playing, he transformed. It became sexually charged and very direct. I had the feeling he was playing just for me, which, since the place was empty, probably was the case. I'm such a fool; I should have hung around and seduced him. But typically, I ran away.

In March of 1967 I was in rehearsal for my part as Irina in Chekhov's *Three Sisters* at the Royal Court. It was freezing and dreary in London and I had the weekend off, so Anita and I decided to fly to Tangier with Brian. Mick and Keith were already there as were the rest of the crew: Christopher Gibbs, Robert Fraser, Michael Cooper.

Anita and I had dropped acid and stayed up all night. We had a wonderful time. We had such fun together. In the middle of all this we went to get Brian, poor baby, from the nursing home. He was having a nervous breakdown, and a drugs breakdown, too. Also a spot of pneumonia. You had to have an incredibly strong constitution to do as much acid as Brian was doing. It takes a lot out of you physically, and Brian wasn't in good physical shape to begin with. Not to mention his mental state! (God only knows what that was like.)

The pneumonia, along with his asthma, meant that he could hardly breathe. He'd be gasping for breath with his inhaler, and we'd tell him, "Do stop!" We thought he was putting it on, gasping and choking just to get our attention.

He was beautifully dressed, very solemn looking in a black-and-gray suit and a white shirt and a tie. Not at all his usual flamboyant clothes with spots and stripes. Elegant and understated, he also looked pale and washed out. We all got on the plane, at which point we shared our acid with Brian. Real smart. There was a stopover at Gibraltar. Brian was terribly excited about this. He'd brought a tape with him. It was of the sound track he'd just finished for Anita's film *A Degree of Murder,* and he got it in his head that he wanted to play it to the Barbary apes who live on the Rock of Gibraltar.

So at Gibraltar the three of us got into a cab and off we went to play his music to the monkeys. We approached the troop of monkeys very ceremoniously. Bowed to them and told them we were going to

play them some wonderful sounds. They listened to all this very atten-
tively, but when Brian turned on the tape recorder, they didn't seem to
care for it. They seemed *alarmed* by it and scampered away shrieking.
Brian got very upset. He took it personally. He became hysterical and
began sobbing. Anita and I had been on this trip for many, many hours
and we were in another place altogether.

Anita had a very disconcerting habit of turning to me and giving
me little asides, which she was awfully good at anyway. I didn't think
anything of it at the time. I was in that nonjudgmental, nonanalytical
state you get into when you're tripping. But later I realized what she
was doing. She must have known what was about to happen — she was
planning to leave Brian — and she was talking herself into it. While
Brian was frenziedly playing his music to the monkeys, she would say
"Don't you think Brian looks very pale and so *dull,* and not very alive?
He's very *bloodless,* wouldn't you say?" And I looked at him and had to
agree, "Well, yes, he does look a bit peaky." He didn't look too well,
but I *liked* the way he looked. He had that romantic pallor of the very
sick.

I couldn't even hold up my end of the conversation, much less
help Brian! But I remember looking at Anita and it seemed that I had
never seen anybody so gleaming and alive and vibrating. She was dazzling. And next to her was the fading, pathetic Brian, looking very
sickly indeed. He barely made it through another year after that. Maybe
a little longer. He wasn't quite on his last legs yet; he was still trying to
hold it together, trying to hang on to the woman he adored.

The flight was getting quite intense. With Anita on one side of me
and Brian on the other and a very disturbing vibe going on between
them, I was beginning to feel very jangled. Then I got a brilliant idea. A
very Eva idea, actually. It's just what my mother would have done. I had
brought a beautiful new edition of the complete works of Oscar Wilde
with me in my bag. I got it out and said, "Why don't we read *Salome*
aloud, the three of us? We'll each take parts and act it out and it will pass
the time." So that's what we did. It was absolutely great. All the way
from Gibraltar to Tangier we read *Salome*. Brian played Herod, I read
Salome and Anita was Herodias. She was wonderful: "You vill not
dance, my daughter!" all in her Marlene Dietrich inflection. We *were*
Herod and Herodias and Salome (it was really good acid!).

When we got to Tangier, they stopped us at the airport. Obviously they were going to check us out. We looked absolutely insane. Anita and I were wearing feather boas in brilliant colors — reds and purples. We were giggling. Brian, by this point, had cheered right up. He was having a great time. The customs officials opened my suitcase. They were speechless. All I had packed were some shells, an Indian sari and an Edmond Dulac picture book. It looked beautiful. The sari was a soft, silvery, purple material. We all gazed at it. A suitcase packed by someone on acid. Exquisite little things; more a collage than a suitcase.

That may have been the best time I ever spent with Brian, but it didn't last long. The next day Brian broke his arm. He had tried to hit Anita and instead hit the iron frame of the window. We dumped him in the hospital in the Clinique Californie and went off to have a cup of chai and some hash. In the souk we saw this wonderful man carrying a white Chinese pot on his shoulder. We thought he looked interesting so we followed him. He led us down some steps to his tiny shop, which was completely empty. There was *nothing* in it. But it was a beautiful pale blue, as if you were under water. His name was Ahmed and all he had in his shop was a little wooden box with four bracelets and a ring and a lot of hashish. We sat down and smoked a few joints. We made friends with him and every time we were in Tangier we went to see him. He got very big at one point. Over the next four years, the shop grew into six shops, all in a row. And lots of assistants. And a huge white car with Swedish au pair girls falling out of the side of it. He became a local celebrity covered in jewels and all that. Then he got put in jail and now he's poor again and has returned to the bosom of Allah, I hear.

We smoked a lot of hash, to the point of immobility. It was so liberating to be out of England. It had been Allen Klein's idea that we should leave the country until things blew over. Go somewhere where smoking hash was routine. Well, here we all were again, getting high and speechless — but in Morocco. Now Ahmed's shop was beginning to feel like a claustrophobic Chelsea drawing room. I had to break the hashish-smoker's spell. I was feeling quite light-headed. As soon as I stood up, all ties to our mortal coils vanished. I began to dance to the Arabic music on the radio. I was wearing my sari. I was Salome dancing before the court of Herod. I spun faster and faster until my sari began to unwind. I kept twirling until I was completely naked and, much to

Ahmed's delight, kept dancing. He clapped his hands and shouted. Mick was not so enthusiastic. He got up and left the shop.

Later Cecil Beaton turned up to shoot some pictures of Mick around the swimming pool. Cecil was bitchy and fussy and too hot. Although he was curious about Mick, you can see from Stephen Tenant's biography that only the young men of his *own* day were really beautiful to Cecil. The extreme dazzle of the thirties. He couldn't see what Robert and Christopher saw in Mick. I found Beaton insufferable. After a few minutes I left Mick and Cecil Beaton to their little dance and went off to flush out Anita. She had cornered William Burroughs in the depths of the hotel lounge. Anita was obsessed with Burroughs and that's when I got the Burroughs bug. Not that he paid the slightest heed to me in those days. To be honest, he never spoke to me until 1987. They completely ignored me; I was just an empty-headed little girl with not a thing to say.

Enchanting as it all was, I can't say this was a simple uncomplicated holiday in the sun. One day while walking in the Atlas Mountains with Mick and Christopher I burst into tears for no reason. Christopher and Mick were astounded: "Whatever on earth is the matter?" they asked in that quintessentially Brit way. Oh, nothing, really, just a spot of existential anguish, I suppose. Carry on! I used to have a lot of those crying jags when I was with Mick. He brought out all my feelings of worthlessness.

Here I was with the whole gang, all in Morocco together — all anywhere for that matter — and I was ill at ease as usual. These were our best friends, Mick enjoyed their company and they adored him. But we were *always* with them. We were never alone. For years I'd been trying to get away from all those people once in a while and spend some time alone with Mick. I didn't like living my entire life from morning till night in a fishbowl. Mick, on the other hand, liked nothing better. Quite oblivious to my ingrained agoraphobia Mick would dash into the bedroom with an opened letter and exclaim: "Look at this, Marianne! Paul and Talitha Getty have invited us to Sidi Mamoun for five weeks in March. Too fuckin' much, *innit?*" I've never been crazy about social life, and the whole feeling of being on display all the time began to get to me early on. But for Mick this is an essential part of life. For him life *is* theater.

There was a wonderful night in Tangier where we had been at a club watching a group of Moroccan dancers, beautiful girls in brocaded native costumes. There was one particularly exquisite girl and after the performance I went backstage and asked her what she was called. She said her name was Yasmin. I asked her if she would come back to the hotel with us. I told her, "I'll pay you." It must have been something she did on the side because she quickly agreed.

She changed out of her costume into her street clothes, a short black skirt and a knitted halter top, and we all went back to the Minzah. I did it to turn Mick on, and it did. I enjoyed playing the role of the adventurous one, the one who would do the things Mick wanted to do but didn't dare. In these situations I don't hold back at all, I just go to the center of it, whatever it is.

The room was candlelit. We were fulfilling a fantasy men have of being in bed with two women. Mick did all sorts of things with her but, as usually happens in these situations, the man ends up watching the girls from the other side of the bed. Mick rolled a joint and watched as Yasmin and I carried on.

She began whispering to me in demotic French, "*Je t'adore! Je t'adore! J'allais baiser tout ton corps, ma chère. Parce que nous rendezvous, toute seule, un de ces après-midis, n'est pas?*"

She liked me and I found myself *very* turned on by her. When I emerged from my drug-induced stupor in the mid-eighties, I had to ask myself if I wasn't really gay. I came to the conclusion that I wasn't, although I enjoyed sleeping with women. It was just an intensely sexual period in my life.

Shortly after this I went back with Mick to London and went on with my rehearsals. It was in Morocco that Anita sloped off with Keith. Keith is a very straight arrow. He was appalled that Brian beat her up. Of course, he'd been in love with Anita for ages, never saying anything to anybody. I don't think he ever thought he'd get Anita, and he wouldn't have if Brian hadn't acted like such an asshole.

After the scenes in Morocco, Keith came along like the proverbial knight on the white charger and carried her off in his Bentley. He'd just gotten that Bentley and he'd taken it all the way to Morocco. He'd had it driven there! It's that crazy thing with men and their cars — they couldn't bear to be separated! In some ways it must've become *him;*

Keith and the Bentley were one and the same. Darling, the Bentley will have to come with us. Take it or leave it!

*The Three Sisters* opened at the end of April 1967. My dressing room, which I shared with Avril Elgar and Glenda Jackson, was terribly small, and for my first night Mick sent me an orange tree. Glenda Jackson was very sniffy about that. She thought it was outrageous. "A *tree?* A bloody tree in this poky little dressing room? Couldn't he have sent you a basket of flowers like everybody else?" It did, of course, take up about half the room and everybody's clothes got snagged on it, but it was sweet. A small, perfectly formed orange tree. But a tree nevertheless. I think we had to get rid of it. Mick came every night. Not always for the first two acts, but he would always come for the last act.

After Anita had left with Keith, it looked for a while as if Brian might not continue with the group. A crisis developed because the Stones were already booked on a few European tours. Anita persuaded Brian to go on the Polish tour by telling him that they would get back together after the tour. They went to the Cannes Film Festival together and spent some time in Rome afterward. Anita was there to audition for the part of the Black Queen in *Barbarella.* It was Terry Southern's script and Terry had recommended her for the part. But then Brian beat her up again, which pretty much put an end to their relationship for good.

Mick was wonderful at this time. Really surpassed himself. Loyal, true, proper and just great in every way. Brian, Keith and Anita were behaving abominably, but Mick was cool and honorable throughout the whole business. Always trying to do the best thing. He took the high moral ground. He didn't get involved in petty games. But because of his love for Keith he was unable in the end to sustain this objectivity. When you love somebody, you can't help but take sides. And with Anita and me already very close, Brian soon found himself shut out altogether.

I never went on tour with the Stones. I once joined Mick on tour and it resulted in the most horrendous incident of our entire relationship. After that I never went again.

Things were going well with Mick and me in the spring of 1967, and to surprise him I flew out to Genoa which was midway on an absolutely mad Italian tour. I went straight to the hotel and waited for him to come back from the concert. It had been a very wild tour. There was a lot of haywire energy. I remember reading about it on the flight over: kids rioting, incredibly violent clashes between fans and the *carabinieri*. Thousands of young, Italian male groupies attacking the limo, rocking it, trying to overturn it. Grotesque photos from inside of hands and faces squished up against the glass like animal faces, Bacon paintings. At the concerts girls pulled off their panties and threw them on the stage. It was their first taste of the big time. Not just screaming fans but your actual Italian aristos and movie stars paying homage to them. There were riots in Rome when Brigitte Bardot and Gina Lollabrigida attended the Stones concerts there.

Evidently there had again been riots at the show that night. People had been trampled. Mick came straight from the concert to the hotel. I was waiting for him in the bed in my negligee. The minute he walked in he was a different person. It was as if he were someone I didn't know. He was absolutely *possessed*. As if he had brought in with him whatever disruptive energy was going on at that concert. It goes both ways. From the performer to the audience and then it comes back at you *magnified*.

He didn't say hello, he didn't even acknowledge me, he just walked over to the bed and began slapping me across the face. Not a word was spoken. I was absolutely terrified and I fled into the big white bathroom. He followed me in there and continued to hit me. He beat me quite badly and I didn't have a clue why. My first thought was "Oh, shit. He must have found out I had a little night with Keith." Such a ridiculous thought! In any case, I knew Keith would never in a thousand years have told anybody. Even Anita didn't know.

Nothing brought it on. It just erupted out of some inner turmoil as if a demonic force had taken him over. When it was over, it was like a hurricane that spent itself and stopped. We never, ever mentioned it. To this day I don't know what it was about. He never did anything like that again. He's not the kind of person who would. I don't think it was anything to do with me or him. He didn't know what he was doing, a victim of mob lunacy. It was on that tour that it all started to change. The Stones had been big in England and the States for years but now they were becoming symbols. Something critical was happening to them and, along with the strain of the bust and the trials, it caught Mick unawares. He hadn't had time to develop the proper defenses or an adequate persona. He was still very raw. The laid-back, aristocratic persona all came later.

After this, Mick took that volatile energy and controlled it, put it into another form. He harnessed all the negative forces and materialized them. Out of these destructive impulses he created the incredible personae of the late sixties — the Midnight Rambler, Lucifer, Jumping Jack Flash. All manifestations of malignant and chaotic forces, the ungovernable mob. Chaos, Pan. That frenzied power caused many of the casualties of the sixties. Certainly Janis Joplin, Jimi Hendrix and Jim Morrison. But Mick didn't destroy himself; he learned to channel it. He *is* a control freak, after all! I don't know whether it's there anymore. Probably now sedated by money and fame. But at that time and with all those doors being opened and all the acid we were taking, it came out quite a bit.

The potential for violence was latent; it was always there in the Stones. The English are just very good at repressing it. And, of course, when you repress something like that, you put it under pressure and it becomes explosive and when unleashed very violent (as we know from the Dionysian rites, the Baccantes tearing people limb from limb in ecstasy).


In the summer of 1967 Mick and I went to Rome to see Keith and Anita. Anita was playing the Black Queen in *Barbarella.* The city that the Black Queen rules over is built on this atmospheric fluid that allows her to suck the life out of everybody in the city. There's a wonderful scene with Anita lying in her dream chamber at the center of the city tapping into everyone's dreams.

Anita got lost in her part. How demented you get all depends on the part, and it was a very nutty part that Anita was playing. Jane Fonda got all the sensible stuff in that movie and even that was pretty silly. The scene in Rome gravitated around Keith and Anita. There were Christian Marquand, Terry Southern and Julian Beck and Judith Malina of the Living Theatre. Terry was very funny about Anita's immersion in her role. He teased her a lot: "Ah, by my troth, here comes the Black Queen! Rats scurry across polished marble floors, and little snakes hiss at her baleful entrance." There was a lot of that going on.

Then there's that line between put-on and reality, which is never quite clear in these situations. That one got crossed by our Anita a great deal. Early afternoon there'd be "Darling, sometimes vhen I am at Cinecittà I really do *believe* I am the Black Queen." As a joke, naturally. Then eight hours later and a lot more stoned: "But you know vhat? I really *am* the Black Queen"; and then another eight hours later a scary: "I AM THE QUEEN OF ALL I SURVEY!"

Now it's true that at this point Anita was doing a few lines of coke as well as the hash but it's a cop-out to put everything down to drugs. She'd been working on *Barbarella* for months and months. Over budget, over deadline, everything. And on top of that there's the overwhelmingness of Cinecittà. You can't believe what it was like. And Anita was in costume *all* the time. She had the most wonderful clothes. All her own clothes began looking like the Black Queen's outfit, so even when she wasn't in her costume she just looked like the day version of the Black Queen. The Black Queen's casual wear. Wonderful. Even better in a way than the costume in the movie, which was the most boring, obvious bit of stuff. She put herself together in the most exotic way. She was at her most beautiful.

Anita was just doing what many actresses do. I'm the same way. It's true you can play Ophelia and not want to drown yourself in the Thames every night, but that would be too sensible an approach. You *want* to get carried away by it. It's a great relief to be someone else for a while. Anita was just getting into her part more than some might consider sane — but I don't think it can be simply written off as drug-addled behavior. For one thing, they weren't doing that much. Not yet.

One day the four of us were strolling around Rome when we were besieged by a gang of kids who appeared out of nowhere and recognized Mick and Keith. Swarming over us, grabbing us. We began running from this mob of fans, fleeing up narrow cobbled alleyways. It felt like that scene in *Suddenly Last Summer*. Teeth, hair, glistening eyes, hands reaching out for us. They were out of control. Anita was so terrorized she almost had a heart attack.

We ran and ran until we came to a dead end. To the right was a tiny alley that led up the hill. Tripping over steps and cobblestones, we stumbled on. Damn these heels! At the top of the hill was the Villa Medici, the home of the French Academy in Rome where Stash was staying with his father, the painter Balthus. Stash saw us coming and let us in. The huge Renaissance door shut behind us. We heard their fists pounding on the door behind us.

Stash invited us to stay the night. He *sneaked* us in actually. He was not on very good terms with his father at the time. We all took acid. It was moonlight, a full moon. There were Baroque staircases and a beautiful, formal, eighteenth-century garden with citrus trees. And with the sort of mood that conjures up, we all became someone else, we all became characters out of the past. Later that night Anita and I saw a ghost. A distraught courtier in boots and a white embroidered shirt who walked about the halls whispering *"Nessuno puó trovare l'uscita."*

We walked about the gardens all night in the moonlight waxing poetical and metaphysical. In the morning Mick sat in the garden strumming his guitar to a dirge like tune, *dun-dun dun-dun-dun, dun-dun dun-dun-dun.* It was the melody to what would eventually become "Sister Morphine."


Mick and I were blissfully happy that summer. We were in love, we were young, rich, protected and the world was at our feet. Mick wanted us to get married and have children. He felt that after the bust and the trial, this would be a good move. And he probably was right. It certainly would have been a good PR move. But in my normal, perverse way, I just wouldn't hear of it. I wasn't even divorced yet. I was wary of getting married again. Anyway, I didn't think we needed to get married. I thought we would just stay together forever. What did the state or the church have to say about it? It never dawned on me that there would come a time where I didn't love Mick and would want to leave him. I was twenty when all this happened, Mick was twenty-four. What did we know?


After a year or so at Harley House we moved to Chester Square. I never liked Harley House. It was Chrissie's place. It was right opposite the

Marylebone Hospital with the ambulances wailing all night long. I couldn't take all that pain!

It was the first very social phase of my relationship with Mick. There was a lot of staying up all night and Mick holding court. Anybody who came into town would come and see him. The house in Chester Square is where Gram Parsons got nabbed by Mick and Keith to work on *Beggars Banquet* and *Let It Bleed*.

It was a big posh house. Neither of us cared for the decor, but since it was rented there wasn't much we could do about it. Christopher came up with a way to get around this with masses of Moroccan hangings that I draped all over the sofas, the walls and the floor. Not too good for the hangings but it was wonderful for what we wanted: a lot of lying about looking great. In the middle of all this North African splendor was a huge glowing green Perspex flying saucer that I had bought from Robert Fraser's gallery in Duke Street.

We went out almost every night dressed up in our finery — to the ballet, a club, gallery openings, the theater. It was the peaking of the London fashion parade and there were parties every night. We missed not a one. Mick was, in John Lennon's words, the "king of the scene."

Mick was obsessed with Rudolf Nureyev and we saw a lot of him. We went to all his first nights. I remember one particularly. It was a ballet he had made for himself called *Paradise Lost*. At the climax he dived like a cannonball through a drawing of a huge pair of bright red woman's lips that resembled a vagina — they looked very like Mick's lips actually — breaking the paper. (Those lips were to show up quite prominently on subsequent Stones tours.)

One night we went to see Jimi Hendrix at the Speakeasy. This was a few months after I'd seen him at the Seven and a Half Club. He was by now the toast of the town and on the verge of displacing Mick as the great sex symbol of the moment. After the show, Jimi came over to our table and pulled up a chair next to me and began whispering in my ear. He was saying anything he could think of to get me to go home with him. All the things he wanted to do to me sexually. Telling me he'd written "The Wind Cries Mary" for me. Saying "Come with me now, baby, let's split! Whatchya doin' with this jerk, anyway?"

I wanted more than anything to go off with him, but I was a coward. And Mick would never ever have forgiven me. Throughout this whole scene Mick remained a model of Brit sangfroid.

Becoming involved with me did not simplify Mick's life. He'd taken on me and Nicholas. And I was still married. Just after we moved in there was a wonderful-awful scene between Mick and John Dunbar at Chester Square. John and I had split up ages ago but John apparently had never entirely given up the idea that we might come back. One day he showed up at Chester Square. He had a big row with Mick and at the end of it, just before he walked out, John said to Mick, "You're nothing but a ten-cent Beatle." Mick didn't say a thing. He was flabbergasted. It sounds very funny now but it stung in those days. Especially for Mick. Mick idolized the Beatles. He always wanted to be John Lennon.

Nicholas was the big bone of contention for John. He was furious that Mick had me *and* his son. He hardly saw Nicholas again for years. And that, of course, is the thing that John is very bitter about. Rightly so.

Despite all the socializing, family life was one of the best things about living with Mick. We did the typical things families do. Michael Cooper and his son, Adam, virtually lived with us, too. Mick was very fond of Nicholas and Nicholas loved him. Mick's wonderful with kids. He has that quality Hitler and Göring had: nice to dogs and children.

As much as Nicholas may have loved Mick, he naturally missed his father. One evening, while we were at Chester Square, Nicholas wandered off in his dressing gown and slippers and somehow got himself on a Green Line bus to Kent — presumably on his way to see the Dunbars. We were frantic, but soon located him at a village police station — happily drinking tea and eating biscuits with the local policemen.

My most indelible memory of this period is of an idyllic afternoon I spent with Mick and Keith in Ireland. We had gone to look at a beautiful, gemlike little eighteenth-century house called Castle Martin. We went inside briefly to see the split staircase in the great hall but we didn't stay. It was such a beautiful day. There was a lawn leading down to a stream and trees overhanging the stream. It was a very hot day. We lay on the moss by the stream and slept and dreamt. We didn't speak for hours.

And then, as the sun was setting, I looked up and saw Keith in the middle of the stream with his shoes off, poking about in the stones, looking like an old Gypsy man, in one of his manifestations — as a poacher. And Mick lying there looking as he always did in those days, like a multicolored, medieval boy.

There was a routine to it, even in the drugs. We were rarely alone. There were always masses of people milling around. They wanted to be near Mick. Mick loved that. A dazzling, scintillating group of people — all in love with him.

Living with Mick I learned early on to disregard myself as a sexual entity. *He* was the sex object. To everybody! It's much easier to appreciate somebody's erotic fascination, their homosexual appeal, when you're a *long* way away from it, believe me. To feel all that charge and to know it mustn't come to you is a funny feeling for a woman.

In London in the late sixties there was a great honoring of the homosexual side of life. It didn't express itself overtly. It was just in the air everywhere. It created some very odd situations. I remember one quite vividly involving Mick, Robert Fraser and me.

I was at Robert's flat. It was a lovely summer evening. We smoked a couple of joints. Robert, so elegant in his pink suit. We used to call him Strawberry Bob because he loved pink. And out of the blue Robert made a pass at me. He was gay, of course. But the times being what they were, it was all very blurred. He leaned over and kissed me quite passionately on the lips. And just at that moment the bell rang. It was Mick. I figured it was a blessing in disguise — some things are better left to the imagination.

Mick was wearing a beautiful silk jacket with a large hand-painted face on the back. He saw immediately that something was going on between Robert and me. He just picked up the vibe and proceeded to go completely berserk. He was so angry he sort of swelled up like a bullfrog. And being so strong and athletic and the jacket quite tight-fitting, he split the thing to shreds. We never did find out if he was jealous of Robert or me.

This blurring of sexual lines was part of the creative mix of the era, but it also had its dark side. The homoerotic subculture had as a nasty by-product a virulent strain of misogyny. And Mick and Keith were hardly immune from this. Their overt misogyny of the *Between the Buttons* period reappeared in disguise with songs like "Midnight Rambler" and "Brown Sugar." To me it was a further example of what Anita and I have often talked about — their utter hatred of women. Compelled to have them and can't bear them! Very English, actually.

The trial and acquittal bonded Mick and Keith — but it created a very odd dynamic. For Keith it was just an alliance within a group, but for Mick it was a lot more than that. It has all the irrationality and passion of a love affair. It's a pity that the things people put Mick down for are what make him Mick: his narcissism and his queeniness.

Lennon and McCartney had a similar bond between them. Not as strong, of course, but both groups had these duennas, these strange bisexual — almost witchy — figures as managers. Brian Epstein and Andrew Oldham.


We went to see the Maharishi with the Beatles that summer of 1967. All the Beatles. And all their wives. When we got to Bangor in North Wales where the Maharishi was in residence, it suddenly felt as if we were back in school again. It was actually a boarding school that was empty because of summer holidays. Very austere and Spartan for us rock hedonists. We were the only people there. There wasn't any press.

There were already some misgivings being aired about the Maharishi. We'd heard from Miles that the word in India was that the Maharishi was suspected of certain financial improprieties and sexual peccadilloes. Also an obsession with fireworks.

We went in separately to see him. He gave us each a mantra and a few flowers and we had brought flowers for him. He giggled a lot and had very cheerful, light vibes, which was a relief. It wasn't heavy at all. He slightly reminded me of the sort of guru that might appear in a Beatles *movie*.

And then in the middle of all this the news came from London that Brian Epstein had committed suicide. The Beatles were desolate. All of them. It was as if a part of them had died. It was a dreadful moment, and the Maharishi acted so badly and so inappropriately.

"There was a death in the family. There are many families, there is one family. Brian Epstein has moved on. He doesn't need you anymore and you don't need him. He was like a father to you but now he is gone and I am your father. I'll look after you all now." I was appalled.

That summer Allen Ginsberg came to London with the Italian poet Giuseppe Ungaretti. He came to read Ungaretti's poetry in English at Queen Elizabeth Hall. I hadn't run into him for ages and I was dying to see him again. I invited him to come and see us at Harley House. Allen was ushered into the bedroom and sat on the bed. Mick and I were in bed naked under a fur coverlet. *The* infamous fur rug. We sat around talking about music, the Marquis de Sade, *The Bedroom Philosophers*, William Blake, Dante, drugs, Vietnam, mystic convergences, magic, politics. Small talk of the day.

Allen, as usual, was on a mission. It was at the crescendo of the Vietnam war, and Allen was trying to persuade Mick to put William Blake's "The Grey Monk" to music. He felt he had a calling to convert the rock 'n' roll scene to William Blake.

"Who could speak more eloquently of our condition than Blake?"

"Waall, my thoughts exactly, Allen." A wink from Mick.

But at the same time he was interested. He respected Allen, poets in general. After all, he was one himself. The Rolling Stones do *Songs of Innocence and Experience* would have been pretty silly, but in the heat of the moment I was all for it. We nearly got him to do it, too.

It was these sort of encounters — with poets and painters and mad scholars ranting about *Les Mystères des cathedrales* — that broke down Mick's barriers. You can imagine having Allen Ginsberg going on at you about Blake and Hoderlin. Burroughs rambling on about soft machines and the thought police. It all sunk in. Mick was interested in everything in those days. He was insatiably curious. He read Eliphas Levi, the 1870s French hermetic magician who had influenced Rimbaud and later the filmmaker Harry Smith.

I remember one particularly odd merging of American academic poets, rock stars and West Coast hippies. Panna Grady was an heiress and a patroness of the arts, especially the literary underground, and at the time she was romancing the poet Charles Olson. She gave a party to which she invited all the poets and writers in London. Burroughs was there. R. P. Blackmur, William Empson, Patrick Cavanaugh along with Pig Pen from the Grateful Dead and Emmett Grogan of the Diggers and Mick and me. Mick among the poets!

In came Allen with a great flourish. He was wearing big, showy Shivaite beads. He went over to Mick, looped them over his neck and asked had he ever heard of Hari Krishna.

"Allen, darling, he *is* Krishna," I said. "But only on acid."

Then we all went and sat down in a little alcove in the front room. Allen had a harmonium with him and began chanting mantras to Mick, accompanying himself on the harmonium. Just as he began singing, a drunken Chris Jagger, Mick's brother, stumbled in, saying: "What you sayin'? What you *sayin'* that for? What you pooftas tryin' to pull then? Who the fuck do you think you are? You think you're *somebody*, eh, do you?" And on and on, breaking it up. So Mick never got to hear the end of it. Who knows, Mick might have written an opera based on the *Mahabharata*.

A few days later Mick sent his chauffeur over to get some Owsley acid that Pig Pen and Emmett had left with Allen. We took the acid, then we went to Primrose Hill where the ancient ley lines are supposed to have run. The stars lined up. We didn't see, as Blake had done, a "spiritual Sun" on Primrose Hill but we did see *something*, a great face in the sky whose voice may have been just traffic and city noise, but which we managed to convince ourselves was the singing head of the god Bran awaking from his thousand-year sleep on Tower Hill.

I think all that acid in the sixties did Mick a world of good. He transcended all his pettiness, his guardedness. Mick became much more open and bloomed and everything went brilliantly for him. Now when I read interviews with Mick, he says he regrets it all terribly. He says that during this time he wasn't really himself. And, of course, something did take us over! Mick allowed himself to be a channel. And in the end that bothered him. LSD burned away all the dross. Ultimately he completely rejected it.

We all did acid for ages and then we all stopped. It was as if the mission was accomplished. Whatever had to happen with the head opening and the mind opening was finished and that was that. Looking back, I see that all this peeling-away of layers was a perfect set-up for hard drugs later on. But that didn't happen for a while. Heroin came with the disillusionment and suffering, later on.

I had made a fateful compromise when I met Mick, and it now began to cause tremors in our lives. I thought that I could stop the endless tours and appearances, but I now saw that stopping was a mistake. When I was working I could get up to all kinds of mischief that I couldn't while I was at home.

I soon found myself in a very odd state. I wanted more. I craved new experiences, and they soon appeared.

I made a couple of terrible movies that year. *I'll Never Forget What's 'is Name* with Oliver Reed in which, appropriately enough, I have the distinction of being the first person to say "fuck" in a legitimate movie. And the soft porn *Girl on a Motorcycle*. It took three months to make. I was away a lot and Mick visited me on location in Zurich and Heidelberg and the South of France.

Alain Delon was the star, and very early on in the film he tried to pull me in the same desultory way that Roy Orbison had. When I turned him down, he became very sullen and nasty and difficult. He was such a pompous ass, in any case, and every time he said that ludicrous line "Your body is like a beautiful violin in a velvet case," while unzipping my leather suit, I would crack up. It was dozens of takes before I could do it with a straight face.

During the making of *Girl on a Motorcycle* I began having an affair with Tony Kent, who was a magician, a card sharp and a photographer by profession. He was an American living in Paris. It was a wonderful romance but very complicated.

I went to his studio to have some pictures taken. Tony began to talk about magic. We smoked a couple of joints and then I left for Orly Airport to get my plane to Heidelberg, where we were about to begin shooting. They'd just called my flight when Tony appeared. He'd followed me out to the airport. He simply got on the plane and flew to Heidelberg with me. It was such heaven. I didn't think Mick would ever find out, but I'm sure he knew. He was sending me roses daily, and that could only mean he knew I was having an affair.

My relationship with Mick was completely public so I loved my extramarital affairs. They were as private as you could get. They were secret!

Whenever Mick and I felt we were getting onto rocky ground we'd go away somewhere and spend time together and fall in love again. We took our first trip to Brazil right after *Girl on a Motorcycle*.

Off we went, Mick, Nicholas and I. It was our first long trip on our own. We went first to Barbados, which I really hated. It was the mid-sixties, and Caribbean resorts were still very tacky. This was before we learnt to appreciate tacky.

We were thinking of buying a big old house on a Caribbean island. This involved a lot of hopping around on little airplanes. I got it into my head that we were going to crash. I had taken along with me a tape of the Dylan bootleg album that came out later as *The Basement Tapes*. It had a lot of heavy songs on it (along with comic surreal stuff) "too much of nothing," "waters of oblivion," "wheels on fire." I drove Mick crazy playing it over and over and over again.

After a couple of weeks we decided to see what else we could find in the world. Finally, we caught a flight to Rio de Janeiro. We never emerged from the hotel until the evening when it got cooler, then we would go out and eat caviar and drink champagne. But we didn't need to travel halfway around the world to do that, did we? We were looking for a change.

We met a black couple from New York and they told us about a wild and strange place on the coast north of Rio called Bahía. And off we went. That's when it began to get hairy. We were quite on our own. There was no Alan Dunn, no Tom Keylock to arrange things for us. We found a hotel and settled in.

That first night there we got stoned and went to watch a fantastic folk religious ceremony in a little town. It was absolutely riveting. It all took place outside a beautiful Portuguese cathedral, although it has nothing to do with Christianity. The entire outside of the church was lit up with colored bulbs like a Broadway theater, and all the adjoining streets were strung with lights. Wild dances, drumming. There were no other white people there at all. None. For some reason the participants took offense at us. I think it was because we were white; perhaps we looked like the Holy Family! Mick had a beard and very long hair, I had long hair and was carrying a little child. Whatever it was, we *enraged* them, spontaneous hatred out of nowhere. We had to get the hell out of there. It was this experience that I've always thought led Mick to use a samba as the basis for "Sympathy for the Devil."

It was in that little town that I read *Naked Lunch* for the first time. William Burroughs was a cult figure among my friends. We were all the children of Burroughs. And I had a blinding flash. This was something I was going to have to pursue. I would become a junkie. Not in that high-life way like Robert — little lines on expensive mirrored tables — but a junkie on the street. This was to be my path.

We met some Brazilians who found us a little hut by the sea on the edge of the most beautiful tropical forest. (With maid service!) No beds or cots, just hammocks. Nicholas had a terrible time falling asleep in a hammock. Making love in a hammock was quite interesting, too.

My relationship with Mick was still romantic. We were very happy in this place, on our own. While we were living in the hut another saint's day came along, this time dedicated to the goddess of the sea. Only the women of the village participated in the ceremony, and this time they invited me to take part. It concluded with a ceremony where all the women brought flowers and threw them as an offering into the sea. I got hold of twenty-four red roses, I don't know how (Mick probably). I broke the petals off and threw them into the sea. It was absolutely glorious, the flowers floating on the sea, the sun setting, the women chanting, the goddess rising up out of our collective devotion!

# Through the Looking Glass

AT Christmas, Dirk Bogarde gave a very grand party at the Connaught Hotel and all the luminaries of British theatrical society came. Maggie Smith, Paul Scofield, Julie Christie. Essentially people Robin Fox represented. He was my agent, too; it was through him that I got the part of Irina in *The Three Sisters* at the Royal Court. He was also the father of the actor James Fox.

It was a terribly stuffy affair. The hippest person at the party was Julie Christie. You'd have thought a theatrical gathering of this kind would have been bubbling with witty repartee and wicked anecdotes, but one forgets these people are *actors* (poor darlings!) and nothing at all like the characters they play. Instead, it was a stodgy bunch of actors talking shop. Only in England could the leading members of the theatrical profession carry on like the upper reaches of the clergy.

Across the smoky room I spied James Fox and his new girlfriend. James was a beautiful young man on the scene and I knew him, of course, through his father. James Fox became famous for his portrayal of the feckless upper-class character in the film *The Servant* and that's where his persona came from. But it was James's girlfriend, Andee Cohen, who caught my eye. She was an exquisite little thing. A vivid, fluttering creature, very thin and androgynous, with dark hair cut short like a boy's, and big, big eyes. The guests at the party were people James normally associated with, but James and Andee were off by themselves, due perhaps to the horrified reaction James's family had to his taking up with Andee. An evil witch come to corrupt the young matinee prince. Which was, of course, was just what the young player prince had been hoping for.

We were relieved to see two other people in the room we could relate to. Kindred spirits! Let's go over and talk to them. It was instant rapport.

We were laughing, gossiping, flirting, making catty asides about the other guests, talking much too loud, and generally carrying on. The more raucous we got, the more uptight the others became.

I saw at once that though James was very much of this scene, he desperately wanted to be understood by a different group of people. That's why he was with Andee in the first place. She was an unrepentant bohemian, obviously an artist of some sort and outspoken in everything she said. Preposterous and profound observations flowed out of her as naturally as some people breathe. I adored her at once.

After that evening we started hanging out together. It was a *folie à quatre*. James was fascinated by Mick as if by some genie of mimicry and energy, and Mick was equally taken with James. Mick has always had a thing for upper-class folk, especially when he suspected they might enjoy a guided tour of rock slumming. Mick's curiosity about James had a professional element as well. James was a fine actor and Mick had begun to think about acting as a possible career for himself. Well, here was a famous actor whom he could observe at close range. He wanted to see how James ticked.

We'd often go out and wander about together. There was a place on Fulham Road called the Baghdad House with curtained booths run by two Moroccan brothers. People smoked hash openly in the restaurant and listened to eerie chromatic *maqam* music. But the best times were the long white nights spent lounging about at home.

We'd go over to James's flat or they would come over to Harley House and smoke hash and drink wine. These were enchanted evenings. Everything unfolded with magical ease. We sifted through the past, selecting exquisite bits and pieces from other eras: furniture, books, ideas, art, other lives. Andee would talk effusively about her past lives. Egypt, Samaria, the court of Louis I, the Tang Dynasty.

Mick was an impeccable host, always jumping up to get things, juggling conversations, finding something new and amazing to dip into. And, of course, he always had fantastic records.

"Listen to this one, man. Knock your socks off. Albert far-fuckin'-owt Collins and 'is tawkin' git-tar!"

He'd play wonderful old blues and Motown, Hank and Audrey Williams duets, Sun Ra and Joe Tex. He was the greatest in-house dee-jay in the world.

"Now, fer all you submarine watchers out there . . . Cuh-zen Bru-skie commin' atja at one o two point fi-uhv on your ray-dyo dial . . . wassamatta baby? . . . Turn me loose!"

He loved Smokey Robinson. He would act out the steps *à l'anglais,* sing along, miming the clockwork footwork, coming right up to your face as in an extreme close-up doing his R&B vaudeville of Slim Harpo or Carla Thomas.

"Oooooh! Oh, mah soul! Ya *gotta* hear this track. Please girls, a little reverence for the Godfather of Soul."

I'd have all my fairy-tale books spread out on the bed: Edmund Dulac, Arthur Ransom, Rossetti, Heath Robinson, all those bizarre Victorian illustrators. Faces coming out of trees, talking fish, the King of the Mountains of the Moon and his bewitched court. Andee would peer down with her big eyes into these old children's books. Moss-encrusted caves of goblins and elves that she could leap into. I think she really *did* fall into one, and never quite came out! I'm sure that's what happened because she's *still* into all the nuttiness we then swore by: the Zohar, Castañeda, Madame Blavatsky, Aleister Crowley, Charles Fort, John Michel, Escher, Druids, UFOs, Tantra. The hippie canon. Mick was totally absorbed in all this too. Celtic fairy tales and *The Secret of the Golden Flower.*

James was a Dylan freak (not quite as bizarre a pairing as Dylan and General Schwarzkopf, but still . . . unanticipated). Dylan was one of the absolute necessities for tripping along with Ravi Shankar and Ali Akbar Khan and — Steppenwolf (the band). Dylan was the voice of God, after all. (But then, a lot of people were the voice of God. The first time I heard Aretha, *that* was the voice of God; the first time I heard Otis, *that* was the voice of God. Percy Sledge was the voice of God. But Dylan was the voice out of the fiery furnace.)

These were the years when all life transpired on the bed. Listening to records, talking on the phone, rolling joints, playing guitars took place on and around the bed. The bed was a sort of charmed island. Acid and hash induced a Lotus-Eaters' indolence and languidness. You wanted to drape yourself on the bed, lie around on stacks of pillows and vibrate. Scarves over the lamps, tiger balm, worn ballet slippers, picture books of weirdness, incense and tapes all over, albums stacked leaning against the wall. A Gypsy's life.

When I saw the scene in Coppola's *Dracula* with the three girls lying on the bed and Dracula falls on the bed with them, I thought, "Oh my God, it's the sixties!" Hanging around in someone's bedroom — all over their house — was what you *did* in those days. It was all hazy edges and blurred lines. Today if someone invites you into the bedroom it's serious, a sex scene. You don't even go upstairs in people's houses anymore.

Our bed was enormous. I don't think such a bed existed before the late sixties! It never occurred to me that furniture might have much of an effect on anything, far less that it could seal one's fate. But this was the sort of bed that in fairy tales leads their owners to do strange things. It might be said that it was this bed that began the decline and fall of the drug-drenched Duchy of Chelsea.

When Mick first bought it, I remember asking him:

"What the hell is *this*? I spend months trying to furnish this flat with the most exquisite things and you go out and buy a bloody battleship to sleep in. Why can't we have a lovely old four-poster or something?"

"Because they don't make king-size four-poster beds."

"King-size beds are for fat middle-American couples with half a dozen kids. Why do we need a great monstrosity like this?"

And he said quite sweetly: "One of the worst things about living with Chrissie was that the bed was too small and I could never get enough space."

I thought, "Well actually that makes sense." I never have liked *sleeping* with people. I much prefer to have sex and then leave and go to my own bed. I've always been like that.

One day Andee came over by herself. Mick and I were spending the weekend in bed swathed in newspapers and magazines. Mick always flirted outrageously with Andee but it was all very camp and fun. It's so British to flirt. It's part of the relationship — kissing, petting, hugging. Mick and James flirted with each other, too. We were all laughing and giggling and carrying on.

By and by James arrived. He walked into the bedroom and when he saw the three of us, by now piled up together on the couch, he stood there and went quite blank for a moment, like someone who'd forgotten his lines. He was the man in the bowler hat come to sell mining shares at a house of ill repute. James had actually forgotten who he was. He did not know the rules to this game. A big, wicked smile came over Mick's face.

"'Ello, James, you're late for the orgy, *again*. What's your excuse this time?"

"I picked up a bottle of this exuberant Sauvignon that Dirk recommended. Would anyone care for a glass?"

"Did you happen to bring any *cocaine* to go with it, James?"

"Well, no, actually, Mick . . . I, uh . . ."

"What bloody use are you, then?"

"Shall I get some glasses?"

"Now, James, *Dirk* always told *me* that he and Princess Margaret wouldn't dream of touching a drop of Sauvignon without a little coke aperitif."

"Did he really?"

"Well, of course he bloody didn't, James, now go and get us some glasses and a rolled-up twenty-pound note, there's a dear."

"Oh, well . . . yes . . . right."

"Kitchen's *that* way, James, but never mind. Come 'ere and give us a kiss, luv."

James had fumbled the ball. Mick'll do anything to keep the game rolling; he loves to instigate. James was the perfect straight man, the classic stooge. In the plot Mick was hatching, all he had to do was pretend he was having a torrid affair with Andee, and James would earnestly write the rest of the sketch himself.

When Andee came into the room Mick would put his arms around her and steer her off into a corner.

"Come 'ere darlin', come in 'ere a minute. Excuse us, we have some very *private* business we *urgently* need to attend to."

And then he'd drag Andee over to the bathroom, lock the door and start making loud lascivious noises as if an incredible sex scene were taking place in there. This could go on for twenty minutes with James sitting stiffly outside in a chair just freaking out. He hadn't the faintest idea this was all a lark. Only very recently did Andee tell him that Mick was pulling his leg all the time.

Mick kept everything buoyant and light. He'd retained his childhood playfulness and mischievousness. Mick was a flirt and a tart, and his androgynous quality gave him an edge. He was always trying to throw people off balance. Testing, probing. . . . Stir it up!

If Mick ever got to James and Andee's flat while they were out, he would quickly cook something up. As soon as Mick heard the door opening he'd say: "It's bloody James. Quick, girls, under the sheets.'"

We'd get under the covers and wiggle about, as though we were screwing. When James came in, we'd all stop and look stricken — as if we'd been caught in the act, trying to straighten the sheets.

"Andee's soooo good at hospital corners," naughty Mick would say. "I could just watch 'er at it all fuckin' day. You're a very lucky man, James, y'know that? If I weren't a married man myself . . ."

"But you're *not*, darling, are you?" I'd point out.

It all went right by James. It was as much as he could do to keep his head above water. Trying to be very proper and gentlemanly about it all. There's three people in your bed, apparently all fucking, including your girlfriend, you've caught them *in flagrante* and you're trying to pretend it isn't happening.


One night Mick, Andee and I had taken acid — James didn't use psychedelics. We were high as kites. I don't think it would have happened if we hadn't been tripping. It was great acid, it just exploded. Torrents of images streamed through my head. The bottleneck guitar was telling me we were in a deep dense muddy bayou, but when I looked down a second later I saw we were in Egypt. The looming bed was a barge on the Nile and we were all on it.

My beside lamp was turning into Tatlin's *Monument to the Third International*, the shade unscrolling itself up to the ceiling in a flat curl containing little reliefs that like a loquacious Trajan's column mimicked and commented on what was gong on.

Andee had become the Pythoness of the world, revealing the mysteries of the millennium:

"There are these subatomic particles coming through that could change us. They've been predicted on the Maya calendar for ten thousand years. *That's* what we've been looking for in all these drugs!! Don't you see, it's all just *bad reception*."

The carpet undulated in little ripples of apricot and ivory. Andee and I were slave girls of the great pharaoh languidly reclining on the royal barge. The pharaoh was fondling James. (It was going to be a very tactile trip.)

We trailed our feet over the edge of the bed into the madder red ruby rosettes of the carpet. Indigo petals floated by like lily pads randomly bearing tiny detached heads of people I had known. I could now read our Persian-Kurdish rug in a way I had never been able to before. It was a mythological map of Samarkand with interlacing arabesques of mechanical peacocks, saffron pavilions, orchards and gardens and cypress trees.

We lived these lives a thousand years ago as courtesans, as opium-eaters at the court of the Kubla Khan. We had drunk of the milk of Paradise and its transforming liquidity made us all quite porous. There were no boundaries where Alph the sacred river ran. No genders, no time and space. We simply sparkled and vibrated. We were all pulsating little Bodhisattvas. I was in love with everybody. Actually, I *was* everybody. I was becoming confused as to who I was and who was who but what did that matter anyway? In such a blissful state as this you could easily fall in love with a chair, with your own shoes. What an absurd thought, someone *belonging* to someone else! God, and to think they started the Trojan War over stupidity such as this!

Sooner or later something was going to take place on this bed, and tonight was evidently going to be the night. It was the raison d'être for the bed — if Mick couldn't get Keith into bed, this was the next best thing.

I caressed Andee, and as I touched her the flesh melted and rippled under my hand. Beneath her skin her phosphorescent heart glowed in pulses of light. I felt as if I could just reach into her body and touch it. I began kissing her, undressing her, licking her breasts. She sighed very ardently and pretended to swoon as if she had suddenly gone limp under the heat of passion and fell back on the bed. We were two odalisques in a Beaux Arts painting of harem girls. As I leaned over her she began to laugh. It was so exquisitely absurd, a mixture of eroticism and kitsch.

I lay naked beside her. I took her nipple in my mouth and began to rub it against my lips. We glanced over to see what effect our little performance was having on Mick and James. They had stopped talking and were watching us with obvious voyeuristic interest. We giggled. It turned us on and we began extending our repertoire. The more aroused they became by our lovemaking, the more it egged us on.

No one else knew about our little evening, of course, not a soul. But somewhere out there in that damp London night, the chief Dracula of this scene, the director Donald Cammell, must have opened his window and snatched it out of the air. Without apparently knowing what happened at Harley House that night, Cammell re-created it in *Performance*.

The Redlands bust and trial as well as problems with Brian kept the Stones from touring much during 1967 and 1968, so by the spring of 1968 Mick had become restless. He was beginning to feel his role as lead singer of a rock 'n' roll band was too confining. This role was something he would later be forced to re-invent, but in the meantime he was casting about for something new. As a culture hero Mick could have become almost anything he wished. For a while, he flirted with the idea of becoming a Labour Member of Parliament!

It was that pivotal moment in the late sixties when all our fantasies of taking over the world seemed to be coming true. Unfortunately, Mick wasn't really that interested in politics. Certainly not in left-wing politics. But *I* was! I'd come from a socialist background, my mother and my father were both Labour supporters. So when the flamboyant

Labour MP Tom Driberg decided to court Mick, I was delighted.

If anyone from any political party could have persuaded Mick to go into politics it was Driberg. Tom was utterly charming, beautifully dressed. Such a perfect model for Mick, too, because he had a lot of money. He had a country house, he was a homosexual, and he was a Labour MP!

He came to Cheyne Walk one afternoon with Allen Ginsberg to ask Mick to run for a seat in Parliament. And, at this point, Mick really could have done it. He was very principled for a while there. And he had been taken aback by the vindictiveness of the Redlands bust. Mick was going around saying a lot of semiradical things at that time: "Teenagers the world over are being pushed around by half-witted politicians who attempt to dominate their way of thinking and set a code for their living."

This was the period when he wrote "Street Fighting Man." He let go of his middle-class hang-ups. Mick Jagger, Leader of the Labour Party in England! And me, the little anarchist in the background, pushing.

It was all taken quite seriously for a while. He went into all the possible objections and conflicts: "What about touring and all that? My first commitment is to my music, so I wouldn't want to have to give any of that up to sit behind a desk."

And Tom said, "Oh that wouldn't be a problem. You could carry on with your music same as you always have and still do something very important for the party."

"Ah mean, I don't exactly see meself *scrutinizing* the Water Works Bill inch by inch, if ya know what I mean."

"Dear boy, we wouldn't expect you to attend to the day-to-day ephemera of the House. Not at all. We see you more as, uh, a *figurehead,* like, you know . . ."

"The Queen?" said Mick, completing his sentence.

"Precisely!"

The first meeting with Driberg got off to a good start — lots of funny chat and zinging questions — and then almost foundered with a very out-of-character, maladroit gambit on Driberg's part. We were all sitting on cushions on the floor, Mick was wearing a jerkin and tights of some kind and in an awkward moment of silence Driberg looked at Mick's crotch and suddenly said "What an *enormous* basket you have."

Oh, well, it probably wouldn't have worked out anyway. I think Mick sensed that the Stones had a more pervasive influence than any politician's. He also knew that it would be unbelievably dull!

I suppose on the most banal level it must have come down to them wanting to get the youth vote. I don't think Mick liked that idea, being bait.

Anyway, Keith finally did the idea in. When Mick asked Keith what he thought, Keith told him it was the stupidest thing he'd ever heard.

He was clever, Driberg, because he could see exactly what Mick wanted, which was a form of respectability and had these overtures come up during a fallow period like the *Goat's Head Soup* era, it would have been one thing. But this was Mick and Keith's most creative period. The time from *Beggars Banquet* to *Exile on Main Street*.

All of the anarchy and hedonism which the Stones personified finally burnt out by the time they got to *Goat's Head Soup*. There was a total breakdown of the vital spirit, of the soul, due to the use of heroin and cocaine. That's decay, not anarchy.


When Mick's flirtation with politics began to fade, a more obvious solution presented itself. He would simply become a movie star.

And why not? Of all the rock performers of the sixties, Mick was the most likely candidate. Over the years a number of projects based loosely on Mick's charisma had been proposed. For as long as anyone could remember, Andrew Oldham had claimed he was getting (or had) the rights to *A Clockwork Orange,* and everybody agreed there could hardly be a more perfect Alex than Mick. In fact, a number of people actually signed petitions to this effect. Then came the next best thing: *Only Lovers Left Alive,* a sort of poor man's version of *A Clockwork Orange.* Mick began taking acting lessons. Then there was *The Man Who Shot Mick Jagger* and a whole slew of hippie projects. Christopher Gibbs and Nigel Gordon had written a script based on the mystical Middle English romance *Gawain and the Green Knight.* Mick was going to play the Green Knight. Mick and Keith do the Middle Ages! Who was going to cut off whose head was a subject of much discussion, but at least they could both wear tights. Another of these daft film projects was called *Maxigasm* and involved sky people and flying saucers. Nothing came of any of them.

And then in the spring of 1968 Donald Cammell started talking about an idea he had: a film about a reclusive rock star and a gangster on the lam. The film would be specifically built around Mick. *Performance*.

All the conditions for this project seemed auspicious. Mick was at his most beautiful, the directors Donald Cammell and Nicholas Roeg were friends of ours, and we knew just about everybody in the film in one way or another. Anita Pallenberg, James Fox. Everyone would be playing themselves, more or less. That couldn't be too difficult, could it? What a colossal misreading *that* would turn out to be.

They were making a film out of what the public imagined our lives to be. It was voyeurism that got the financing for the project from Warner Bros. I should think they envisioned a Hollywoodized version of our circle complete with moral and retribution.

Even before the first day of shooting, *Performance* was a seething cauldron of diabolical ingredients: drugs, incestuous sexual relationships, role reversals, art and life all whipped together into a bitch's brew. All I knew was that I wanted to be as far away from it as possible. I moved to Ireland with my mother and Nicholas.

I was expecting a baby, after all. Mick and I were ecstatic. We both hoped it would turn out to be a girl, and in anticipation gave her the name Corrina.

While looking for our own place, I stayed the first few weeks with Desmond Guinness at Leixlip Castle. One weekend Mick and I flew to London, then back the next day to Leixlip Castle. And in the time I'd been away the nanny I'd hired to look after Nicholas had locked him in the nursery, taken an emerald ring of mine and left. Nicholas was not discovered until the next day. He was peeling the wallpaper off the walls by the time they found him, trying to get out. Nicholas was three at the time and I resolved not to leave him again. *Performance* seemed very remote; I didn't want to think about it.

I eventually found a lovely old house in Tuam, County Galway.

Mick would spend every other weekend with us. While he was at home we read the script together. It was an excellent screenplay. But as the project moved to the final shooting script, Mick became apprehensive. He realized he didn't have the faintest idea how to do it. He knew hardly anything *about* acting.

My reading of Turner was as a symbolic figure. Vaguely tragic, a little pathetic, but still with an edge. He was the archetypal sixties rock apocalypse character. A pre-Raphaelite Hamlet. We worked it out very carefully and put it together, element by element.

I suggested he start forming his character based on Brian. Also his hair should be a very strong, definite color. To do Turner as a blond would have been too much. In the end he dyed it black, very black, a Chinese black, like Elvis's hair. Brilliant. Straight off it gave him a strong graphic outline. His tights and costumes gave him a tinge of menace, a slight hint of Richard III.

The idea of using Brian as the basis for Turner was a good start, but as soon as he began rehearsing the script it was obvious that this was too simplistic. Characters on the stage and especially in movies are composites, like dream characters. So we thought, "What about Brian and Keith? Brian with his self-torment and paranoia and Keith with his strength and *cool*."

Mick's personality was not dark enough or damaged enough to support a mythic character such as Turner. Turner was a sort of jaded Prince of Denmark Street, but Mick was no Prince Hamlet. There's nothing truly mythic or tragic about Mick. He's too normal, too sane for any truly bizarre fate to befall him. Brian and Keith seemed, if not actually tragic figures, at least *fated* personalities, human beings with fatal flaws caught in the tow of deep undercurrents.

Underneath all these overlays a lot of Mick bled through so in the end you had a wonderfully complex characterization. He did his job very well, so well in fact he *became* this hybrid character. What I *hadn't* anticipated was that Mick, by playing Brian and Keith, would be two people who were extremely attractive to Anita, and who were in turn obsessed with *her*.

In a sense most of the people in *Performance* weren't acting at all. They were exhibiting themselves. Real gangsters, real rock stars, real drug addicts, real sirens.

One of the quirkiest things Donald did was to switch Mick's and James's class roles. It was brilliant. Mick played the aristocrat and James a working-class hood. James became the archetypal servant, while Mick was the ineffectual blue blood, the very qualities that he always taunted James about.

Let's face it, we were all pretty lightweight, pretty naïve compared to Donald Cammell. Donald was older and more devilish. This is why Andee was afraid for James's immortal soul. She was very chary of Anita, too. Anita was the dark queen under an evil spell, so gorgeous and dangerous. But the sarcastic, sophisticated and decadent Donald was the major Dracula.

Donald's method of directing was to set up a vortex. Into this vortex went every disorienting thing you could imagine. God knows what drugs were being taken on the set, and then add to that all the indiscriminate sex. James Fox was, of course, very fearful about sex and drugs and rock 'n' roll, but he was even more terrified of his *own* dark side. From a very proper and respectable British theatrical family he was suddenly plunged into a den of iniquity filled with drug-snorting, hedonistic rock 'n' rollers and decadent, sexually ambivalent aristos. His sole bearings depended on Mick, someone with whom he already had a problem gauging the genuine from the put-on. He was totally out of his depth. *Performance* exposed a lot of things and exposed a lot of people to things that they had (wisely) stayed clear of.


While *Performance* was being filmed, I felt, quite erroneously, that I had nothing to worry about. I never imagined Mick would be fucking Anita.

I see Anita as very much a victim of all this, the vulnerable one who should have been looked after and protected. Her breakup with Brian over the previous year had been devastating. It was only natural that she would find Mick's incarnation of Turner irresistible. Their characters were propelled toward each other, and she already had a hard time distinguishing what was real and what was imaginary.

The only person who was never out of control and might have showed some restraint was Mick. But poor Mick was on a bit of a high wire himself. He was somewhat cowed by Donald, who had a ferocious temper and would go off like a firecracker, unleashing blistering tirades. Mick found the whole process of filming very bewildering. Compared to performing in a rock 'n' roll band, it was excruciating. The repetitiousness, the retakes, the out-of-sequence performing to thin air. Mick was losing control!

I tried not to think about it at all. I concentrated on living with my mother and Nicholas in Ireland and pretending everything was okay. Anita was my dearest friend and Mick was the man I loved. I was expecting his baby. I guess I knew by then that things weren't right between Mick and me, but I didn't know what to do about it. It was terrible.

And anyway, who was I to talk? I'd had my blazing affair with Tony Kent the year before. It was like that then. . . . If it felt good, you did it. That was part of our creed. It would have been *hypocritical* not to sleep with someone simply because he or she was involved with someone else!

Mick and I in our usual manner never discussed it. It just stayed there hanging between us in the air. I knew nothing then about talking things out, and even if I had I wouldn't have had the courage to bring it up. It would probably only have made matters worse.

Even the customarily fearless Keith couldn't handle this one. While filming was going on Keith deliberately stayed away from the set. To go up there would have meant a head-on clash with Mick. Keith knew that if he had ever done so, it would have been the end of the band.

It was just before they started filming that Keith wrote "You've Got the Silver." He and Anita were staying at Robert's flat. Robert had rented his place to Anita for an exorbitant amount of money and then refused to move out, creating yet *another* quasi–ménage à trois.

Keith's method is to take the germ of a song and nag at it, all the while keeping it to himself. He played his guitar constantly. I never saw him without it. He's the lute player sitting in the window, that's Keith exactly. Always gnawing at a song. And very secretive about this process. It stays in his head until it's finished. And then out of the blue he'll drop it on you. A dazzling thing to do. It knocks people dead.

We were sitting on Robert's beautiful seventeenth-century four-poster bed. Robert leaning against one post, me against another and

Keith and Anita entwined at the other end of the bed. Keith began to play "You've Got the Silver." He sang it in a very drony and nasal twang as if the song were still somewhere deep inside him and only just emerging. We were speechless. It was a love song for Anita, obviously. The depth of his attachment to her was just flowing out of him. Very romantic, very consummate love. Which is why Anita and Mick's betrayal during *Performance* was so devastating to him.

So what he did instead of confronting them was to hang out at Robert's flat in Mount Street pouring all his turmoil and hostility into songs. What came out of that was *Let It Bleed*. All that pent-up anger. It turned out to be one of the Stones' most uncanny tappings into the zeitgeist. In "Gimme Shelter" Keith's mind spun out into a mythical take on where we all were heading. As an album, *Let It Bleed* allegorized the themes of *Performance*. Took its toying with the occult and made it into satanism and turned its flirtation with the gangster netherworld into anarchy.

*Performance* was truly our *Picture of Dorian Gray*. An allegory of libertine Chelsea life in the late sixties, with its baronial rock stars, wayward jeunesse dorée, drugs, sex and decadence — it preserves a whole era under glass. By some sinister exchange of energies, the film took on a florid and hallucinated life of its own while those involved (and on whom it was based) began to fall apart almost as soon as the film was finished.

The fusion of life and drama in *Performance* had some deadly aftereffects. People who fall through sugar glass skylights often end up falling through real ones. If ever a film set off a chain reaction, *Performance* was it.

Certainly Mick came out of it splendidly, with a new, shining and impenetrable suit of body armor. He didn't have a drug problem and he didn't have a nervous breakdown. Nothing really touched him. In the same way that some actors get to keep their wardrobe, Mick came away from *Performance* with his *character*. This persona was so perfectly tailored to his needs that he'd never have to take it off again. This *is* Mick Jagger as far as most of the world is concerned and by this point probably to himself as well. He came out of *Performance* with two new characters, actually. The one we know and feel whatever it is we feel about it — *that* Mick — and another, more sinister one: the gangster figure, heart-of-stone type. This character first appears when Mick sweeps his hair back and becomes the ruthless thug who will do *anything* (including killing people) for money. The money-mad Mick, devotee of Mammon.

If one person comes out of a situation like this very strong, someone else is likely to come out very badly. It seems to go like that. This was James Fox. He gave the best performance of his acting career in the film and then went nuts.

Michele Breton didn't fare so well either. She became a heroin dealer in Marseilles shortly after the film and is, I think, probably dead by now.

It was soon after *Performance* finished shooting in the fall of 1968 that drug use among our inner circle took a quantum leap. It's when things become completely unacceptable to the human spirit that you turn to alcohol, to drugs to help you get through. It's a form of self-medication, an act of self-preservation.

It was right after *Performance* that Anita really went off her rocker. For years. Into an abyss.

Our world like a magician's box collapsed inward on itself. It was as if we willed it to happen, peevishly wanted to wreck it. Let the walls come tumbling down, not like the battle of Jericho, but the house of Usher.

We all forgot Dylan's Dictum. We should have left it all behind and never looked back. That's what Paul McCartney and Linda did by going to Scotland to live on an island with sheep and chickens and not see anybody after the sixties. But *Performance* changed everything. For one instant we looked back and, although we didn't become pillars of salt, I found that when I turned round again there was no ground beneath my feet.

# If I'm Mary Shelley, Where's My Frankenstein?

WHEN I finally got back to England at the end of 1968, I found our new house on Cheyne Walk in Chelsea filled with free-loading liggers. Mick had hired a cook and invited half of the Kings Road to come and stay. We would have a vast dinner at about seven o'clock, *en famille,* with all these mad people still involved in their messianic, desperately futile film projects. It was the sort of ménage that Mick fantasized about in songs like "Live with Me." I put up with this mad scene for about four days and then I threw such a tantrum that the walls shook. I began to throw plates and saucers at Mick. The cook was sacked; Tony Fuchs and his boyfriend were thrown out. Finally, peace reigned. Mick loved it when I did that. He rarely got to see me rant and rage!

Domestic life was still enormously exciting, but it was now on more of a mental level. The sexual side of the relationship had all but disappeared, and since we didn't want to break up we had to cast about for other things to take its place. For Mick it was his work; he was doing his best work in this period. He would get up, read the papers, go to the theater and then work in the studio till eight in the morning. On the nights he was at home we would stay up reading in that lovely old bed together. Me with my Arthur Machen's *Great God Pan* and Mick his M. R. James. He'd say "You've got to 'ear this one, Marianne.

It'll *chill* yer bones!" And he'd read me a ghost story. That kind of thing. We no longer leapt into bed to make love.

A very agreeable intimacy developed between us; the nice feeling that your partner doesn't expect too much of you! I liked that very much, the camaraderie, the easy understanding between us, but there were long periods of boredom.

Mick is a great conversationalist, but discussing any of my real fears or problems with him was quite out of the question. However hip or enlightened they are, Mick and Keith are also very English, and in England you just don't talk about emotional things — even with your lover. Personal feelings and anxieties are taboo. Anything unpleasant has to be hidden. I was just as much to blame. I held back. I was no more willing to talk about these things than Mick was.

We talked less and less about things that mattered. One of the biggest barriers was hip protocol. I was the victim of cool, of the tyranny of hip. It almost killed me. A lot of that had to do with smoking too much dope. All that hash precluded talk altogether, except of a very general nature. Subjects of any seriousness or personal concern were totally *verboten*.

The most serious unspoken thing between us was the loss of our baby, Corrina. I had miscarried after returning from Ireland. I was too anemic for the baby to come to term. I felt devastated and guilty and it took me ages before I could even begin to grapple with my feelings about it. I began turning to drugs (chiefly barbs and alcohol) to block it out. It was at this point that it all becomes a feminine morality play.

I was somewhat surprised how quickly Mick seemed to be able to snap back from the loss. He just plunged into his work, and now that Keith lived next door there was nothing to stop him working day and night. Whenever Mick felt he'd been ignoring me, he would turn up with roses or jewelry, but I always lost the jewelry and I've never cared much for out-of-season roses.

Mick was around less and less. He was working all the time. I was back to my old routines. I often used to go out alone. Sometimes I would go out to events I particularly wanted to go to as a proxy for Mick.

I remember going to a dinner with Tom Driberg and W. H. Auden. In the middle of the evening Auden turned to me and in a gesture I assume was intended to shock me said, "Tell me, when you travel with drugs, Marianne, do you pack them up your arse?"

"Oh, no, Wystan," I said. "I stash them in my pussy."

I was so high most of the time, and in that state you're extraordinarily aware of things going on around you, but often wonder whether you're imagining them. Acid is a very sexual drug. The whole idea of two sexes that mate exclusively with their opposites seems an absurd concept on acid. The conventional taboos seem completely ridiculous.

I didn't mind Mick sleeping with men at all and it wasn't as if I was always walking in on him *in flagrante* with some man. Unlike myself. Mick was always coming in on me and finding me in bed with a girlfriend. He would laugh, then he would pretend to be upset.

Saida had been my girlfriend for years and, in any case, I always felt that having a girlfriend wasn't exactly being unfaithful. Mick seemed to feel the same way. It wasn't another man, so that was all right. But Saida thought of Mick as a rival.

Saida's drug of choice was Mandrax, which led to some funny incidents. I remember once at Cheyne Walk, getting high with Saida, who, as usual, had taken far too many of her little pills. Many more than even I had taken. Saida had a little Mini, and in our incredibly wobbly condition we got it into our heads to drive to some club. We managed with great slow-motion deliberation to get into the car. But Saida was so stoned she was driving at about five miles an hour and even at this snail's pace we managed to have a crash. The police came and we were talking to them like a record played at the wrong speed. Things like this were always happening to us.

With Mick in the studio all night, I was left on my own most of the time and began to get involved with other men. I was expected to be Caesar's wife. I don't think he had any idea how promiscuous I was and would have been shocked. He came to know, eventually. And it embittered him.

My first affair at Cheyne Walk was with Prince Stanislaus Klossowski de Rola, known to all as Stash. Stash had a crush on me for ages, going back to the time I was married to John. One night Stash climbed up the wisteria on the front of the house to the balcony of Cheyne Walk. He got into the house and came up to my bedroom making a grand entrance in his cape. Well, that deserves a fuck, I thought. It was terribly dangerous. Mick could be very jealous. But Stash knew exactly where Mick was. He'd just left him at the studio. Mick was at Olympic and was going to be there till six in the morning.

Mick would stay out in his studio in the garden until six or eight in the morning; he had his friends, the other musicians he was working with. He was writing very productively with Keith. For Mick the impetus to work is very strong. He was learning to play the guitar. Eric Clapton was giving him lessons and he was getting better and better at it.

Meanwhile, I'd be pacing around the house alone or with Anita, both of us bored to tears and feeling rather useless and ornamental.

It wasn't as easy a gig as it sounds. It's a bit like life in the seraglio. Luxury, drugs and a lot of waiting around for the sultan to make an appearance! Anita and I dealt with it very well, under the circumstances. What we had in common was magic and books. But mainly we talked about things that people talk about when they don't want to talk about what's really happening. We would take acid and dress up a lot. Anita's idea of help in those days was to give you drugs. And there's nothing quite like drugs for making time pass.

We did what girls do. Kissed. Took baths together. I was madly in love with Anita. She was so gorgeous. The one time we began to make love we were interrupted *in flagrante* by Mick and Keith. We were upstairs at Anita and Keith's house, caressing each other and kissing on the bed and in the middle of our lovemaking Mick and Keith walked in. Mick's attitude was, "Let's join 'em." But Keith put a stop to it right away. There's quite an old-fashioned side to him.

I had a great deal more in common with Anita than I did with Mick. Anita and I would spend the day reading passages from *The White Goddess* out loud to each other. That's what we loved to talk about: phases of the moon, alphabet dolmens and mnemonic finger poems. That was *our* stuff. We didn't speak about it in front of other people.

Anita eventually took the goddess business one step further into witchcraft. There were moments, especially after Brian died, where she went a little mad. This was the period when the filmmaker and self-styled warlock, Kenneth Anger, was on the scene. There were a lot of crazy West Coast magus types around. All this occult stuff had been percolating out there for ages. It existed in England, too, but it was all very hermetic and gothic and secret. Hidden in Crowley, and much more dark and dire.

Kenneth was obsessed with the Stones. He claimed to have seen Brian Jones's supernumerary witch's tit and believed Mick, Keith, Anita and I all had one. He clearly had a crush on Mick and for a while Mick indulged him. He was entertaining and appropriately creepy, but when his protestations went unanswered and he took to hurling copies of William Blake through the windows of Cheyne Walk, Mick took all our magic books and made a great pyre of them in the fireplace.


There was still acting, love affairs and drugs. I'd had my first line of coke at an apartment in Kensington. Robert put out six large lines of cocaine for us and gave me a hundred-dollar bill. I said, "What do you do?" And he said, "You put it in your nose and you snort it." I knelt down and snorted all six lines. His face was a scream: half amazed that I'd done it all and half appalled. I didn't know the drug etiquette. I quickly learned it.

The first time I did smack was when Mick and I went to see Stargroves, a great grim Victorian house that Mick bought later in the year, with Christopher Gibbs and Mason Hoffenberg. On the way back to London we had to stop a few times for Mason, who was very unwell. The last time we stopped to "freshen up" Mason was at a coaching inn in Newbury.

I was playing Irina in *The Three Sisters* at the time and I was sure that I was going to miss my entrance. I had to get to the theater by half past six, and I was in a panic. I decided I had to have a line of smack.

Mason kept saying, "You don't really need this, baby, you know."

"But Mason, I really *want* it."

"Believe me, you don't. Why are you doing this, you stupid bitch?"

"'Cause I'm going to be late. And if I'm late I, I'm just gonna die."

Marianne, ever eager for fresh experience! It wasn't enough to be whirling toward an unknown universe. I needed that something extra.

I found myself taking a curious but detached interest in what was going on around me. As if I were watching a movie of my own life as it took place. Whatever happened seemed to have nothing to do with me personally.

Heroin was different from any other drug I had ever tried. The other drugs had been taken in a quest for sensation. This was the cessation of all sensation. What is so seductive about heroin is that there is an absolute absence of any kind of pain — physical or otherwise.

It made me so sick I almost missed the performance *altogether.* Every time I came off stage I had to throw up in a bucket.

The director Tony Richardson had seen me in *The Three Sisters* and asked me to play the part of Ophelia in his production of *Hamlet* at the Roundhouse, which opened in March 1969. Tony Richardson, like everybody else, was in love with Mick.

He had a Machiavellian streak. He wasn't just a bisexual narcissist living his life; he was a *director,* which gave him a license to indulge in serious game-playing. He was bitchy, sarcastic and ruthless; in other words your typical director.

I got very little direction from him — he just let me walk out there and vibrate — but I did get a lot of manipulation. Directors will do almost anything to extract the reactions they want from you. Never mind the havoc this might cause in the lives of the actors. At some point I figured out that my affair with Nicol Williamson had been set up by Tony. Nicol played Hamlet, and Tony wanted to get that charge out of the two of us on stage. We would make love in Nicol's dressing room before going onstage.

Nicol was very mad and possessed and helped me a lot, especially with the technical stuff, the Shakespearean meter. Nicol read his lines in a run-on North Country lilt meter, but for that to work the rest of us had to do ours in iambic pentameter.

When I started to play Ophelia I was getting deeper and deeper into drugs, much to the despair of Mick. I was also getting involved in a long affair with Tony Sanchez, dealer by appointment to the Stones. I can't believe I did that! I didn't get enough pocket money from Mick and I didn't have any money of my own, so how else would I have been able to get my own drugs? That was the level of my thinking. Not a pretty picture. I had charge accounts at every shop, but I never had any cash. I now realize that if you do want drugs, then you have to make your own money and buy them! To live outside the law you must be honest, but I didn't understand that yet. For years I simply charmed and seduced people to get what I wanted.

He was a dreadful person. You only had to see him eat to know how loathsome he was. He was a lowlife, a small-time spiv, but a weakling at the same time. He was as enchained as anyone else, completely hung up on his own particular sickness. It's odd to realize that the person you're sleeping with is there only because you're Mick Jagger's girlfriend. Or were!

Mick never knew too much about my affair with Spanish Tony. If he had known, I imagine he would have found it measured up perfectly to his contempt for women. He has a very low opinion of them.

For years I had been babbling about death in interviews. That was play-acting. There came a time, however, that it stopped being a performance. The combined effect of playing Ophelia and doing heroin induced a morbid frame of mind — to say the least — and I began contemplating drowning myself in the Thames. I was acting as a child does. I *became* Ophelia. I had fused with my part the way Anita had done in *Barbarella*. The difference, of course, being that Anita had been playing a dragon lady out of a comic book, too operatic a role to really infest your daily life (even for Anita), whereas I was playing a teenage suicide. I would indulge myself in lurid pre-Raphaelite fantasies of floating down the Thames with a garland of flowers around my head.

Little by little, but in such tiny increments that I didn't even notice it, drugs were destroying me. The progression happened over a period of years from my first taste of heroin with Mason. I went through times when I didn't do any drugs at all, especially when Mick and I went away. By the time I began doing *Hamlet,* I was still doing rather little. But then Spanish Tony started arriving every night during intermission and giving me a jack of heroin. Right before the mad scene!

It was easy for people to put my strangeness and my lack of engagement during this period down to drugs. But drugs simply made it easier for me not be involved in life itself. I really didn't feel involved anyway. The ability to be there and not be there was something I learned long before drugs. The little stony place I retreat to. Drugs just gave me a way to *explain* my withdrawal, but what was behind that detachment was a lot more than the drugs.

Mick and I had regaled Keith and Anita with tales about our wild adventures in Brazil the year before, and now they wanted to go. All of us together in the tropics. The subsequent trip was much more controlled and of course a lot less interesting. It was really just like being in London or Rome or anywhere you like. Our little group on another set; only the scenery had changed.

The insect life was astounding. We had a monstrous mosquito problem. They were huge; the size of your thumb. The attacks became more and more violent. They ruled us. Around six o'clock every night Keith would take a rolled-up newspaper and embark on his mosquito blitzkrieg throughout the house. But by the end of our stay, even Keith capitulated. We just sat on the porch covered in them.

In self-defense I draped myself from head to toe. I wore large hats with veils, long-sleeved dresses that trailed along the ground and high red boots. And this is how I would walk around in the jungle, an apparition with a persistent cough.

There were wonderful moments — for Nicholas's birthday I filled the swimming pool with little floating candles — but the vibes were weird. It was right after *Performance*. It was supposed to be a chance to heal the wounds (and cool out our accelerating drug habits). Keith and I still were feeling very jangled from Mick and Anita's affair on the set. There was no residual emotional link for Anita. Like all her affairs it was a fling, and when it was over that was it. But Mick obviously did not feel the same way, and the shadow of *Performance* cast a pall over the whole trip. Mick was continually whispering come-ons in Anita's ear, but for Anita it was over.

Anita was beginning to cool it with drugs, too, because she was now pregnant with Marlon, but Keith and I blazed on. Smoking the powerful Brazilian grass, *macuña*, guzzling cough mixtures, anything we could get our hands on. It was on this trip to Brazil that Mick wrote "You Can't Always Get What You Want." He could see it was getting out of hand. Mick knew that if I went on along the path I was on, we weren't going to be together much longer, but he never talked about it except in songs.

In Brazil the situation among Mick, Keith and Anita seemed to boil up into a lethal brew. I never understood quite what was going on. I felt I was there for some psychic, magical reason, but what the hell it was I never understood.

When we got back from Brazil we put our attention to fixing up 48 Cheyne Walk. Our new home was a sixteenth-century house that had belonged to a shipwright and had wonderful wobbly floors and a crooked staircase. It was much less refined than a proper Cheyne Walk eighteenth-century house like Keith and Anita's house down the road. I tried to find things that fit the mood of the house. No carpeting, for instance. Just wooden floors with oriental rugs on them. And walls each painted in a different pale color. Very simple, not a typical Leo house. It was in a more austere style, not quite the palatial manner that Mick later adopted at places like Stargroves.

The next serious rift in my relationship with Mick came about over "Sister Morphine." After "Sister Morphine" I began to lose my way.

My dilemma as a pop singer had been that I felt my career was a dead end. I was bogged down in the banality of the material. I had neither the resourcefulness necessary to ring changes on it nor the will needed to surmount it. My career had been a fluke and I had run with it as best I could. All I could do was go on and on making slight variations on a theme that was becoming monotonous. At best I was a curious anomaly in the mechanics of pop. As a performer I was only average.

My last pop song, "Is This What I Get for Loving You?" had been released in February of 1967. But by the time it came out I had lost interest in it and the whole wretched pop music business along with it. The music business had become a nightmare, with endless disputes and lawsuits flying about between me and my various managers, Andrew and Tony Calder and Gerry Bron. I hated the tawdriness of what I was doing. As soon as I fell in love with Mick I began to see pop music on an entirely other level. Since I no longer had to work, I could let the whole damn thing go. Until "Sister Morphine," I didn't have the slightest interest in writing songs.

I had felt I was never going to transcend the trivial level of pop songs. And yet this was all I knew. If I was ever going to tell my own inner tales it would be through pop, the prodigal bastard that my generation had made into high art. I was envious of Mick and Keith. They had moved far beyond the boundaries I was still locked in; they were stepping on the posts of life itself. I had seen what the Stones were doing, what pop music could become. "Sister Morphine" was an attempt to do that myself. To make art out of a pop song!

People tend to assume that "Sister Morphine" comes from an incident in my life, that it is a parable of a junkie's last hours. But at the time I wrote it I'd only taken smack once. I was still far from becoming a junkie. "Sister Morphine" was in my *head* — my feelings about what it might be like to be an addict.

"Sister Morphine" is the story of a man who has had a terrible car accident. He's dying and he's in tremendous pain and the lyrics of the song are addressed to the nurse.

By 1972, when it came out on *Sticky Fingers,* I *was* the character in the song. You have to be very careful what you write because it's a gateway, and whatever it is you've summoned up may come through. It happened to Mick and Keith.

Mick began writing the music for "Sister Morphine" in a garden in Rome where we were staying with Keith and Anita. It was just a riff, essentially. He had the melody for about six months and he would walk around the house strumming it. It got to the point where I realized that if someone didn't write the lyrics, we'd be hearing this for the next ten years. Mick seemed to have no idea what kind of words would go with the music. Maybe he was waiting for me to do it. That wouldn't surprise me. Even on the guitar it was mournful, but it became even more lyrical. I used John Milton's "Lycidas" as a model.

I do believe in inspired bursts. These things come through you. Mick was a major conductor of electricity, but this particular day the lightning struck me. A vivid series of pictures began forming in my head, and a story about a morphine addict.

What may have triggered the idea for the song (and "the clean white sheets stained red") was an incident on the boat to Brazil with Mick, Keith and Anita. Anita was pregnant with Marlon at the time and after a few days at sea she began bleeding badly and she panicked. She called the doctor and he eventually gave her a shot of morphine. I remember that Keith and I were very proud of her in that idiotic junkie way. "Wow! You managed to score a hit of morphine!"

I was a big Velvet Underground fan. I played their records around the house continually. I knew "Sister Ray" and "Waiting for the Man," and these also must have drained into my brain somewhere.

The first person I showed the lyrics to was Mick, who was impressed. Also frightened. Only then did I dare show them to Anita and Keith and, eventually, to Robert.

It was all there complete from the very beginning. I heard it in my head and just wrote it out. It was obviously a moment lived on the beam. But, as often happens with me, I didn't really understand it. The result of this effortless creation was not to inspire the writing of more songs but the use of more drugs! I became a victim of my own song.

Mick knew that if I had no outlets I would soon become edgy and fretful. A pest as well. It was important, too, that the relationship remain mutual and reciprocal. He taught me about black music and the blues. He played me James Brown, Howlin' Wolf, Sam Cooke and Skip James and acted them out, *danced* them for me. They were incredibly wonderful sessions, where he would tell me all the things he knew and, more important, instill in me his own enthusiasms for things that until I met him I'd not even heard of. And I hope I did the same for him, with books and art and ideas. There was a mutual exchange of experience, energy. And then he became very, very involved in his work, and the work got better and better.

I am very competitive; I always want to come out on the top, and a relationship by its nature is a compromise. Nobody's going to be the winner, but I couldn't accept that. I began to become very jealous of Mick. He tried his best to cope with the situation as far as he understood it. He knew I needed to have my own work and he encouraged me to keep making records.

It was beginning to dawn on me that if I was Mary Shelley, where was my *Frankenstein?* I was very contemptuous of women who just hung around groups like the Rolling Stones. I wasn't doing anything. I began to complain bitterly, so Mick decided to record my version of "Sister Morphine."

It was his idea to set up the recording session for "Sister Morphine" with Jack Nitzsche. And the fact that he went to the trouble of doing this while the Stones were mixing *Let It Bleed* shows that it was taken seriously.

We put down the instrumental tracks in Los Angeles (the vocals were done in London). Mick produced the session and Ry Cooder, Jack Nitzsche, Mick and Charlie Watts played on it.

Jack Nitzsche was a very funny, neurotic guy having problems with his marriage and talking a lot about the fault line in California, the earthquake. They were all going on about it, everybody who lived there. It was the time when there was the theory that half of California was going to fall into the sea any minute.

He was very intense and arrogant. He saw me drinking and doing coke, and he was furious. "How can you call yourself a singer and do coke? Don't you know what that stuff is doing to your vocal cords and your mucus membranes? Forget about Keith and Anita. Everyone in the band can get wrecked except the drummer and the singer." I said, "All right, sir, I won't do it again, sir," and I didn't — until the session was over.

"Sister Morphine" was released in England in February of 1969. It was out for a mere two days when Decca freaked and unceremoniously yanked it off the shelves. There was no explanation, no apology. Mick went to see Sir Edward Lewis at Decca to protest but he got absolutely nowhere. I was crushed. It was as if I had been busted again. Decca, I assume, wasn't going to allow me to contaminate the minds of young people! When it came out on *Sticky Fingers* two years later, however, there wasn't one peep about it, so perhaps it was the timing. Perhaps it was because they were men. Perhaps it was my cursèd image.

The song must have come as a bit of a surprise to the old dears up at Decca. My previous album, *Love in a Mist*, three years earlier, had not signaled that much of a departure from my other records. I felt trapped; I wasn't going to be allowed to break out of my ridiculous image. I was being told that I would not be permitted to leave that wretched, tawdry doll behind. If I went on doing my nice little folky songs I could go on making records. Otherwise, I would not be permitted to do so.

"Sister Morphine" was my *Frankenstein,* my self-portrait in a dark mirror. But, unlike Mary's, my creation wasn't going to be allowed to see the light of day. Mine was a very pop *Frankenstein,* just a song, but in my mind I had painted a miniature gothic masterpiece, my celebration of death! I blamed Mick; I didn't feel he'd fought hard enough. For almost a year he fought with Decca over the lavatory album cover for *Beggars Banquet,* but for me he had one meeting with Decca and left it at that.

I began to lose heart. I felt that "Sister Morphine" was my inner vision and no one would ever know about it. That was the most depressed I've ever felt. At the moment when "Sister Morphine" was taken off the shelves, our relationship began to shatter. I, too, was now caught up in the gathering gloom of the late sixties. My *Frankenstein* had been denied its own life and I began to wither and brood along with it. It was one in a series of calamities that included *Performance* and the loss of the baby. And once things began to unravel, there was no way they would ever go back together.

Since the beginning of 1968 Mick and Keith had been working to create what Keith called the Stones Mach II, and they saw that it was now within their grasp. It would be a new incarnation — without any of the elements from the past that they felt were dragging them down. The bit was now going between the teeth.

After Andrew Oldham abandoned ship, the next logical step was to lose Brian. And — finally — they would rid themselves of Allen Klein. Brian, of course, was doing a good job of eliminating himself. Allen Klein would prove a little trickier.

Mick's strategy in dealing with Allen Klein was fairly diabolical. He would fob Klein off on the Beatles. Mick called up John Lennon and told him, "You know who you should get to manage you, man? Al-len Klein." And John, who was susceptible to utopian joint projects such as alliances between the Beatles and the Stones, said, "Yeah, what a fuckin' brilliant idea." It was a bit of a dirty trick, but once Mick had distracted Klein's attention by giving him bigger fish to fry, Mick could begin unravelling the Stones' ties to him. It was just a matter of time before the relationship was severed.

In my perceived role as a mystical being (which I took incredibly seriously), I used to throw the I Ching a lot. Actually, Anita and I both did! What a combination. . . . This has all been blown up and made to sound satanic, as if we were involved in the Hellfire Club. Step right up! Witchcraft! The black arts! But it was just the usual hippie stuff: Tarot cards, ouija boards and so on.

As 1969 plunged on, I was becoming increasingly worried about Brian. I could feel something very nasty coming. So I suggested to Mick that we throw the I Ching about Brian and see what we should do.

It was just dusk when I threw the coins. The reading I got was: Death by water. I turned to Mick and said, "It's very odd, isn't it?" And he said, "My God. Do it again." I did it again, and I got the same thing. We just looked at each other. Finally I said, "Look, this isn't good at all. We've got to do something." And he said, "We ought to phone, see if he's all right." And he actually did. Guilt, maybe.

Brian was at Redlands with Tom Keylock. He must've been astounded to get a call from Mick, the cynical, mocking Mick whom he hated. But there was another side to Mick, and that was the Mick who was on the phone to Brian saying, "How have you been, man?"

Brian was just delighted. He was always pathetically grateful for any tiny crumb of kindness and he responded effusively. He opened like a flower. "Oh, Mick, how lovely, please come down and have dinner with us." So that's what we did. We got into the Bentley and off we went. The intention was fine.

We got down to Redlands and there was Brian with Suki Poitier. She was very beautiful but perfectly silly. She was wearing her hair in those pretty long blond twists or falls or something. A nice poor little thing. But she was very suspicious, and our sudden concern did look a little like Greeks bearing gifts. I think we *were* bearing gifts, actually.

They'd cooked dinner, but Mick is fussy about his food and drink. Everything has to be perfect. A Leo *and* a star! So we walked in and without warning Mick had one of those terrible mood changes that he had on occasion, and he turned to me and said, "I can't eat this shit. We'll have to go out." So after coming down on a friendly visit in care and concern, we ended up mortally offending Brian.

I wish I could say I hadn't, but I did the only thing I knew then —

which was to acquiesce. I could have said, "Why don't we *all* go out?" But there were so many things going on at once, so many factors to consider! I think Brian may have been too ill to go out or too paranoid. It would've been quite typical; he was very frazzled. Perhaps that was why they'd cooked dinner there in the first place.

Brian got like that in the end; he couldn't deal with a lot of things. And I say that without judgment because I've been in that state myself. Often. But Mick doesn't get like that. The worst Mick ever gets is really drunk. He's awful when he's drunk, but he doesn't get mentally twisted.

So Mick and I went *out,* if you can believe it, and had a perfectly dreadful meal where we hardly spoke. When we got back to the house, Brian was a in rage. The insult had burned him like acid. It was awful. Mick and Brian ended up in a fistfight. About everything, I suppose. Nothing was said, they were just flailing about, hitting each other. I think in a way that must've been Mick's chosen form, the physical, being such an athlete. It was a sort of courtly thing to do, like jousting, except that here it was a rather ungainly punching and shoving match.

What a joke. There was Mick in perfect physical condition and Brian, who usually could barely move. But swelled by rage he became quite agile. Until in the midst of battle Brian fell into the moat. That ended it.

I thought, "Death by Water must be a *symbolic* message. What a relief!"

Two weeks later I got a call from Tom Keylock. Brian had drowned in his pool at Cotchford Farm. He had quietly slipped away.


Brian died in a drunken muddle, with no one trying very hard to look after him. A puffy, bewildered, raging, depressed muddle. When the phone rang at four in the morning it was always Brian. A thin, faint voice with labored breathing like a ghost who'd looked up your number in a call box. Someone fading away before your very eyes.

One of the things that keeps you alive when you're on the skids is that people care what happens to you. It's your life line, and with Brian nobody really cared anymore. He would test levels of endurance, and no one had any patience left. He did it all the time, endlessly. For Brian, relations with other people always took place in the extreme. The only kind of affection or friendship he could tolerate was unconditional love. From men, women, girlfriends, chauffeurs, waiters. Even with that, he could only just about cope with life. Anything less he found a bit tricky.

Brian's death unnerved me terribly, perhaps because I identified with him so strongly. He was the emblematic victim of the sixties, of rock, of drugs, of Mick and Keith. His fate could easily have been mine.

During the sessions they were doing for *Let It Bleed,* Brian was always very out of it; it was near the end of the road for him. They'd pretend to be recording him, pretend to hook him up, and then they wouldn't patch him in. We'd watch Brian, in his stupor, fumbling with his guitar, biting his lips, leaning over his fretboard so intensely, and we'd all laugh. He knew, but not properly because he was so stoned. It must've been awful, it was that thing where you see a little bit of the truth and you think: "Did I really hear that? Am I imagining it?"

Brian was no more able to articulate what was happening to him than anybody else. He *talked* more than Keith but never about his own feelings. He was at his best in nonverbal situations, as with the musicians from Jajouka, just playing their instruments together. He loved all kinds of music. He was one of these extraordinary people who, if there was a basket in a room with twenty-four different musical instruments from twenty-four corners of the world, could pick them up and find out in a minute what they did and how they worked, and he would play them and get really beautiful sounds out of them. He was at his very best when no words were needed.

I've often wondered what caused Brian's disintegration. Maybe it began on that day in Tangier, when Anita left him for Keith. It could have been anything with Brian. Drugs, obviously. And that very competitive thing — being in a group. Who's the leader, who's going to be in control. The tension between Brian, Mick and Keith — but especially between Brian and Mick — came from an ancient feud between them that had been going on for years, since before even Andrew had entered the picture. Brian had once told a reporter that he was the leader of the band. Something as childish as that. And for Brian to come out and *say* something like that was absolutely taboo.

Brian was so far ahead of them. When Mick and Keith were up on stage trying to learn how to be sex objects, Brian already had two illegitimate children! Brian was acting on it faster than anybody else; he knew his stuff very well. In the beginning, Mick and Keith were still schoolboys. Brian was the one who did the hustling, getting people together and believing it, knowing it, unlike Mick who couldn't make up his mind whether he wanted to be an accountant. Brian was the one saying, "Look, it's going to happen!" At the same time, he had it in his hand; he could control it, so he *did* control it. And when they found out he was right — that they were going to make it and they *did* make it — instead of appreciating what he did they resented it. And that's when Brian's doom really started. They had a vendetta, Mick and Keith, a real vendetta.

We all saw Brian's death coming — an OD, a car crash — there wasn't a great deal of remorse about it. And, in any case, it just isn't in Mick's nature, or Keith's either, to dwell too long on this sort of thing. Brian dying was something of a relief; it solved a terrible predicament for them.

After Brian's death I thought we were all in trouble. I didn't know that it was *I* who was in trouble.


At the concert in Hyde Park July 5 — which Mick dedicated to Brian — I was in very rough shape. I was dope sick coming off smack, anorexic, pale, sickly and covered with spots. Looking like death. I should never have gone in the first place. I was obviously a woman in the middle of a big pickle. And there was Marsha Hunt bursting out of her white buckskins. She was stunning. After the concert I went home with Nicholas and Mick went off with Marsha. If I'd been Mick in that situation, I might have done exactly the same thing.

Mick and I were still trying to keep it together, in spite of everything. That is in part why we'd agreed to go to Australia to make *Ned Kelly*. When Tony Richardson offered Mick the part of Ned Kelly and me that of the outlaw's sister, I was thrilled. We would be together and away from all the temptations of London, principally, in my case, drugs. What I liked to do best with Mick was going to faraway places on our own.

And so just six days after Brian's death we left for Australia. I was pretty much gone by the time the plane landed.

I was scared of flying. That's what I had told the doctor.

"I've got a long flight and I need some downers . . . and I'll be away for three months." He gave me three months' worth of Tuinals. I must have taken fifteen Tuinals during the flight. By the time we got to the hotel, I was in a trance. We got our room and I went straight to sleep.

When I woke up I couldn't remember who I was.

# Suicide by Mistaken Identity

BY the time we got to the hotel in Sydney I'd forgotten not only *where* I was but *who* I was. I looked in the mirror. What I saw was a very thin, frightened face. I'd cut my hair, I was anorexic, and my skin looked cadaverous. I saw someone literally falling apart. Someone with blond hair and looking very scared. In my drug-induced stupor I dimly recognized the ravaged face of Brian Jones staring back at me. I was Brian, and I was dead.

You might think that at such a point of stupefaction I had reached the nadir of my willful descent into self-destruction, but you would be mistaken. It was only the beginning.

At that moment Brian was my twin. I identified with him because he had been a public sacrifice; it was a role I understood.

Quite logically, I thought I was Brian.

It was all very rational in the way these things are when you're unhinged. I reasoned that since I was Brian and since Brian was dead . . . I had to take the rest of the pills so I could be dead too. I took the pills.

Mick was asleep. I walked around the room. I looked out of the window. Our hotel room was on the forty-fifth floor; and it looked out over Sydney Harbor. I attempted to open a window but the windows didn't open. Had I been able to open a window, I would have jumped. The Tuinals were taking forever to kick in. I looked down and saw things on the street that shouldn't have been there. I recognized a number of people and waved to them. And then I saw Brian Jones. At that moment I went into a coma that lasted six days.

When I first spotted Brian he was far below at street level, but greatly enlarged. A blowup of himself. Various parts of him — his face, his hands — expanded and extended toward me as he spoke, and then he rose straight up as if on a shaft of air until he was directly opposite the window of our room. He was boxy, with a wan face, dressed in Kings Road medieval in lace and fur, with red and yellow striped pants. His hair was green, and Buddhist lightning bolts were tattooed on his palms. As he raised the palms of his hands to me he smiled that Pan smirk of his.

He beckoned to me the way spirits traditionally beckon to mortals in the movies. I passed through the plate glass and found myself outside. But instead of standing suspended above the street, I was now in an unstable landscape that pulsed and shifted as we spoke. I had, I assumed, gone over to the other side.

There was no weather, no wind or rain or sunshine or darkness. There was nothing recognizable at all. The grandeur and enormity of the place had the phantasmagoric mood of illustrations by Edmund Dulac or Dürer's engravings of Hell. As we were walking along, I realized that Brian had no more idea of where we were going than I did. Obviously he had woken up dead, not known where he was and decided to call for me!

It was the nicest chat I ever had with him, actually. He told me how he had woken up and put out his hand for his bottle of Valium, and about the panic that had seized him when he found nothing there. He said he had been lonely and confused and had brought me to him because he needed to talk to someone he knew.

We strolled blithely along as the quivering earth crumbled away on either side of us, and he told me about his miniature coronation set with the Beefeaters and the coach and horses. He said he liked books about railway bridges, guides to switching boxes, George MacDonald's fairy stories and *Fox's Book of Martyrs*. I said I'd get them for him when I got back to London.

Afterward he became weepy like the Mock Turtle in *Alice in Wonderland* and said he was very sorry to have put me to all this trouble. He didn't seem to know he was dead. I'm sure this happens frequently when people die violent, unexpected deaths. They don't know where they are. Hence ghosts. There was, I realized, a distinct possibility that I might already be one myself.

"Brian, dear, isn't this *lovely*," I said, trying — as usual — to distract him from grisly realities. But my sudden descent to small talk must have tipped him off that something was wrong. I was speaking to him in the patronizing way people talk to mad people, children and small dogs. Nevertheless, he plunged ahead in typical Brian fashion.

"Death is the next great adventure," he said portentously. This was something I used to go around saying myself, so I nodded wisely.

"Oh, yes, I quite agree," I said fervently, as if we were speaking of a new religion. Or a new drug. His mood changed abruptly. Was it beginning to dawn on him where he was? Had I, perhaps, transferred the thought telepathically to him? He turned and put his hands on my shoulders.

"Welcome to death!" he said brightly.

I wasn't quite ready to be *that* enthusiastic about our situation and tried to treat it like a joke.

"Oh, is *that* where we are?" I asked.

"Well, you won't find any hotels here, darling, or any restaurants either. You won't need 'em."

I didn't like the drift of this conversation.

We came to the edge of the Dulac landscape. It dropped off abruptly and completely. There was a very obvious point where you chose whether to go over the edge or not. Brian said "Coming?" and slipped off the cliff. I drew back. I heard a chorus of voices calling to me, but I wasn't ready just yet.

Getting back took a long time. I was stranded in a deserted town. The color had been drained from everything. The houses were empty. I was in Albania! Wandering down long, deserted streets with names like the Avenue of the 17th of October. Looking utterly incongruous, people I knew floated by (their feet didn't quite touch the ground). I called out, but they hurried past as if they hadn't seen me.

I was lost in an airport. People came up and asked me the sort of questions you ask a child stranded at a railway station. "Are you lost, dear?" "Do you know your name?" And I would answer, "I'm waiting for Mick to come and get me." Which, in a sense, he did. If he had not woken up and got me to the hospital as quickly as he did, I actually *would* have gone over with Brian.

When I opened my eyes six days later, I came back to life in an upside-down country, Australia. Whatever season it is in England, in Australia it's the opposite. The trees in Australia don't lose their leaves, they lose their *bark*. I remember being told as a child if you dug straight down through the earth, you'd come out in Australia where everybody walked upside down and everything happened topsy-turvy. I had woken up in a land where everything was inside-out.

The first person I saw was Mick. He held my hands in his and said, "You've come back!"

"You can't get rid of me that easily," I replied (there's a little bit of truth in all kidding).

"Don't be so silly, darling. God, I thought I'd really lost you this time."

"Wild horses," I said, "wouldn't drag me away."

My mother was there, too. I think she'd been by my side the entire six days. Mick had been drumming back and forth from the movie location. Nothing stops Mick when he's working, not even an attempted suicide! I wouldn't expect different.

Mick was loving and compassionate and wrote me beautiful letters every day from the film set. The letters were full of remorse: "Please forgive me for causing you all this pain. . . . I'm utterly devastated to realize that you felt you were in such agony you had to kill yourself."

I haven't had many psychotic incidents in my life. I'm usually very much *there* — in my own way! — even when I'm very fucked up. And I know that when I took my hundred and fifty sleeping pills, I did it out of revenge. I remember doing it and I remember why. It was the only way I could make my point. It had something to do with Brian. Everyone was taking his death so *in stride,* for God's sake! Well, I thought, I'll show you! You want pain and suffering? I'll show you pain and suffering!

The circumstances of Brian's death precipitated in me morbid thoughts about my own fate. I saw myself as a very likely stand-in for the sacrificed Brian. Of course, for the whole thing to complete itself, the sacrifice must be willing. And Brian was. And I was feeling very sorry for myself — something I'm now loath to admit. Just before I went under I clearly remember thinking all those classic, horribly infantile things: "This will show them!" Or even worse: "When I'm dead you'll be sorry!" But it wasn't purely a theatrical gesture. You don't take a hundred and fifty Tuinals if you don't mean it.

I didn't think about brain damage when I took the overdose. I was unconscious for six days, and there was quite a good chance that I could have come back a vegetable. I think I actually did sustain some loss! The six days of unconsciousness heightened my psychic abilities — as every near-death experience does — but there is definitely a price to pay.


In anguished relationships like the one I had with Mick it's much easier and more satisfactory for all concerned if the one playing my role dies, after which I would turn into a sainted, mystical figure — like Brian — and no longer be a threat to anyone and — more important — no longer be a *bother* to anyone. The martyred Marianne. Perhaps that's what I had in mind!

But, inconvenient as it may have been, it turned out not to be my time to go. And although I was absolutely set on a particular ending to my story, over the years I began to accept that perhaps there was something else. It's very corny, but people who "come back" from death all say the same thing: "There's a reason I didn't die." That's exactly what I realized. There was something I had to do that I hadn't yet done and I'd just have to stay alive to do it.

If I'd had any doubts about the possible advantages my death might have for others, they were quickly dispelled. Within days of my overdose Andrew Oldham had issued a greatest hits album of my records, the cover framed by a black border and the title in gothic letters.

An inevitable consequence of the Australia business was a widening split between Mick and me. The novelty and romance of my return to the living wore off rather quickly, and Mick drew back. He really didn't have any choice — once my mother was there she took up all the available oxygen. There was simply no room for Mick.

Although my mother always liked Mick, the things she liked about him — that he was rich and powerful — were the things I liked least. I didn't mind the perquisites of that life, but what endeared him to me were his kindness and his intelligence. He also had the kind of psychic power I've always been drawn to. What I fell in love with (on acid) was the god I saw doing that dance. Shiva. Eventually I fell in love with him as a real live human being, but by then it was too late. And by the time of the "incident in Australia," I'd already made my decision to leave — by any means necessary!

On almost every count Mick behaved like a paragon. He was good to Nicholas, he treated my mother wonderfully. He gave her a thatched cottage called Yew Tree (near Aldworth) to live in. You couldn't fault him. Maybe *that's* what irritated me. I couldn't see any way out, except the one I took. I'm ashamed to say that one of the attractions of that way out — suicide — was that I knew if I managed it, it would make Mick look particularly bad! The odd thing was that, without any justification, people already thought he was a monster. The Sydney police had such a diabolical picture of him they actually believed that Mick had stuffed the pills down my throat. They actually asked me: "Did you take them yourself or did someone *force them down your throat?*"

I said, "*What? Who?*" And they said, "Well, I mean if it was that, uh, Mick Jag — you can tell us, miss."

What really galled me about that story was not the wicked old Mick business but the image of myself as a hapless damsel. I may have been a feckless twenty-two-year-old but I wasn't quite *that* non compos mentis. If I was going to take pills, I could quite easily take them myself, thank you.

Their attitude reflected the almost pornographic image of me in the popular imagination. Angelic innocent ravaged by corrupt, degenerate satyr. Although by 1969 I had exchanged the maudlin pop-angel figurine for a sort of doomed Lizzie Siddal-like creature, the Australians hadn't quite caught up with me yet.

My mother went into high-gear religion (during my coma she had extreme unction performed), and being in a weakened state I was powerless to resist her. After I got out of the hospital, she had me moved into an infirmary run by nuns. My cure was all done on that level: religion. Catholicism no longer worked for me by then but it was the only way my mother knew to exorcise my demons. Finally, after the nuns, we moved to a ranch near where they were filming *Ned Kelly* — in the wildest, most beautiful part of Australia. I fell in love with the country and began to feel alive again for the first time since my "return."

What Mick did throughout all this — what he always did — was pay for everything. After a month or so in Australia I went to Switzerland and saw a very good doctor, a woman psychiatrist who really did help me. But not once did anybody suggest I stop using drugs. The cops, I suppose, had they been consulted, would have recommended I stop, but among my friends it was assumed, I think, that I was incapable of stopping.

Months later I finally made it back to England. I was bursting to tell all my friends about my extraordinary experiences in a coma, but no one wanted to hear about it. It was a subject to be avoided at all costs. I can see now why Anita would not be that excited to hear that I had conversed at length with a dead Brian Jones! I admit it *was* somewhat tactless of me, but I thought as my best friend she would be enthralled by this strange and otherworldly adventure. Keith wasn't that interested either. Nor, of course, was Mick. Christopher and Robert had no interest in the thing at all. They considered it, I imagine, an indiscretion on my part — an instance of paranormal kitsch! Besides, Brian's death was turning out to have been quite convenient for any number of people. Like an Agatha Christie mystery where *everyone* has a motive!

Brian's death acted like a slow-motion bomb. It had a devastating effect on all of us. The dead go away, but the survivors are damned. Anita went through hell from survivor's guilt and guilt plain and simple. She developed grisly compulsions. One of them was that terrible business of cutting out pictures of Brian and sticking them up on the wall and then in the morning tearing them all down. It was a recapitulation of what Brian used to do with his tapes. It's a psychotic thing people do when they've gone over the edge; they create something and then destroy it. Camille Claudel did it. She made beautiful sculptures in the night and then smashed them in the morning.

Keith's way of reacting to Brian's death was to *become* Brian. He became the very image of the falling down, stoned junkie perpetually hovering on the edge of death. But Keith, being Keith, was made of different stuff. However much he mimicked Brian's self-destruction, he never actually disintegrated.

My suicide attempt and my stroll with the posthumous Brian were put by all concerned in somewhat the same category as Brian's death. It was something that made them nervous and from which they wanted to distance themselves. Something best not dwelt on too long. It was around this time that people started to think me completely mad, and due to the Undead Brian business I've been considered pretty much mad as a hatter ever since. But I don't really care. It did happen, and I'm not going to change my story just because it doesn't suit other people's views of reality.

In families there's always one person — almost always a woman — who is designated to be the mad one. In my circle I was the one elected, and since we lived our lives on the pages of the tabloid press, I became famous for it.

# Let It Bleed

WAS in very rough shape when I got to L.A. in the summer of 1969. Phil Kaufman, Gram Parson's roadie, met me at the airport. He must have seen this strange white apparition staggering off the plane and thought, "Blazing tumbleweeds, I can't let her blow into Babylon like *this!*" He knew what was awaiting us in Los Angeles, what people were expecting of the Rolling Stones.

He put me in hibernation for three or four days, and then I was okay again. Keith and Anita were in about the same shape. We were all chipping at heroin. It was still just a recreational drug; no one had major habits yet. It was just that smack has a particularly pernicious effect on me. More so than anyone else I knew.

Mick knew what I'd been up to and he had obviously told Phil to go pick me up at the airport and get me back into shape. Not shape as we think of it now — the gym and jogging and aerobics — but back to *life*. Phil put me back together. (He's the one who stole Gram's body from the funeral parlor and burned it in Joshua Tree National Park.) He gave me a four-day course of fruit juice, vitamins, Percodans and massages until I returned to the land of the living. This was the first time anybody had ever done this for me (but not, alas, the last). I didn't see Mick for the first week — I was in some little bungalow in the Hollywood Hills. When I had recovered, I was wrapped up with a bow and delivered to him.

The Stones were in L.A. finishing *Let It Bleed*. Mick rented a house in the Hollywood Hills. Mick and Keith were recording, leaving Anita and me with time on our hands. Never a good idea! Our job was to enjoy ourselves, which we did. Anita had a chauffeur and limo outside her house twenty-four hours a day to take her anywhere she wanted to go. She would stumble into the limo, go and get some acid, then come back and trip. I also spent a lot of time with Pamela Mayall and Andee Cohen, just sort of swimming and lounging by the pool, doing a little coke and a lot of raving around. But no smack. Andee and I had cocktails in air-conditioned bars. Anita didn't come out till later. We were having a high old time.

But wherever we went, I never mentioned my name. The Stones, I knew, were looked upon as gods of deliverance in L.A. They'd reached mythic status by the time they went on that tour in 1969. People had lost faith in the Beatles, they seemed phony and hollow. One of the few times I saw fan frenzy at first hand was when I walked into the Roxy with Mick and Keith and Anita. It hit us with full force. The boys had a couple of hours off. Wot should we do, man? I know, let's go to a club. We walked in and it was like the Aztecs seeing their first horses. A hush fell over the room. The band stopped playing. Like that moment in *The Day the Earth Stood Still*. Mick, who always knew what to do in these situations, made a funny little curtsy and everybody laughed and we could all breathe again.

At that moment the Stones were the Bearers of the Vibe. I knew this would be an epochal tour for them, but I was damned if I was going to tag along like the team mascot. Mick kept saying "Why don't you come? It's gonna be a gas!" But I wouldn't go. I hated going on tour, still do. I didn't like being trapped. When they were recording, I was free. I could go to the studio and leave, get out, do what I wanted. On tour I wouldn't have been able to do that, I wouldn't have had any life at all.

I was far too disorganized, in any case, to go on tour. You have to have your head screwed on to handle a tour. Packing, unpacking, travel, makeup, finding your hotel at night, for chrissakes! Also I had another wee problem. I was jealous. Jealous of the groupies, of course, but also of the Stones.

Michael Cooper came out for a while and we all went out to the desert, to Joshua Tree, and did mescaline; it was wonderful. Staying up all night driving out to Joshua Tree and walking along as the dawn came up. We would leave the car somewhere and then just go off. I don't know how we ever managed because we didn't bring *anything.* In that state we could have gone off in the wrong direction and gone round in circles forever, but somehow we didn't. We got back to the car and went home the next day. Generally what happened is we would go a little way into the desert and then get totally hung up on something, a *cactus* or something. If we had been walking in a straight line we might have got lost, but there is no such thing as a straight line on mescaline. It didn't take very long to get totally immersed in the face on a stone, a boulder turning into the head of Sitting Bull. There's a lot of sacred ground at Joshua Tree!

In the middle of the night we were on a high precipice somewhere in Joshua Tree. We made a fire and the moon came up and suddenly out of the blackness I heard this unearthly sound, a sound I'd never heard before. It was so thrilling, like being in India with the wolves howling. And I remember turning to Gram and saying, "God, what's that?" And he said, in his funny Southern accent "Why, Maryanne, don'ja know that's just a li'l ol' coyote."

Michael Cooper took a very spooky picture of me in Joshua Tree. It was cold and I was wearing a black caftan from Morocco. The strange thing about this photo is it's of something that hadn't happened to me yet. There I am as the shady lady I wound up as. That was what was coming. The card had appeared in the deck. And I went right with it. To go to the bottom of the ocean and not drown.

*Let It Bleed* was being made, mixed and fixed. They'd done most of the tracks in London already. Charlie and Bill were adding a bit of bass and drums and there was a lot of overdubbing with Ry Cooder and people dropping by to play. For me the sessions were not the point. I generally passed out after an hour, so all I saw was Keith laying down the bass track. Over and over again. With Mick periodically chiming in, "A bit faster, don't you fink? We don't wanna put 'em to sleep just yet." Back then, Keith often did the bass lines. It seemed to me then that the reason they had Bill Wyman in the band was because they needed someone to play bass on tour.

*Let It Bleed* is my favorite Stones record. All those great songs:

"You Got the Silver," "Moonlight Mile," "Salt of the Earth," "Prodigal Son," "Monkey Man," and of course "You Can't Always Get What You Want." Every time I heard that song I would burst into tears. It was about my romance with drugs. It is about a few other people as well. Jimmy Miller, the Stones' producer, is in there. "Mr. Jitters." He wasn't in *too* bad shape yet, but in Mick's eyes what Jimmy was doing to himself was horrifying.

One of the extraordinary things about *Let It Bleed* was how of-its-time it was. After Altamont, "Gimme Shelter" was so in sync with the zeitgeist that it seemed almost supernatural. People were amazed at how prophetic it was, but it had actually come out of the past. Most of it had been done almost a year earlier. Mick and Keith were, in any case, not that conscious of what was happening on the street. We were all somewhat removed, to say the least.

"Gimme Shelter" came out of the hell Keith went through during *Performance* and all the other stuff that had happened in the last few years: the bust, the trial, Brian's death. The album happened to come out at the end of the sixties when the culture was obsessed with an impending apocalypse, but many of the songs had been written much earlier. What had happened to Mick and Keith at Redlands was now happening to the culture as a whole. Keith was also picking up the edge-of-the-volcano vibes in L.A. The real darkness came down much later.

Mick and Keith have always been very good, in any case, at tuning in to the psychic radio band. *Let It Bleed* was a kind of confirmation of the accuracy of their antennae. When you are as synchronized as that, you have to be careful what you write about. Even for the allegedly worldly and sophisticated Mick and Keith, the experience of the last couple of years, with all the jumps that were happening, had been mind-boggling.

It was totally different from the days of Andrew, when they'd all sit about waiting for the press clippings to come in. What did Keith Altham say in the *New Musical Express*? None of them gave a fuck what anyone thought of this record! Other people's opinions were beside the point now. In any case the Stones were already wrapped up in the *next* record.

Years earlier Mick and Keith used to fantasize about the day they would outstrip the Beatles, and now it was happening. By the time they were doing *Let It Bleed,* they were just . . . flowing. They were no longer controlling it, they were riding the beam. I think L.A. was such a happy time because we all of us had this exhilarating feeling of being on time, a feeling of the spirit streaming through you. We knew that something momentous was happening.

I think one of the reasons the chaos at Altamont happened was that nobody was paying attention. All they were thinking about was the next thing, about how they would look in *Gimmer Shelter,* the documentary the Maysles brothers were making about the tour. By then Mick and Keith felt themselves immortal and untouchable, as if they couldn't put a foot wrong. They hadn't thought about the consequences of what they were putting out, the random acts of madness.

They'd forgotten that violent disturbances are also part of the time stream and are called out by strong emotions. They had no idea of the demonic forces that were gathering. They made jokes about this stuff, because in England the apocalypse is a *biblical* concept. In the States, given the mix of fantasy and real life — especially in the hippie culture — it seemed a definite possibility. The Stones took none of this seriously. Kenneth Anger they thought laughable. Mick and Keith were utterly contemptuous of his satanic hocus-pocus. They thought it was idiotic, which is why they could play with such ease. Anita and I, being women, were a bit less cynical about these things.

When the horror erupted at Altamont it must have looked to many people like the demons coming home to roost, but not to the Stones. They were just playing a dangerous game that came to life. It was only *after Let It Bleed* that weird things began happening to *them.*

The most indelible misconception to come out of *Let It Bleed* was the silly notion of Mick as the disciple of Satan. A devotee of satin, perhaps! Mick is far too sensible and normal ever to have got seriously involved with black magic. "Sympathy for the Devil" was pure pápier-mâché satanism. I had given him Mikhail Bulgakov's *The Master and Margarita* to read — he devoured it in one night and spit out "Sympathy for the Devil." The book's central character is Satan, but it has nothing to do with demonism and black magic. It's about light, if anything. The plot consists of two stories happening simultaneously: Satan coming to

Moscow to give a ball and St. Matthew on the road to Calvary with Christ. The most sensational part, Satan's ball, is terribly funny, beautifully written, and absolutely brilliant. Mick wrote a three-minute song synthesized out of this very complex book. By putting himself in the mind of the central character he was able to animate the somewhat labyrinthine and prolix plot. Mick was attracted to the character of the devil because he is — naturally — the most entertaining person in the book. As he always is in any work of art where he appears! Mick liked the *glamour* of the character. The *role*. He recognized immediately that this was a great part for him. I've noticed people don't like to hear this. But like any artist, Mick is a master scavenger, constantly picking up things and trying them on for size. The consequences never even cross his mind.

It's a simpleminded point of view, the idea that your icons really are what they appear to be. A peasant, religious attitude, basically. America is much more religious than we are in England. All their films are passion plays, and they believe that the person playing the part should *live* it. You see this every week in the *National Enquirer*. All those hot items about so-and-so and the blonde in the hotel room have, at their basis, the belief that this person *should* be the character they play. In Mick's case, this isn't even remotely true. Keith and Anita later got into this black magic stuff, but Mick never got into magic any more than he got into drugs. He's a dabbler.

The only reason that the Stones were not destroyed by the ideas they toyed with is that they never took them as seriously as their fans. Mick never, for one moment, believed he was Lucifer. It was always "this is all a game." Eventually the game turned and started to become reality. For Keith and Anita it certainly did. Especially Anita. Now she just reads occult fiction. It's such a hoot that all that flirtation with the black arts should end up with Dennis Wheatley novels. They satisfy her now and would probably have satisfied her then. She was never a staunch devotee. It's just that drugs inflate you to the point where you start to believe you really do have arcane powers.

This may have been the Rolling Stones' finest hour, but things were not going well between Mick and me. I remember listening to takes of

"Sister Morphine" and "Sympathy for the Devil" with Mick at the house in L.A. I was sitting in the bedroom and Mick came in very forlorn and put his head on my knees like a child. He was trying to hold on to me. I could see how much he loved me, and it broke my heart. I patted him on the head as if he were a little boy. I felt badly for him and wanted to take away his pain. I felt great empathy for him, but I wasn't in love anymore. There's always one person in a relationship that's a little more in love. I was retreating, and he knew it.

By this time I don't think he knew any longer where his image ended and the real Mick Jagger began. I wasn't quite sure either. Much of the turmoil for me had to do with Mick's inability to separate himself from this image, his compulsion to see life in a perpetual Sunday supplement. Where you watch yourself leading your life, but you don't feel anything. It's spooky. But what I didn't know then, and I can see it very clearly now, was that this was always the arrangement. The pretty girl, the beautiful house, the well-turned-out children and dah, dah, dah, dah. Make everything *look* right. Everything has to look right from the outside. It's a much harder deal than it seems. I mean, it must be hard if *Bianca* couldn't take it anymore. Because she'd been bred for this.

His damn image pervaded everything. I can see now that even the way he dealt with the bust at Redlands was an extension of his obsession with his image. The *theater* of it took over almost immediately. It was priceless stuff. He could be noble and suffer and be martyred and have marvelous photos taken of him handcuffed in his ruffled velvet suits. Like bloody Charles the First on the way to his execution! He got the full exposure out of it that he always likes to get.

The whole Redlands business gave a patina of gravity to his personality that really wasn't there. Like Ronald Reagan, he had learned to play a character more complex than his own. When he needed a new Mick to go with the new Stones of *Beggar's Banquet* and *Let It Bleed,* he took the character he played in *Performance* as his own. It wasn't really him at all. Turner was a composite and complex character. Mick selected his new persona as carefully as he would a new suit. He has good taste. It was a perfect role for him.

Mick grew tired of his Jumping Jack Flash persona — perhaps he suspected it was going to be presenting him with a set of demands he didn't want to deal with — so he just created another one. After the

Hyde Park concert, the carapace grew like a shell around him. I began to feel as if I was living with a monster. The last year or so I would wake up in the morning — I know I was taking too many pills and doing too many drugs — but my intuition was that I was living with a vampire. A hollow, voracious entity that constantly needed to replenish itself with things, people, ideas, souls.

Mick's genius was in his lyrics, but his great talent has always been artifice, inflation and swagger, and gradually he developed his by now well-known pneumatic personality, a flexible and cartoonlike envelope that eventually became his all-purpose self. All celebrities become burlesques of themselves in the end. Mick has his lips, Dolly Parton her tits. I've watched it for a long time, wondering how I could do it myself!

Not only was Mick having a hard time keeping track of his different selves, he was becoming confused about me. When I was with John Dunbar, I had been able to keep my performing identity separate. With Mick, it was becoming a strain. I started using coke and that drove a further wedge between us. I would be raging about while he took tea in the parlor. With Mick, it was everything in moderation — including drugs.

It was a nightmare for Mick, the whole experience of my getting into smack. But he never did anything to stop me. The most he would say was "Don't you think you're doing a bit much of that stuff?" I would lie to him and tell him I was only chipping and he would believe me. Mick is the classic codependent. He gets his energy from being around drug addicts. Like Andy Warhol. He'll do drugs with addicts if he *has* to, to get their trust and affection. Like an undercover cop.

Drugs — especially psychedelics and speed — had once propelled the scene. They were the very engine of so-called Swinging London. Eventually, however, drugs *replaced* the scene. It became internalized. And hard drugs (essentially the same drugs-of-choice preferred by the doomed Romantics) brought with them their own dark, compulsive realm. Many creative dabblers were soon caught by the foot and dragged into the pit. And there's more than a bit of self-destructiveness in me.

I did love Mick in my own way but somehow the more I loved him the crueler I became. It was awful. Altamont was the moment I chose to run off with Mario Schifano.

I have a vague recollection that my affair with Mario Schifano was set up by Anita. And I was obviously the willing victim.

He was an old boyfriend of Anita's. Anita rang me and said, "Can he crash at your place?" Probably thinking, "Poor Marianne, so lonely and in need of a good fuck." So Mario stayed at Cheyne Walk and, needless to say, we had sex. Mick was away on tour. And by then, I was really hurting. Not that Mick was neglecting me. He was charming, even in the midst of an American tour. Ringing me at all times, telling me he loved me, sending me on little errands so I would feel involved. I went down to the Chelsea Antique Market and got him the studded belt he used in "Midnight Rambler."

When I read Pamela Des Barres's book, *I'm with the Band,* I found out that during this period they were having a torrid affair. People coming on to Mick — women, men, groupies, debutantes, my best friends — was one of the things that whittled away at our relationship until it deteriorated into chronic retaliation. This is inevitably what happens when you have infidelity in a relationship. *He* would have an affair with somebody and I would find out about it and I would think, "Oh well, now *I* have to go and get him back for that." We were soon involved in playing an endlessly destructive game of payback. "Oh, you fucked her? All right, I'll get you for that one. I'll see you one and *raise* you one." It started with Mick's affair with Anita during *Performance*. That was real betrayal. She was my closest friend. She was my *only* friend!

I went to Rome with Mario and Nicholas and it made the front pages of the papers. Mick, who was still on tour in the States, had to find out about this through the press. At Altamont. There I was looking up at him from the *San Francisco Chronicle* saying things like: "I am happy. I am absolutely penniless. I am going to start from scratch. People can help by just forgetting me." He must have thought he was hallucinating. When he got back I was gone, taking Nicholas with me.

Mario was a great painter and an even greater cocaine freak. He was a great love of Anita's, and I'm sure that's one of the reasons I liked him. I think Anita was just trying to give me a nice Christmas present. She never thought I'd actually pack my spotted handkerchief.

Mario and I did a lot of coke. And Nicholas got more and more unhappy. He loved Mick and my betrayal of Mick was terrible for him.

The crunch came one day when Nicholas was in his room. We were in another part of the house, a huge place in the country. It was winter and an electric fire was on. Mario had given me a sable coat (or got somebody to give it to me) and Nicholas took the fur coat and put it on the electric fire and stood there to watch it burn. And just after it caught fire, Helen, our nanny, walked in, thank God. After that, it hit me that I had to *focus* on Nicholas. The next day we went back to spend Christmas with my mother at Yew Tree cottage. Me, Mario and Nicholas.

Mick was back in England calling me at all hours saying "Dunno wot 'appened but it's gonna be different now, innit? I'll see to it. You 'ave me word. I mean, we gotta at least *try* don' we?" And to whatever he said I kept saying no. It was time to let go, obviously. Mick, too, must have known we couldn't go on together. Maybe he didn't want it to *look* as if I had left him. You know, like there's something wrong in this picture.

Mick showed up at Yew Tree. There were a lot of operatic scenes between Mick and Mario, but in the end Mick prevailed. Mick spent the night with me and Mario slept on the couch, and in the morning Mario departed, never to return. I went back to Cheyne Walk with Mick, who was very pleased with himself. He had *vanquished* Mario.

# Ahmet's Curse

MICK had been spending a lot of time in Los Angeles, where bevies of *wahinis* fawned over him and catered to his wildest fantasy. These girls would do *anything*. He was *the* rock star par excellence — the whole *point* was to please him. So when he came back to Cheyne Walk he quite naturally wondered whether he couldn't get some of the same stuff at home! Unfortunately for Mick, I'd only recently read Germaine Greer's *Female Eunuch,* from which I had discovered that the whole point was the orgasm. Mine, not his. It must have been a bit of a comedown for him reentering normal life with me — normal as I could manage, anyway.

One night shortly after he got back, Mick suggested that I start using ice cream–flavored douches. I'm not stupid. I realized that this must be the sort of thing that American chicks did. But I didn't put two and two together till I read *I'm with the Band* (Pamela has a whole rap about strawberry- and peach-flavored douches).

I was flabbergasted. "Listen sweetheart," I told him, "this may be what you get from your groupies in America, but you're talking to me now. So fuck off!" A very alluring approach, I know.

Of course, privately I was curious about these exotic ice cream–flavored douches, so I inquired at the local chemist. He gave me some sort of surgical appliance — made of rubber. It was huge and the douche that went with it had a decidedly medicinal flavor (obviously *not* what Miss Pamela had been using in L.A.). I ended up substituting jasmine florist bath oil, but I don't think Mick noticed.

Once in a while I did find out about these affairs, but I never said a word. Getting upset about a little fucking around was unhip and middle class. I told myself he was "Mick Jagger," a national treasure, but I began nonetheless to feel inadequate. I knew I couldn't compete with *groupies,* for chrissakes, I didn't even give anyone a blow job until I was in my late twenties.

Sex, in any case, had long ceased to be our primary bond. After the first six months Mick seemed to lose interest, and it wasn't entirely his fault. Sex has always been problematic for me; and it takes ardent strangers like Tony Kent to break through my barriers. Anyway, a good fuck just doesn't do it for me. I need a lot more than that. I'm not really that *interested* in sex. I've noticed that this upsets men. They want women to think about sex a lot, and always be wanting it. Sometimes one does, of course. I have my moments, even now at the ancient age of forty-seven.

It was the seventies, and Mick had made a real resolve to hit the high life. His social calendar now revolved around events that he had once taken such delight in jeering at: debutante balls, flower shows, petromillionaires' brunches and formal dinners with indiscriminate members of Burke's Peerage. I enjoyed socializing with the Kings Road aristos now and then, but Mick was infatuated with the aristocracy *per se.* He would attend dinners given by any silly thing with a title and a castle. He was as smitten as any American millionaire in the movies! That's when things started to get weird for me.

I didn't fit in, and I had no intention of trying. Making small talk with humorless bores was my idea of hell — someone else's hell! I would much rather find my own, thank you very much.

Out of bloody-mindedness and perversity, I tried to frustrate Mick's wish to pull me into these tiresome scenes. When he did manage to drag me to one of these affairs, disaster inevitably followed.

One incident at Warwick Castle was fairly typical. Mick and I had been invited to dinner by David Brooke, the Earl of Warwick, known affectionately as Brookie. This invitation was terribly important to Mick. The Earl of Warwick! Dinner in a castle! So off we went.

It was the grandest thing we'd ever seen. A footman in full silk uniform behind every chair. But it was an insufferably stuffy scene, and I soon found myself swooning from boredom (and a few other things).

I didn't know the Earl of Warwick from Adam. I didn't like him. I didn't care a flying fuck about him. He was, in fact, a raging bore, and in those days when I became desperate I took whatever I needed to alter my frame of mind. I took five Mandrax and passed out in the soup. Mick had to carry me upstairs. This at an event where using the wrong fork was considered uncool!

After the face-in-the-soup incident, Mick stopped insisting I accompany him to these things. Instead of passing out at expensive dinners, I'd take a bunch of Mandrax and go to Pamela Mayall's house and pass out *there!* I'd come round the next morning and I'd be perfectly all right. Meanwhile, Mick went off to his Country Gentlemen's Club or the party for the Supremes at Lord Whatsit's or the christening of some dim bulb peer's new grandchild.

Clearly, I wasn't the right person for the job; I wasn't good at details, never have been. There even came a point where I even stopped trying to dress for dinner. I've never been all that interested in clothes, anyway, and I've certainly never wanted to get dressed up to please others. The only time I like to dress is when I'm performing. It's a ceremonial thing; an offering. What Mick needed was someone glamorous and fashionable. Like Bianca.

Mick is always starring in an endless movie. He feels that he has to look great all the time for the great director in the sky. If they wheeled in the cameras and lit the scene at any minute, we would all look wonderful. I was becoming someone you couldn't take anywhere. I was a wreck, physically. I was talking to myself, an unmoored boat slipping away down the Thames.

My form of retaliation was especially vicious. Mick idealized me. Every time he saw another flaw in me, he couldn't bear it. I knew that to destroy myself in his eyes would be the worst torment I could inflict on him. I wanted to destroy my face. A systematic, cold blooded self-desecration. Since he saw me as an extension of himself, it would be much the same as desecrating Mick. After everything we'd been through together, to leave him for drugs!

In my catalogue of regrets — it's quite a long list! — I used to think that if I could do it all again the only thing I would do differently would be not to take drugs! Silly, but from day one, it was quite clear to me (it would have been to anybody) that smack was like poison to me. I always had a horrible reaction to it. Almost immediately my skin gets very strange and vile spots appear and all sorts of strange things happen to me. I don't know why I liked it! I suppose I was in pain, and it did stop *that*.

The drugs progressed slowly, but inexorably.

I was beginning to fragment unbearably. Once I really started to hit my stride, Mick was out of his depth (although he was too, well, po-lite to actually say anything about my condition). He also knew that, in some funny way, I knew what I was doing. At one point my mother decided to put me in the loony bin. I made one call to Mick and he came and got me out — he didn't think I was crazy, just high.

Sometimes I think I self-destructed because that's the only way Mick would let me go (and the only way I could get up the courage to). I saw myself doing it in slow motion. I pushed him away and pushed him away until in the end he was so weary.


It was spring and we were out in the garden at Cheyne Walk. Andee Cohen had come to visit. Mick was strolling in and out of the house, chattering. He was his customary affable self, but there was tension in the air. For one thing, I was ignoring him.

"Would you care for a glass of wine, Andee?" Mick asked.

"Of course she would," I said.

"Owabowta joint? A line? A good fuck?"

"Just bring me whatever's the special today, thank you."

Mick disappeared into the house. After he had left, I turned to Andee.

"Why don't you take Mick home with you?" I said. "If you want him, you can have him, you know. I won't mind a bit. He's yours."

Andee was in shock. "Whatever are you *saying?* Why are you treating him like this?"

"Oh, I don't know, I feel somehow it's my obligation as resident ghost of Cheyne Walk."

It was the beginning of my world-weary period. Like the Lady of Shalott I had "heard a whisper say/A curse is on her if she stay. . . ."


One day, you see, I had heard Mick and Ahmet Ertegun talking downstairs at Cheyne Walk. Ahmet was the head of Atlantic Records, the Stones' new label, and since I was by now a virtually taboo subject of conversation, I was surprised to hear my name. They must have thought I'd gone out. I crept to the top of the stairs and listened.

Ahmet was saying, "No, no, Mick, we *do* have to talk about Marianne."

"*Christ!*"

"I know it's going to be tough on you, but she could jeopardize *everything.*"

"But wot to do, man, wot to do?"

"There's only one thing *to* do. I've seen a lot of heartbreak with junkies. Believe me, old friend, it wrecks the lives of everybody *around* them, as well. It's a bottomless pit, and she'll drag you into it unless you let her go."

I could hear Mick saying, "Yeah, yeah, I know, man."

"If we're putting up thirty million dollars, we want some guarantee that the whole deal isn't going to be blown because of Marianne. You can understand that, can't you?"

"I just have to think for a minute. Let me think."

There were Ahmet and Mick in my living room discussing my fate as if it was some business matter. Like distribution or foreign rights. Sitting at the top of those stairs like a child listening to her parents, the precariousness of my situation hit me full force. This was writing on the wall that even a junkie could read!

I never mentioned to Mick that I had overheard his pact with Ahmet. If I'd just once told him, in the normal, human way: "You fuck. I heard you talking with Ahmet about getting rid of me." Oh well, I guess I'd had enough. It was just a question of *when.*

When the Stones' money manager Prince Rupert Lowenstein came into the picture, I knew my days were numbered. I wasn't appreciated because I didn't pitch in. At all. According to the new Rolling Stones order, I wasn't a "team player."

Early on in the new regime, Lowenstein's wife, Princess Rupert, or whatever her name is, gave a White Ball, where everybody was expected to come dressed in something white, and I, being contrary, showed up in black from head to toe. I thought it would be amusing, but it didn't go down well. They were *incensed*. They took this stuff very *seriously*. It was a White Ball, and when they said white, they meant *white*. And so — on such a symbolic, frivolous note — things finally fell apart. That black outfit was the beginning of the end!

In any case, it wasn't long until the Stones camp, on Prince Rupert's advice, decided to transplant lock, stock and barrel to the south of France. I knew it was time to bail out. (And from what Anita has since told me about life at Keith's château, Nellcôte, it would have been hell, especially for me. I was already hanging by a thread.) It was in the south of France that things really began to go haywire. The drugs that we were doing in London were nothing compared to what went on at Nellcôte. The Stones were making a lot more money; the lifestyle shifted gear. That's when the big-time consumption of hard drugs started. I would have been dead in a matter of months!

I wasn't about to leave England with Mick. I had a little child. I didn't want to be that far away from my mother. Ultimately, I must have not loved him enough, or trusted him either. I felt he might at some point betray me. Better to get it over with as quickly as possible! And in England.

Mick knew I was slipping away, and he made one last courtly and romantic gesture. Mick, being a Leo, is a master of ritual and symbolism. Every time we would start to break up he would write me another song.

This time he said: "I have something I want you to hear." He went over to the stereo and put on a tape. Then he knelt down in front of me, took both my hands in his and looked into my eyes. And on came "Wild Horses."

> *Graceless lady, you know who I am*
> *You know I can't let you slide through my hands*

I hugged him, and I cried. For what might have been. But it was going to take more than a song to put Humpty-Dumpty together again. Mick didn't understand. He didn't know what to do. It was a tremendous bother to him, my being that way, and I hate being a bother. I'd rather just go off and be a bother by myself.

In the turbulent crosscurrents of the Stones, someone has always had to be "*it*." Now it was my turn. The stability of the group from the very beginning has always depended on Mick's demonization of someone in the inner circle. First it was Brian, then Andrew and now it was happening to me. After I got out, Anita suddenly became the malevolent evil-doer. She was demonized beyond belief. People, to this day, suspect all this dark stuff about Anita. Ridiculous. After Anita was gone it was only a matter of time before Keith became "it."

If I didn't know him, if I was just observing these things, I would have to say, "This man is acting in this way because he has been bitterly disappointed in love." And I think he must have been, but when and by whom I don't know. Who was the great love of his life? Was it Chrissie or Bianca or Jerry or me? (Actually, I think it was Keith.)


I was already seen as an unrepentant Jezebel and druggy when the vicious court case between John Dunbar and me came up in the summer of 1970. He divorced me citing adultery, with Mick as the corespondent. "MARIANNE WASN'T FAITHFUL!" screamed the papers. Almost overnight I had gone from helpless victim to wanton "Miss X" to national witch. The Archbishop of Canterbury was saying intercessionary prayers for me.

Eventually I twigged that you could actually manipulate this stuff to your own advantage. I did an interview for the *New Musical Express* in 1973 in which I portrayed myself as a ruthless adventuress with headline-grabbing statements like "I slept with three Rolling Stones. . . ." It *was* somewhat of a perverse thing to do, but fun.

I hated the way I'd been cast, as this victim, this pathetic mad creature in Mick's soap opera. To call someone mad is an easy way of dismissing them. The minute you say someone's crazy, they stop being human. It's the same process whereby women were made into witches in the Middle Ages. Old women who were a drag on the village economy and lived alone were made into demonic entities and then disposed of without any guilt.

That's I suppose where the shadow comes in. For every bright, beautiful thing we throw out there, there's a dark one. They exist together. I know the dark side of Mick, but the other side is a legendary great romance. So I can see why Mick thinks I'm a she-devil, and I can quite understand why he would say, "It wasn't me that almost killed Marianne, it was she that nearly killed me." I put him through such hell. I took on all the negative attributes, I made all the trouble. And through all this he really acted practically like a saint (which only provoked me further).

The last phase with Mick is difficult to navigate because I don't want to justify my bad behavior, I'm not trying to blame anybody, but I also know I was never quite as rotten as I was made out to be. I was in a bad dream made all the more nightmarish by the illusion — to outsiders — that I was living a fairy tale.

Every little girl in Kansas wants to know what it's like to be there, to be a fairy-tale princess, the girlfriend of Mick Jagger. But life with Mick was never a fairy tale. Toward the end I cried all the time. I would have inexplicable moments of anguish. I remember once, after the screening of *Candy*, bursting into tears for no apparent reason. I was miserable and nobody could bear it, nobody could even *understand* it, least of all myself. I would tell my mother how unhappy I was and *she* would get furious with me!

People had a tremendous investment in believing my life with Mick was one long idyll of love and happiness. It seemed terribly important to people that it be that way. It was fate all right, but only in the tabloid meaning of the word. And when I left Mick it was as if I committed some terrible crime in the eyes of the press and the eyes of Mick and the eyes of the world.

Extracting myself from Mick was really a case of saving myself. I didn't want to become another Rolling Stones' sacrifice. I don't know what was expected of me, but I felt it was a distinct possibility. If I was going to become a human sacrifice, it was going to be for something else!

For Mick, the awful thing was that I wasn't leaving for any reason he could see. He didn't know that I'd heard the exchange with Ahmet. I left him for a romantic ideal. I wanted to be a junkie more than I wanted to be with him. That was my idea of glamour!

# The Wall

IMAGINE it's all been built up now, but in 1972 Soho still had a few bombed-out buildings left over from the Blitz. I passed my days sitting on the partly demolished wall of one of them. I sat on a low wall that must have once been the wall of a house, and leant against an adjoining wall. The middle of this bombed-out building was a shell filled with rubble where the derelicts and meth drinkers would get a bonfire going every night. Meth is vile stuff, pure ethyl alcohol, the cheapest drunk there is, practically free. Even in the lower depths there were class distinctions. The junkies and the winos. We bummed cigarettes and waved, but we remained in our own spheres.

I did as close to nothing as I could. As I sat there day after day, high as a kite, I must have seemed a strange apparition among the ruins. I was still wearing the exquisite clothes from my former life. A bedraggled White Queen whose tatterdemalion finery was gradually getting frayed, worn away from sitting on walls and sleeping in squats. I was rail thin. I hoped I was becoming invisible.

Ever since I'd read *Naked Lunch,* I'd wanted to be a street addict. And there was no doubt that I had achieved my goal in a spectacular manner. But underneath the literary aspirations, I was broken-hearted, devastated and defeated. When I was high, however, things didn't seem too bad at all!

Just a few months earlier, in May of 1971, Mick had finally given in to his narcissism and married . . . *himself!* I wasn't invited to the wedding, but I celebrated anyway and ended up spending Mick and Bianca's wedding night in the Paddington Police Station.

It began with one of my little sorties up to London. I was living at Yew Tree, the thatched cottage near Reading that Mick had given my mother. Once a week or so I would go up to London on the train to see Doctor Dally, who would shoot me full of Valium. Then I would get the five o'clock train back to Goring. That particular day I was on my way back to Paddington when through the window of a taxi I saw a huge headline banner: MICK AND BIANCA WED IN FRENCH FRACAS.

I immediately went into the station bar and had three vodka martinis. Got blind drunk. Problem was, I didn't know that you simply don't drink when you are shot full of Valium.

I went lurching and staggering to an Indian restaurant. (For some reason I thought I'd be safe if I was near the train.) There, I did my famous falling-into-the-curry trick. The owner of the Indian restaurant called the cops and they came and locked me up. Just for the night, they said. To sleep it off.

"That must be quite a hangover you're enjoying, miss," the copper said as I tottered out of my cell next morning. I was not just hung over, but strung out as well.

This was a new police station; it had just been opened by Princess Margaret or somebody and they were very proud of it. And as I was leaving this copper comes up to me and very formally presents me with their "visitors" book and says: "Miss Faithfull, as you may know this police station 'ere was very recently inaugurated and you bein' our second celebrity guest, we would consider it a great honor if you would sign our book." I thought I was dreaming. This really was the beginning of the end. A precipitous build-up of horrors that just got worse and worse.

I hadn't played my role properly. I hadn't died my long-anticipated death and I hadn't been thrown out. I had simply packed up and left the palace. What I did simply wasn't allowed. It's just not acceptable to a narcissistic personality like Mick for the *other* person to leave. It's completely *verboten*. But being at least as narcissistic as Mick, I didn't understand any of this. I was just trying to walk before they made me run.

Well over a year before Mick and Bianca's wedding, I had already made up my mind to go. I had been looking for an "honorable" way out for some time when I met Lord Paddy Rossmore. I used Paddy, but I figured he was a grown-up and knew the score.

Mick and I were staying in Ireland at Glin Castle near the Shannon River with the Knight of Glin, a dear friend with one of the sweetest and oldest of Anglo-Irish titles. There I met the delightful Lord Rossmore. He was so Anglo-Irish: long legs that curl up in that English aristocratic way, a bit like an old lady. In short, the sort of man my mother always wanted me to marry! He was very clever and bookish. He loved William Blake; we talked endlessly about Blake. He gave me a copy of *Songs of Innocence and Experience*. In our enthusiasm, the two William Blakes — Paddy's pre-Raphaelite Blake and my decidedly more psychedelic Blake — managed to coexist quite effortlessly. The relationship was on that sort of level.

Under normal circumstances, my interest in Paddy would have been nothing more than flirtation, but these were not normal circumstances and flirtation became infatuation. I don't know if I really loved him or merely saw a way out. A *respectable* way out. Mick and I were still together, but barely. And here was Paddy Rossmore, who seemed to be in love with me, and I used that as a way of extricating myself. At the time I wouldn't have had the guts or the integrity of spirit to just get up and leave and leap into unknown space. He was nothing like Mick. Monkish and spiritual, the product of many years of civilization! Anyway, because I was desperate I decided this was it. I left Cheyne Walk with Nicholas, a couple of rolled-up carpets and a box of books. A few weeks later Paddy and I announced our engagement.

At the point when Paddy met me, he knew nothing about my drug habits. He couldn't fathom what was the matter with me. And it wasn't just heroin. In an effort to curb my heroin addiction, I'd developed a horrendous barbiturate problem. I was substituting alcohol and barbs for smack. Poor old Paddy was engaged to a zombie. I was comatose on sleeping pills the entire year. The whole scene was complete insanity.

Paddy's solution to this state of affairs was a perfectly practical one: Why don't you see a doctor? So I went to a specialist, Doctor Dally, in Devonshire Place, one of those very grand houses where twice a week this woman — without speaking, we never exchanged one word — would shoot me up with Valium. It was eighty quid a pop — what a terrible rip-off! — and poor Paddy paid for this. I had no idea what drug therapy might consist of. There are a number of different methods for weaning addicts off heroin, but even then I had a pretty good idea that shooting you up with Valium twice a week wasn't one of them. I wasn't complaining, though.

Paddy was so shocked by my drug problems and the prevailing method in treating them that after we split up he went on to found a drug rehab in Ireland for addicts, called Coolemine.

Another oddity of my relationship with Paddy was that we did not live together. I went to live with my mother and Nicholas at Yew Tree. And Paddy went back to live with *his* mother! It was all very difficult and felt as if it had nothing to do with me. Eva wasn't going to let me go just yet. She was still acting out some strange inner drama with me at the time, I've never known quite what. When I was at home in those days with my mother, I was no longer myself at all; I became the completely passive daughter. I stopped having a personality altogether, and for many years I was like that. My handwriting became smaller and smaller and more cramped. And then we had Paddy's mother — the eighty-seven-year-old matriarch, Lady Rossmore — to contend with. A tyrant in her own right. It was the Reign of the Dragon Mothers!

I did go off on disastrous weekends from time to time to stay with Lady Rossmore and we were occasionally allowed to go on holidays together — we went to Ibiza and once on a Gypsy caravan — but they were always a nightmare. There were frantic knockings on chemists' doors in search of codeine linctus and barbs to the utter bewilderment of a nonplussed Paddy.

Paddy left me about nine months later. I'd had enough of it myself. Once I'd left Mick and lost Paddy and moved back to my mother's house, I was completely under her thumb. She took over completely:

The supervision of Nicholas (who now lived with her), the running of the house. I became this useless person who just lay around a lot.

After about a year and a half of trying to be good and do what my mother wanted and do what Paddy wanted, one day I split and shortly after went to live on my wall. I still had my beautiful engagement ring, which of course I left in some dealer's sink.

There was one last comical experience with Mick before he finally gave up on me. For a long time after we'd broken up he phoned me constantly, wrote me letters, pleaded with me to see him. But I was no longer quite who he thought I was. I'd been drinking heavily and I had put on a huge amount of weight, fifty pounds at least. I remember doing this quite consciously. I didn't want to be that sylphlike person anymore. The next thing was to cut my hair off, which I also did. Mick had not seen any of this, and one day when he called I agreed to meet him. "Right!" I thought to myself. "We'll see how he likes *this.*" I knew the moment he saw me it would be all over. I took the train up to London and I went to see him. When I got to Cheyne Walk there were all these girls hanging around, soi-disant housekeepers and cooks and this and that, groupies of one stripe or another, and I was turned to stone. He took one look at me — a look of utter horror — and sort of *gasped.* Who *is* this chick? This is not my lady at all. He wanted nothing to do with a ten-stone damsel. That did it. It stopped the phone calls and the letters. I never got another one. I went back to Yew Tree, poured myself a stiff drink and laughed. How silly it all was.

At some point I found myself in Paris with Jean de Breiteuil. He was a horrible guy, someone who had crawled out from under a stone. I had met him at Talitha Getty's house, Jean Paul Getty Junior's wife. She eventually died of an overdose. She was the first person from my old life whom I had gone to see. Jean de Breiteuil happened to be there. He was Talitha's lover, and somehow I ended up with him. What I liked about him was that he had one yellow eye and one green eye. And he had a lot of dope. It was all about drugs and sex. He was just slightly higher on the evolutionary scale than Spanish Tony. Breiteuil was very

French and very social. He was with me only because I'd been involved with Mick Jagger. In that froggy way he was obsessed with all that. To him I was *très le type* rock 'n' roll. I knew this species well, but as I said, he had a lot of drugs.

I went back with him to Keith and Anita's house in Cheyne Walk. They were in the south of France, at Nellcôte. They had given Jean their house. He had showed up at Nellcôte with a lot of smack, so Keith and Anita were happy to see him. "How wonderful! Listen, man, when you're in London, stay at Cheyne Walk." I lived there with him for months and then we went to Paris for a weekend.

We were staying at L'Hôtel when he got a call from Pamela Morrison and he had to leave very suddenly.

"Jean, listen to me," I told him. "I've got to meet Jim Morrison."

"Not possible, baby. Not cool right now, okay?"

"You are an idiot *and* a fucking prig!"

"Not now. *Je t'explique* later, okay? Be right back."

He slammed out of the room.

But he didn't *come* right back. He returned in the early hours of the morning in a very agitated state and woke me up. I was fucked up on Tuinals. Then, for no apparent reason, he proceeded to beat me up. I've noticed that men particularly seem to get violent (in a detached sort of way) on heroin. When this happened to me my natural reaction was always that I must have done something to deserve this. In another incarnation, perhaps.

I lit a cigarette and asked him: "So, did you have a good time over there? Aren't you going to tell me why you're in such a good mood?"

"Get packed."

"Are we going somewhere?"

"Morocco."

"Very funny. We just got here."

"I want you to meet my mother. Hurry up!"

"Uh-oh. . . . What happened over there?"

"Shut up, goddammit!"

"Oh, shit."

"Yeah. It's fucked."

He was scared for his life; Jim Morrison had OD'd and he had provided the smack. Jean saw himself as dealer to the stars. Now he was a small-time heroin dealer in big trouble. He was very young. Had he lived, he might have turned into a human being.

I was in very rough shape. We were frenziedly throwing things into suitcases the way people do in crises. Jean was taking me to Tangier to meet his mother, the Comtesse de Breiteuil, on Tuinals. *La formidable!* It was a disaster. We stayed a week, both horribly strung out. In a panic before leaving Paris he'd got rid of all his drugs. And all we found in her house was some ether.

Subsequently I read in some magazine that I was supposed to have been at Morrison's when they broke down the bathroom door and found his body floating in the bath with the big purple bruise over his heart. Or alternately that I gave him the *coup de grace.* (I never gave anyone a fix in my life. I only learnt how to shoot *myself* up in the last few months of my addiction.) It's just my role in the mythology, I guess. Sister Morphine.

However hard I thought living with Mick was, the first couple of years without him were harder. I had no idea how much I had been protected by Mick. Then again, if I hadn't left him, I would never have found out what strength I had myself. For once I left Mick, my last protection was gone.

The persecution of me by the press made me fair game. It gave a license to every sadistic little creep in England to vent their vileness on me. Endless humiliating and shameful things. People can really be horrid. I was able to grit my teeth, smile and fake it for many years. I started to do heroin in earnest. I was in the most awful pain, and I figured I had tried everything else. I had even tried suicide, which didn't work. Then my mother tried to kill *herself,* for God's sake. At that point I entered one of the outer levels of hell, and stayed there for years.

Very rarely someone I knew and loved would visit. Andee came to dinner at Eva's one night. I saw the house through her eyes. It was a house drawn by Arthur Rackham. Oversized, dark oak furniture stuffed into this tiny cottage. After dinner I went into the bedroom and fell down on the bed. There was an enormous space between us, a gap she couldn't cross. I had gone somewhere she couldn't go. I just fled down that tunnel.

An American journalist came to see me while I was living at the cottage with my mother, and when he got back to the States he sent me the complete recordings of Robert Johnson and Hank Williams. These were the only records I had in Yew Tree and I played them day and night over and over again. Eventually I drove my mother out. She couldn't take it. It was her or me. She went out and got a job and while she was working I would listen to Robert Johnson and Hank Williams all the time, ponder and think.

One day, into my cheerless routine came a flamboyant figure out of my past. Kenneth Anger, underground filmmaker and soi-disant magician. Having misread Mick's pantomime satanism, he must have assumed that I believed in black magic (and was ripe to be his apprentice). He wanted me to play Lilith in his film *Lucifer Rising*. What could I say?

Anyway, although I never believed Kenneth had any psychic powers I was willing to believe he was a great filmmaker.

Lilith is obviously one of the great female archetypes, another form of the Great Mother like Ishtar and Astarte, Diana, Aphrodite and Demeter. From the point of view of the patriarchy, of course, she is the pure incarnation of evil. Lilith did not eat of the Tree of the Knowledge of Good and Evil, so she never knew right from wrong.

I went to Egypt with Kenneth and my brother, Chris O'Dell, who was the cameraman on the shoot. Chris Jagger was cast as Lucifer. Kenneth's films are always about sexual politics. Kenneth really wanted Mick for the lead in the film, but Mick wouldn't do it so Chris got the part. And being the silly little boy he is, he couldn't take the role seriously. Also, Chris is an incredible loudmouth and smartass bully, and he continually talked back. Everything Kenneth said Chris would ridicule. After one day Chris Jagger was on a plane back to London. If anyone was going to play Lucifer, it was Kenneth.

My part was shot around Giza with the sphinx. When we got to Egypt, I could see Kenneth didn't know what was happening, either as a magus *or* a director.

Even as inept as Kenneth was, I knew he was dangerous in a way. I knew that simply by being in the film I was involving myself in a magic act far more potent than Kenneth's hocus-pocus satanism. Smearing myself with Max Factor blood and crawling around an Arab graveyard at five o'clock in the morning as the sun rose over the pyramids was absolute insanity. To be that passive, to let someone like that make me perform a ritualistic act of such ghoulish proportions, was just mindless. If I'd been my normal self I would have just laughed, but by then I was a hopeless junkie. I used to feel a lot of the bad luck in my life came from that film. I think I've worked *that* out, at least!

The Star Mountain sequence was to be shot last — and now I know *why*. The Star Mountain is an ancient neolithic place of worship in Germany. There are two hundred stone steps cut into the mountain. When the sun rises on the solstice, the rays go through an aperture and hit a sacred spot.

We were filming on the morning of the winter solstice. The sun was coming up. There I was, dope sick, climbing the mountain. When I got to the top I remember seeing the sun shining through the aperture and hitting the rock and then I blacked out completely. What had happened, of course, was that I had run out of smack and had a slight dope fit. I think I lost consciousness for a second and when I came to I realized I was falling off the mountain. I came to as I was tumbling through the air and remembered in midfall that I had to do some somersaults and land on my feet. Which I did. They rushed me to hospital. They thought I must at least have a concussion. But nothing. So there, Kenneth Anger. My magic was bigger than yours! (Kenneth would have liked me to fall off the mountain and die. It would have been a magnificent climax for his film.)

Quite a few years after *Lucifer Rising*, Kenneth sent me a biography of Frances Farmer and a letter telling me I was exactly like Frances Farmer and Eva was just like Frances Farmer's mother. I realized then what he was: a witch out of a Hollywood tabloid. Kitsch occult, wow!

Doing the film was bad enough, but there were further consequences. Pictures came out in the papers with me looking like death in gray makeup and a nun's habit, with pyramids in the background. All contributing to creating a quite fiendish, devil-worshipping image of me. Even old photographs of me outside Yew Tree cottage now took on a sinister aspect! That sweet little cottage began to look like a little witch house.

After *Lucifer Rising* I ended up on the wall and became a junkie. I felt unclean and dangerous to the people I loved. The wall was a very good place because I couldn't hurt anyone while I was there. It's like taking yourself out of the tribe. When you get sick you go into the woods and if you don't get better you don't come back. I knew by heart William Burroughs's mantra THE CURE IS IN THE DISEASE. You go to the source of the illness to heal yourself. I could only get out of my nightmare by going to the heart of the matter. The junkie on the street in Burroughs cosmology is the mythical center. Burroughs, of course, never spent a day on the street and never took off his suit and tie except to fuck. I took the train to London and didn't return home for two years, except for the occasional bath.

For me, being a junkie was an honorable life. It was total anonymity, something I hadn't known since I was seventeen. As a street addict in London, I finally found it. I had no telephone, no address. Nobody knew me from Adam.

When I first left Yew Tree I stayed with friends, but eventually I exhausted the patience of even the most long-suffering. For a while I stayed with my friend Pamela Mayall and did a lot of smack. I would stagger up her garden path and collapse into the lilacs, followed shortly by a cabdriver with hand extended saying to Pamela, "That'll be three pounds seventy-five, missus." Pamela was trying to bring up four children, and I was driving her crazy. Dirty needles on the drainboard, shooting up on the end of her bed. The only good thing to come of my atrocious behavior was that those children grew up with an absolute horror of hard drugs.

I terrified her children and alarmed her guests. One night Pamela had invited her very proper lawyer (with fancy French wife) to dinner. Before they arrived, Pamela had pleaded with me not to embarrass her. "Marianne, I beg you, be on your best behavior, just this once!" This was always a cue for me to do something outrageous, unfortunately. We hadn't sat down to dinner before I felt the urge to excuse myself to go pee and, of course, shoot up. While in the loo my dress somehow got tucked into my knickers. Oblivious of my ridiculous appearance, I tottered back into the dining room, a cigarette nonchalantly listing in one hand, paused in the doorway with what I imagined as great sophistication and said, "Hi, darlings!" A glazed look came over the guests. Never mind. This was faintly amusing in comparison to the epic folly that followed.

I began doing better, despite the occasional lapse, so one day, Pamela decided it was now safe to go shopping and leave me in the house alone. I took the opportunity to shoot up and run myself a nice hot bath.

By the time Pamela returned, steaming water was cascading down the hall steps. She ran up to the landing only to find water gushing even more furiously down the flight of stairs above. It was pouring off the landing like a small waterfall. Finally reaching the upper bathroom, she found me nodded out in the bathtub with one arm draped over the side. She tried to pull the plug out, but the water was too hot and she couldn't keep her arm in the water long enough. It was scalding hot and I, like a lobster, was gradually being cooked. I was quite oblivious to my state. Pamela thought that if she could pull me out of the tub the water level would go down and she could then get at the plug. She grabbed hold of my arm and began to pull, but my arm was so soapy that it slipped right through her hands and she fell backward, hitting her head on the bidet and knocking herself out. Another twenty minutes elapsed before Pamela came to, another twenty minutes while the water poured like a cataract through the house. It was now running out the front door, through the garden and onto the street. By the time Pamela came round and got the plug out, the ceiling on the landing had collapsed, the carpets were ruined, the walls of the children's rooms were caving in and Pamela's face was covered with ugly black-and-blue lumps.

It was after this that Pamela finally threw me out. As I made my way out through the gate I could hear Pamela shouting behind me like a mantra: "I've had it! I've had it! I've had it! I've had it!"

The choice now was between going back to my mother's or the street and, believe me, the street didn't seem all that bad.

My new "home" was a wall in St. Anne's Yard. I had chosen this particular location because my friend Gypsy, who was also my connection, had a tiny room there over a restaurant in one of those strange warren-like places in Soho. It was in St. Anne's Yard that I would wait on my wall for Gypsy to come by so that I could score. It was through Gypsy that I met a lot of street people and local shopkeepers, and all of them were astonishingly kind to me.

Soho then was a very odd place. Full of dodgy clubs and seedy hotels. Very fly-by-night. A lot of "marginal" types: junkies and prostitutes, music-business hustlers, great painters and underworld faces. It felt right to me. It was a long way from Chelsea or anywhere I had any associations with. It was several worlds away from the one I had known. I would never run into Mick or Keith there, or anybody else from my old life. It was not a neighborhood they would frequent. I used to hang about at a tea stand where cabbies would go for a cup of chi at two in the morning. It was all very Dickensian, with of course a bit of Burroughs.

I saw none of my old friends. I did run into the writer Brion Gysin in those odd moments I wandered away from my wall. Brion was very sweet to me. He didn't care whether I was with Mick Jagger or the man in the moon. But other than Brion, not one person had ever tried to find me. Then again, why should they? And to be quite honest I couldn't quite imagine all my old friends going to look for me on a bomb site in Soho.

When I left Mick I thought that humanity was the worst thing ever to have plagued the planet. It was out on the street that I began to see how kind and compassionate people could be. It was junkies and winos on the street who restored to me my faith in humanity. People think that my time with Mick was this glorious moment in my life, but not for me. I knew that the life we were leading wasn't reality.

I threw myself on the mercy of the street people and did they ever come through. They didn't know me from Adam. They didn't give a flying fuck whether I'd been Mick Jagger's girlfriend or the Queen Mum herself. All they knew was that I was very thin and liked to get high. I would try anything. In a whore's flat I almost OD'd on Pethidine (an anaesthetic). At night someone would take me to a squat and occasionally, when I got too grungy, I would go back to my mother's house and get cleaned up. If it was cold, somebody would always get me a cup of tea or cover me up. I had only one set of clothes, which I wore all the time. Gypsy would sometimes take me to the Chinese restaurant where they would put me in a blanket and wash my clothes in their washing machine.

When people hear about this part of my life they imagine that I must have turned to prostitution to get my drugs. I never had to, luckily, because I never would have made it. I was incredibly frail. I weighed barely seven stone, which is about ninety-eight pounds. I never ate. I lost my looks. Aside from doing drugs, the nearest I came to actual criminal activity was hanging out with a group who broke into chemist's shops.

Terrible bits of news kept coming through the haze. "Didja 'ear Jimi 'Endrix died last night?" It was like hearing reports from a distant battlefield. Hendrix, Jim Morrison, Janis Joplin, Sharon Tate, Charles Manson, Kent State. I seemed twitchily in sync with a disintegrating world. We were entering an era of disillusionment, self-destruction and tragedy. Even as a hopeless junkie on the street I can't describe how devastating it was to hear of Hendrix's death, of Janis's death, one right after the other. The awful feeling that we must really have fucked up. The Manson murders as a judgment on us all.

It was the biggest, steepest plunge of my life. A free fall. It was around this time that everybody I knew began to turn to hard narcotics to kill the pain, or alcohol or sleeping pills to obliterate themselves. The days of the mind-opening drugs were over. The world had tilted. A major change in key had taken place. It was a Mahler symphony whirling madly out of control.

I emerged from the sixties carrying a load of other people's baggage and it's taken a hell of a lot for me to put it down. My very life depended on jettisoning these phantoms. It's all very sophisticated stuff, this business of media-generated images. Jimi and Janis didn't understand what was happening to them. They got caught up in the vortex.

Since I had no money, drugs were hard to come by. A friend of Pamela Mayall's took pity on me and introduced me to the writer Alexander Trocchi. He was very Scottish, an addict himself, sympathetic and sensitive to my plight. Alex was just what I needed at that moment — a great drug guru. He introduced me to his doctor, the wonderful Dr. Willis of Bexley Hospital. It was Dr. Willis who got me registered. Prior to this I'd been scoring on the street or at Gypsy's. Alex helped me get on the National Health Program. I must have been one of the last patients; they stopped it soon after that. But in those glorious days, once you registered you would get a script for heroin jacks, little white pills that you could dissolve in water and then shoot up!

Every morning I would go to John Bellencroyden's, the chemists, and get my prescription filled. Then I'd take the jacks of heroin over to Alex's house and he would shoot me up. I always was a hapless junkie. I was a disaster even at that.

Now that I had a prescription I didn't have to depend on Gypsy or scuffle around trying to pop. I got my dose and stayed on my wall. I didn't do much. I had a very large prescription of heroin, twenty-four jacks of pure British Pharmaceutical heroin a day, and that kept me in a trance for most of the twenty-four hours. A thousand thoughts and images passed through my mind. I let them go without reflecting on any of them. I was as remote from them as if they were interesting specimens in a glass case. I was attached to nothing. I was Basho in his straw hut on the mountain side composing haikus out of air.

Whenever I went home I'd end up having a dreadful experience with my mother. By then we no longer spoke to each other. It was too awful; there was nothing to say.

I must have been a terrible mess when I'd go home. My mother couldn't bear it. Why was I doing all this to myself? I didn't know. It culminated in my cutting my face with a razor blade in a fit of cocaine psychosis. I developed a violent hatred of my appearance, of my face, of beauty itself. Didn't it get me into all this trouble in the first place? Beauty was a curse. It stood between me and who I was. It prevented people from seeing what was really of value, if anything!

Meanwhile, all this time I had been living on the wall, the Dunbars — John and his family — had been planning to take Nicholas away from me. In the spring of 1972, when Nicholas was seven, John went to court to get custody of him. I fought very hard not to lose him, but there was no way I could win. How could I? I'd been living on a *wall* for a year. Even my own dear Pamela Mayall came to testify that I was unfit. I felt hunted down.

The most galling part of the custody battle was John's getting up in court and saying I was an unfit mother because I was a drug addict. It was a wicked and hypocritical thing to do. John spent our honeymoon on drugs, for God's sake, when I didn't even know the right *words* for them. I did my utmost to keep Nicholas, but as usual I did everything to ensure I would lose him. All these people making decisions supposedly for my own good and Nicholas's. Not only was I unfit to take care of Nicholas, apparently Eva wasn't good for him either. And it was true Eva was becoming a bit unbalanced by then. She loved Nicholas so much. But it should never have been a question of Eva's having Nicholas. This is the stuff Nicholas and I talk about with horror. The saddest consequence of the trial was that Nicholas thought that because I no longer lived with him, I no longer loved him.

So, Nicholas was taken away from me and he went to live with John and his girlfriend, who at the time was the model Jean Shrimpton. I remember him coming down to Yew Tree with her. I don't know even why they came. I used to have this feeling that people would come up to Yew Tree cottage just to take a look at me as if I were an animal in a cage. It was grotesque.

I hardly saw Nicholas again for years. With the custody trial, John had simply turned the tables on me. After Nicholas was eighteen months old, John hardly saw him and he was very bitter about this.

Losing Nicholas was one of the reasons Eva tried to kill herself. It really put her over the edge, absolutely the last straw. And much as I hate to admit it, I honestly hadn't given a thought to what effect my behavior might have on her. That's the trouble with selfishness of this kind — the drug kind. The *last* thing you think about is "how is this affecting my mother?"

Shortly after the custody case my mother took an overdose of liquid morphine. She had quite a large supply stocked up after my grandmother had died. She'd kept all these narcotics. Just in case. "Just in case of what, Mother?" In case somebody might need a shot of morphine? Sudden bit of cancer in the night?

She was absolutely serious about killing herself. And then, soon after she'd taken the morphine overdose, her friend Carol got a clear psychic message in the middle of the night that told her to drive to Yew Tree cottage as fast as she could because something was wrong. And something was indeed very wrong. Eva — having taken all the morphine and written her good-bye letters — was collapsed on the floor. Carol got there in the nick of time, got her to the hospital and saved her. And when Eva recovered she was unbelievably nasty to Carol. Eva was *furious.* When you really want to kill yourself, the last thing on earth you want is for some meddlesome idiot to come along and save you!

I went back to my wall and stayed as high as I could. With that sort of habit, very little bothers you. You don't feel pain, you don't feel cold and you don't catch cold either. Never caught a cold till I got clean.

Time stood still, ran backwards, and then lurched forward into a murky future. Little patches of my past floated to the surface.

My mind kept reeling back to my days at the convent. I must have wanted to return to a time before I became entangled. To see how it

*Hamlet* with Nicol
Williamson, 1968, just
before Australia

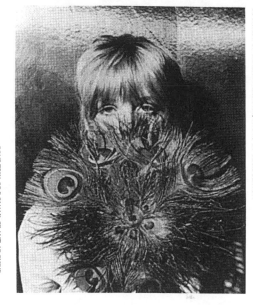

Me, photographed
by Cecil Beaton in
Christopher's flat, 1968.
I'm very, very stoned.

Chekhov's *Three Sisters,*
directed by William
Gaskill, Royal Court
Theatre, 1967. Me,
Glenda Jackson and
Avril Edgar

Nicholas and me at the Rolling Stones concert in Hyde Park

Opposite, above: The game of life with Oliver, in Edith Terrace, 1974

Opposite, below: Bob Potter, Ben, me and Joe Maverty in Danvers Street just before the Masterpiece (*Broken English*) came out, 1979

Leaving for Rome with Mario Schifano. Nicholas is obviously very unhappy.

The squat in Lots Road, where Ben and I lived in 1978

Me in Sweden on the *Broken English* promo-tour wearing Ben's leather jacket

Eva and me in the garden at Yew Tree, 1979

Ben and I get married. *Broken* is finished, true love awaits, 1979, Chelsea Register Office

Dominion Theatre, 1980

Keith and me, 1994.
Bourbon to hand, switch-
blade in his boot, guitar
across his back and the
law at his heels — Keith
Richards is rock 'n' roll

With Allen, at the Jack
Kerouac School of
Disembodied Poetics,
Boulder, Colorado, 1987

And the Irish elk looked
on and said, "Never
thought either of you two
would get here," with
Anita, Shell Cottage, 1993

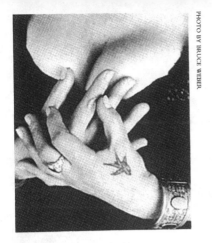

Home at last

had all begun and if there were any point at which I could have stopped it. I thought a lot about the convent. My best friend Sally Oldfield . . . banned books covered in brown paper . . . Mrs. Simpson.

I got a bee in my bonnet that Mrs. Simpson could save me. I had been looking for a key to a way out and one night it hit me that maybe it was Mrs. Simpson. Mrs. Simpson, my English teacher from when I was twelve years old, whom I loved. Mrs. Simpson would know. She was one of those wonderful inspiring teachers. We had studied a book in school called *Prester John* and we'd all had to write an essay on the build-up in the novel. My essay was called "The Climax" and Miss Simpson thought it so good she read it to the whole class. So I decided to call her. It was horribly embarrassing, of course. Poor woman! She had imparted to me all this wonderful knowledge. She gave me my love of Shakespeare, of Keats, of books. She opened all these doors. In my befuddled state I'd made the connection between Mrs. Simpson opening doors and my way out. And of course she wasn't going to know what to do with me, she was just this very straight, nice middle-class woman who'd only *read* about junkies. As soon as she came to the phone I knew I'd made a terrible mistake. I said, "Hi, it's Marianne Faithfull. Do you remember me, Mrs. Simpson? I was in your class at St. Joe." She was dumbfounded and, of course, didn't have the faintest idea what to tell me. After several excruciating minutes on the phone we both — with great relief — hung up.

One day, as I was sitting on my wall, my old producer Mick Leander tracked me down. He wanted me to make a record.

"Well, okay," I said, "but I have to have somewhere to live." Simple as that. Gem Music got me a flat in Russell Square by the British Museum, a very strange part of London. Bloomsbury. It was the year of the power cuts. Every night from seven to eleven all the lights went off. The Heath government was in power; it was part of the breaking of the working class in the early seventies. Strikes and the energy crisis had been going on for months — none of which I'd noticed, of course, while living on the wall with no televisions or electric lights. It went right by me.

I checked myself into this awful private clinic with Ginger, Michael Cooper's girlfriend. It must have been a desperate last-minute attempt to clean up before making the record. I stayed a day and a half and while I was there, supposedly detoxing, got someone to smuggle in some smack for me and got punched out for it by my male nurse, losing my two front teeth. Soon after I went to do the record at Mike Leander's in Denmark Street.

The record itself is very strange and ghostly, but the most bizarre thing about it, given my situation at the time, is the title: *Rich Kids Blues.* People, even people I was working with every day on the record, persisted in seeing me as this glittering, wealthy, high-living chick when it was perfectly obvious that I wasn't anything like that anymore. I'd moved on! I wasn't living in Chelsea, I was hanging out on a bomb site in Soho. I was missing my two front teeth.

The picture of me on the album cover shows how I actually looked then. Pale, thin and sickly. I looked like death. My voice is so weak on *Rich Kids Blues,* I can't bear to listen to it. It's the voice of somebody incredibly high, probably on the edge of death, making a record. It's always like that. Johnny Thunders sounds like that. There's no energy. Anybody who heard that record would have just said, "Well that's that. We'll never hear from her again."

It took no time at all to make the record, then I went back to the wall.


In front of Granny Takes A Trip on Kings Road I ran into Mick, who embraced me as passionately as if we had just been reunited after a brief separation. We held hands and looked into each other's eyes. When he began to caress my back, I realized he wanted to have sex with me. He asked the owner if we could use the room upstairs. We went upstairs and made love. Afterward we got dressed, went downstairs, kissed good-bye and went our separate ways.

The oddest part of it was that neither of us spoke *during* the entire time. It didn't exactly feel all that loving. Maybe it was an inarticulate way of connecting, but it felt more like an exercise of, well, property rights.

Within a week of my encounter with Mick, the new Stones album came out. *Sticky Fingers* was everywhere and it had my song, "Sister Morphine," on it. I proudly dropped into a record shop one afternoon to peek at my name, only to find my song attributed to M. Jagger & K. Richards. The ultimate humiliation, my name expunged even from my own song! I wrote an indignant letter to Allen Klein and went to see him.

Allen explained to me that the omission of my name had nothing to do with a fiendish plot — really! He showed me a letter written by Mick and Keith early in 1969 saying I should get a third of the royalties. It turned out they had not credited me because at the time "Sister Morphine" had been written I was still contracted to Gerry Bron, and none of us wanted to see him get the song's royalties. Apparently the arrangement was that I would get royalties, but no credit. Oh well, that song did well by me. I lived on the royalties from "Sister Morphine" for several lean years.

It was Oliver Musker who hauled me back. Without him I wouldn't be alive today.

I was drifting about, very thin, shooting a lot of dope. And then one day I went to a party in Chelsea on one of my jaunts out. I'd been to see David Lindell at his carpet shop. He told me about a party that night and I suddenly had a great urge to go to it. I hadn't been to anything like that in ages.

Mick was there with Suki Poitier. I spent a great deal of the party in the bathroom talking to Mick and Suki and doing coke. But it was Oliver who was the knight in shining armor that evening. I looked rather good that night, I thought. So good that Oliver Musker fell in love with me. He was delightful, young, good-looking and strong. An old Etonian aristocrat who ran a little antique business.

With the arrival of Oliver in my life everything changed. Oliver had decided to save me. And with grand old Brit imperial flourish, that's just what he did. He came in with new energy and like a clean breeze he swept away all the cobwebs. "We must get you out of this ghastly situation, my dear. It simply won't *do*." Before I knew it, I was in Bexley Hospital.

Bexley was famous for Dr. Willis. He did wonders with addicts of all stripes, but his methods were highly unorthodox, to say the least. He neither told you to stop nor took your drugs away. Quite the contrary. Dr. Willis let me have as much as I wanted. My prescription went up and up. He was waiting to see what would happen.

Finally I went to him and said: "All right, I've had all the smack I ever want and now I want to get off."

To which he said: "Well, Marianne, that's an admirable resolution but at this juncture I'm not sure you can."

That got my back up. Now I was determined to get off. They dropped my dosage a tiny bit each day, half a grain a day. The longest detox known to man.

Oliver came to see me every day. He was dying for me to be over this thing and get out. I was there eight months getting off dope. Only on the National Health Service could you do something like this! I was getting better and therefore became a prime example. Dr. Willis saw that I might be helpful to other addicts and had me talk to them. Willis taught through examples, good and bad. He kept a coke addict in the hospital, an American woman who'd come over in the days when you could get coke on prescription. She was there to make a striking point. A once beautiful and intelligent woman who was now a piece of human wreckage. The addict who gets off drugs is a powerful incentive.

There was a boy in Bexley who idolized me. He was very ill. And one night — he must have known he was dying — he asked if I would hold his hand and I refused. It was a very shameful thing. He called my name all night long but I wouldn't go to him. I was cured of my addiction but I hadn't yet seen the light.

Oliver comes out of this part of the story as truly chivalrous. It was one of those heroic moments where you see people — the cop, the dealer, one's manager — transcend all the dross, the dreadful self-interest we all have to live with, and do something truly noble. And that's what Oliver did. He whirlwinded me into Bexley and then plucked me out of there and whisked me off to India and Bali and Singapore. He was like Siegfried with his blond hair, so beautiful, like a shining creature.

We had wonderful times together. We went to India first because I was making a film called *Ghost Story* there in which I played a girl who escapes from an insane asylum to murder her cruel brother. We landed in Bombay and stayed in the Taj Mahal Hotel on Bombay Harbor, which is the most crazy place. It was designed in the nineteenth century by a French architect. It was his tour de force. A very beautiful, palatial hotel on the bay. The splendid facade was meant to face the harbor where the liners would come in from Europe and see his jewel-like masterpiece. But while putting it up, the Indians got confused and built it up *back to front!* The exquisite facade faces a mean little back street. It's typical of the misreadings that go on in India. The poor French architect was so upset he committed suicide by leaping from the top floor of the hotel.

Oliver had long periods where he was a splendid creature but crucial things were lacking that made me realize I couldn't live with him for the rest of my life. One day we were going by train from Bangalore north to Delhi to see Robert Fraser, who was living there. Oliver was becoming increasingly testy. We had a long ride ahead of us and all I wanted to do was read my novel. He was obviously bored and wanted to talk. Any withdrawal into one's self he considered an act of hostility. Oliver was sweet but a savage, really. Very grand and completely uneducated. I was immersed in *Howards End,* which is all about falling in love with families. I couldn't put it down. Now what Oliver liked to do was gossip about people he knew and my reading so got on his nerves that somewhere in the plains of India he picked up my book and threw it out the window. It was a library book, too. I was astounded.

He couldn't help that he was a very social English upper-class guy, I know. Chitchat was his life. When things like this happen I don't do anything at the time. I say nothing. I just think, "This is unforgivable behavior" and ages later — it's a Capricorn trait — I think to myself: "One day I shall not be with him and he will realize what a big mistake it was to throw *Howards End* on the track from Bangalore."

The feeling of traveling was exhilarating and there was the joy of seeing my Robert again. He was healthy and very spiritual and dressed in white robes, but still wickedly funny. His mother, Cynthia, came out and we went on a trek, climbing the foothills of the Himalayas. She was wonderful. She traveled over the Himalayas with a little vanity case filled with Elizabeth Arden makeup and face creams. And every morning she would sit there and put it on and every night take it all off again. She was a Christian Scientist and having all that mind-over-matter stuff on tap she always knew the right thing to say when I faltered. Eighteen months earlier I had been a junkie and a registered addict. I was clean by then but my muscles hadn't quite knitted yet.

We trekked up into the mountains. It was heaven being in the Himalayas climbing real mountains. I don't know how I managed it, but I did. Now, whenever I feel myself weakening, I say to myself: "Come on, you climbed the foothills of the Himalayas!" It was beyond therapy. That was the way Oliver saw things. Action. He was never much of an analyzer. Reading and talking about the meaning of life didn't interest him, but *doing* things — that was his *metier.*

At the top there was a little tea house. Robert and Oliver were already there. They got on famously. They'd both been to Eton together.

When I was better, David Bowie asked me to perform with him in his "1980 Floor Show" in 1974. I did "I Got You, Babe" in a nun's costume. The nun's habit was David's idea. What I loved was doing my version of the Noel Coward song "Twentieth Century Blues."

David invited me to go to a Rolling Stones concert at Wembley. We weren't having an affair, but that's what it would have looked like. David Bowie takes Marianne Faithfull. I decided to go with his entourage instead, dressed in my wild Mozart costume. Bowie was livid.

Oliver took this sort of thing in his stride. Dressed to the nines as Mozart, I said, "Well, I'm going to go and see what happens." He just said, "All right, dear."

I got backstage somehow, but everybody shunned me like a leper. By then I was a pariah. The only people who were delighted to see me were Keith and Anita, who fell on me: "Oh Marianne, how lovely to see you! We've missed you terribly! And look at you. Right out of a Vatteau, my dear."

Mick was dreadful. I must have been crazy. Without even thinking I went into his grand dressing room at Wembley where he was having his makeup put on and just sat down as if nothing had happened and started chatting and he said to me: "Marianne, really! You of all people should know better. You can't just come in here and start talking to me, I'm having my makeup put on." I was crushed. I was dismayed at how elegantly dressed Bianca was and how out of time I was. I understood what it must have been like to have been Chrissie Shrimpton and hear Mick crowing: "You're obsolete, my baby, my poor old-fashioned baby."

After the concert I stood outside Wembley Stadium in a daze. I was fucked: I had no money, I was dressed as Mozart and it was pouring with rain. Twenty limos drove past, all going to the Rolling Stones party, until finally the last rather modest limo stopped. It was Andrew. He gave me a lift back to town.

Oliver and I saw a lot of David and Angie Bowie. One night we were all a bit drunk at David's house and David began coming on to me. We went into the corridor. I unzipped his trousers. I was trying to give him a blow job, but David was scared to death of Oliver. Oliver does have this Gestapo-officer vibe to him. Absolutely terrified of Oliver David was, and so he couldn't keep it up. But David completely underestimated Oliver. This was not the sort of thing Oliver would have got upset about. He would have laughed.

Oliver wasn't crazy like Brian, but he did have a terrible, uncontrollable temper. For this reason alone I could never have stayed with him. He would become enraged and I wouldn't know what I'd done. I got to the point where I could leave my body behind, rather like meditation. I'd appear to be there, but I'd be gone. He found this infuriating, poor guy. Oliver took me back from being a junkie on the street, got me off smack and took me around the world, but there was a bit of me that didn't come back for years. My life force came back when I started to sing again.

My drifting away caused terrible rows with Oliver. It's one of the reasons I smoke. John Lennon said smoking grounds you. That always rang true to me. Whenever I've tried to stop smoking I've had the sensation of floating away. I work very consciously to keep my feet on the ground. It's not my natural condition. Obviously the right place for the part of me that flies is the stage and theater. Ever since I've taken control of my life — or as much control as I'm going to get — I've consciously had to put sandbags on my feet. I take them off only when I perform.

I loved Oliver but he frightened me. There was something masochistic in my love for him and there was something sadistic in his love for me. My great-uncle Leopold von Sacher-Masoch's strain of masochism didn't surface in Eva, but it certainly came out in me. Not directly, not physically, but psychologically.

I did do a little theater while I was with Oliver. I'd tried reviving my acting career while I was still doing smack but each time I did, it ended in disaster. I was always getting involved in classic fuckups. It was clear to me that I was someone who shouldn't be doing smack. The minute I did, something grotesque would happen. I tried out for a number of parts. All catastrophes. I went up to see Jack Good. He was doing a musical version of *Othello* called *Catch My Soul* with Jerry Lee Lewis as Iago and he wanted me to play Desdemona. I got really fucked up for the occasion and went into the audition — and passed out cold. This would have been passable for the death scene, but they thought, "Well, we need her alive, at least for the first part of the play." So that was that.

I played the victim in *The Collector* at the Hampstead Theatre Club. My career in the theater was becoming something of an irritant to Oliver. He felt I'd proved my point and the thing to do now was to retire gracefully and marry him. I thought so too until I became involved with Bowie and I began to write songs again. None of them was ever used but I was quite fascinated by Bowie's way of writing, which fused autobiographical elements and fictional characters.

Oliver gave me a beautiful engagement ring that belonged to his family and for a while I did consider marrying him. But at the last minute I couldn't go through with it.

I knew I was never going to fit into his aristocratic circle and he would regret marrying me, sooner or later. I'm an outsider and I belong on the outside.

Even to people closest to me I appeared to be at the end of the line. It looked as if Oliver was my last best chance. "How lucky for her. She can marry Oliver and then we won't have to worry about her." I think it was difficult for people while I was floating through London in the anorexic, heroin haze. I was a wraith drifting into their lives, sleeping on their couches, passing out in their bathrooms. It was as if I were haunting them.

I remember friends of mine, my gay friends principally, who knew Oliver, and they would point all this out to me in grim detail. I was so incensed and angry and offended when they said this to me. Someone actually did say, "You should marry him, you know. You'll never have a chance like this again, dear." I didn't say a thing.

# Broken English

THE Baroness's Daughter, Pop Star Angel, Rock Star's Girl-friend... even after the brutal bashing I'd given them, these demon dolls of myself would not go away. You couldn't just shed them by cutting off your hair or getting fat. Even getting arrested or becoming a junkie on the street didn't do it. Those things didn't change the image, they just modified it. I was now the *tarnished* Pop Star Angel: "Baroness's Daughter on Public Drunkenness Charges," "Jagger's Ex Says Drugs Are Behind Her Now."

By the mid-seventies I had reluctantly come to the conclusion that if I was ever to obliterate my past I'd have to create my own Frankenstein, and then become the creature as well.

The reconstruction of Marianne began with a song, "Dreaming My Dreams." That put me back together. For a couple of years I had been involved in the soul-destroying business of going around the record companies. I was something of an albatross. The rejections were gentle, if ludicrous. At Warner Bros. they begged off, saying they were about to sign Emmylou Harris and we were too similar to be on the same label. I had a laugh over that. They were trying to let me down easy: "Poor thing, we must be nice to her or she'll go off and kill herself."

I was finally signed by Tony Calder, my old manager from the mid-sixties. Tony was now at NEMS Records working with Patrick Mehan. They gave me the contract, I thought, because of my notoriety (it sells records). Also, the possibility that I might come up with something great couldn't be *completely* ruled out. I was very grateful, whatever the reasons. I didn't know quite what I wanted to do just yet or who I wanted to work with. I was ready to start making records again, but I needed to do it in an atmosphere that was not too high pressure.

NEMS managed the European publishing of a number of American songwriters, among them Allen Reynolds, who had written songs for Crystal Gayle and Waylon Jennings. And one day a song of his came in called "Dreaming My Dreams." Tony, bless his heart, recognized it as a potential hit and got me to record it.

The first incarnation of the New Marianne was as a sort of country-western Marlene Dietrich on "Dreaming My Dreams." Marlene singing torch songs at the Dodge City Saloon. Probably me German blood coming through. Dietrich had been cast in a number of cowgal roles and, in its own overblown way, it worked. And I remembered those movies and loved the mix of sentiment and camp in them.

"Dreaming My Dreams" is Middle European *weltschmerz* and country melancholy; a swooning country ballad in waltz time. Perfect, dribbling piano music for crying in your beer. (The band used to call it "Creaming My Jeans.") I wanted to have a lingering, smoky quality as if time was suspended while you listened to it. My instinctive tendency with songs is to slow things down. It allows you to hear more, to sink into the sound. Mick's inclination had always been to speed things up.

"Dreaming My Dreams" was released in Britain to a resounding silence. And then, out of the blue, a deejay in Ireland by the name of Patrick Kenny started to play it on his show and it went to number one on the Irish charts for seven weeks. (The Irish love a waltz.) Okay, it was a fluke, but it gave me hope. Getting on the charts was a kind of forgiveness. *We don't care what you did, we like it anyway.* I don't know whether it's the Church in Ireland or the drinking, but these people do know how to forgive.

Now I had a chance to make an album and what I wanted was to do a country album — in my own fashion. At the cottage I'd been listening not only to James Brown and Otis Redding but also to an awful lot of Hank Williams and Jimmy Rodgers. During the sixties everyone had been trying to emulate black music, but I had now begun to wonder what *white* blues would be. I came to the conclusion that it would sound like Hank Williams. After that revelation I felt I wanted to do a new kind of country album, not imitating Waylon or Willy and not recorded in Nashville or Austin but done in England, a sort of country roots album with Celtic vibes. I've got loads of the old Druidic *longing* and melancholy in my bones, on account of my Welsh blood.

When I began making *Faithless* this was my plan: an *English* country album. It would have been an interesting experiment to come at country music from such an elliptical angle, and it would have worked. I still plan to make that album someday, because *Faithless* certainly wasn't it. *Faithless* wasn't exactly what NEMS had in mind. I found myself in the compromising position of having to include a lot of material on the album because they were songs NEMS happened to publish in Europe. Typical music-biz crap. Which is how I ended up doing "Vanilla O'Lay," an absolutely absurd pop jingle.

But it was on *Faithless* that I began writing my own songs again. I hadn't written anything for years. "Lady Madeleine" was the first song I had written since "Sister Morphine." It was also a new kind of song for me. More realistic, more personal. It was based on the wasted life and sad end of a close friend, Madeleine D'Arcy.

I hadn't heard from Madeleine for several days. Her phone was off the hook and I suspected the worst. I had a feeling she'd OD'd, and I might have to smash down her door, so when I went over to her flat in Maida Vale I took with me as muscle a burly Maltese drug dealer and another lowlife friend. We knocked and knocked. No answer. Eventually the boys broke down the door and in the bedroom we found Madeleine lying fully clothed in a long gown on the bed. She was obviously dead and looked bruised and bloody, as if she'd been beaten up. The two dealers split the instant they saw her. I had to wait five hours with the body until the cops came. I got rid of all the drugs and, in the process, took not one speck of anything. I was disgusted by the drug culture — for *that* night anyway.

Madeleine had been a *News of the World* headline the previous year. MISS GOLD-DIGGER 1972. The story was about her having been a hooker and leading this allegedly glamorous life with Spanish Tony, Keith and Anita in the south of France. Those were the days when Spanish and Madeleine would fly down to Nice for the weekend.

By the time of her death she'd gone back to turning tricks in Brighton for fifteen pounds a night. It was a rough deal and it broke my heart. In her combination of low life and grand name she always reminded me of Tess of the D'Urbervilles. Her mother was a little Irish Catholic woman from outside Dublin and when I spoke to Mrs. D'Arcy I knew that for her the most important thing was that Madeleine be buried in the Church — any question of scandal would ruin her chances. That's how it is in Ireland. Even a whiff of suicide would have been a complete disaster, and a murder inquiry would have been equally damaging. There would have been so many ramifications that it would have become another big scandal.

The inspector came to the flat. He walked up and down and took notes. In my most peremptory manner I told him it had to go down as "death by misadventure," and then I told him why. He happened to be a compassionate man and he understood.

When I wrote the song I didn't want to dwell on the sordidness of the situation and on her degradation. I wrote about her beauty and my love for her.

I was constantly reminded during these years of my parasitic status in the pop world. I remember once going out dancing to a club and Rod Stewart came home with me. He thought I was just one of these girls that sort of floated around pop stars and tried to put the whole thing across like that. Pop stars are perpetually on the prowl. They are looking for their particular type, a girly sort of woman with pretty underwear and frocks and the whole female fantasy. And he thought he'd found one in me. He would have been so disappointed! And I laughed and threw him out. It was hysterical. I threw him out very gently, you know, for his own good. He made an honest mistake. He just mistook me for something I wasn't. It wouldn't be the first time.

I met my second husband, Ben Brierly, in 1976. That was the year Thatcher came to power as leader of the Tory Party. I was just about to go off to Ireland with a pickup band to do the "Dreaming My Dreams" tour. Ben was living off the Fulham Road at the time. I think I'd gone round to score some smack. (My cure hadn't lasted very long.) He wasn't dealing himself but he knew where to get it. He was just recovering from hepatitis and he looked very pale and interesting in that leather-jacketed, drug-addicted way. Ben was a find. He was funny, charming, vulnerable and I fell in love with him.

When I got back from Ireland I called Ben up and went by to see him. We sang the old Everly Brothers song "When Will I Be Loved." Our voices melted together.

We began living together in a flat in Fulham that had been lent him. So for a while we clung to this illusion of security, of a normal life together. The flat was quite grand. It belonged to a friend of one of Ben's ex-girlfriends. It was like a country house in the middle of Fulham. Very elegant, with beautiful old furniture and rugs. One day Vivian Westwood came around. Vivian designed the torn T-shirt and bondage gear for the punk mecca, Sex, on the Kings Road. She was a coconspirator, along with Malcolm McLaren, of the embryonic punk scene. They were just putting the Sex Pistols together. Vivian looked around the flat and in mid-camp drawl said: "So this is how you old hippies live, is it?" That was their pose.

But the flat wasn't Ben's and eventually we had to move out. We had nowhere to go and almost no money to speak of. I was getting a hundred pounds a week from NEMS and it went very fast. Even in 1976 you couldn't live in London on a hundred a week. We only had enough money for drugs!

We moved into a squat in Lots Road, which is in the far reaches of Chelsea. It was very romantic, with candlelight, wooden boxes and a mattress on the floor. We had two things in common: music and sex. It was the most passionate relationship of my life and, naturally, the one that caused me the most pain.

Ben was an ideal person for this part of my life and my mother saw that. Eva liked Ben, she understood that I needed to be with someone who was in a similar condition to my own. He reminded Eva of one of her old Gypsy boyfriends from before the war. She had been a dancer in Berlin in the thirties, and had her share of relationships with very wealthy men, who sent her flowers and bought her expensive clothes. That's where she placed Mick Jagger. But there was another side to her, the blazing romantic, and that's where she saw Ben and me.

During that early, happy time with Ben we listened to James Brown and Otis Redding and Bessie Smith and Janis Joplin and reggae and Lou Reed's Berlin album. And loads of country music. Ben loved all that, he got right into what was happening to me internally. I was singing Waylon Jennings and Hank Williams and Willie Nelson.

Whenever I went to a rock concert in those days I was totally overwhelmed by the gear-grinding razzle-dazzle of the thing. It was all sound and fury. I remember going to a Led Zeppelin concert and being amazed at how written in stone our rebel's image had all become. And then, shortly after that, along came punk and changed everything. It was such a great antidote to the excesses of late sixties rock — Rick Wakeman doing King Arthur on Ice.

We mixed a lot with the punks, and I took that energy and ran it through my own circuits, waiting to see what would happen. It was punk nerve that fed right into the rage of *Broken English*. Sid Vicious and I shared the same dealer and I was once actually cast as Ma Vicious, Sid's mum, in Russ Meyer's Sex Pistols movie. What a deluge of new hate mail *that* would have inspired.

In the pre-punk wasteland, however, I saw no way out. I even thought of myself, briefly, as a honky-tonk angel. "That Was the Day (Coke Came to Nashville)," on *Faithless,* is my country fantasy song. Me in a big blond bouffant.

The squat in Chelsea was really a hovel. No electricity, no hot water and absolutely skint. Ben was making a little bit of money giving bass lessons to the guy who was to become Adam Ant. But we loved it and we had a great time. For a while we moved to the flat upstairs — a squat superior to our own — lent to us by an astrologer and all-purpose mystic and fortune teller who had gone off to the country to write his book. All the walls were decorated with signs of the zodiac and runic symbols. Candles and pentagrams.

That was the happiest time for us. The stars must have been right.

It was summer. We often had to sing for our supper. We would take the guitar to people's houses and sing songs and they would feed us. It was a wonderful fantasy of two penniless troubadours and, in the process, we met a lot of people.

We moved in and out of a number of squats. It was getting cold and without heat or electricity the flat would have been a horror. Ben decided we really had to do something: "I'm sure we could get a band together and go to Europe, make some money. We can't just sit here. We're going to starve *and* freeze." So we went to NEMS and they booked a tour to Holland. They gave us half the money up front and six weeks to get a band together.

We held auditions in a rehearsal room in Chelsea off Cheyne Walk. This was to be the first band of my own. It was then, while we were assembling people for the band, that I found the incomparable Barry Reynolds. He's one of the great rhythm guitar players, a dying breed. With Barry I wrote most of the songs on my next three albums.

We got the band together with Ben on bass and went to play the Paradiso in Amsterdam. We were the opening act for Southside Johnny and the Asbury Jukes. On the first night I was standing offstage in a groggy daze watching my band playing the intro to "Sweet Jane." Dun, dun dun, dun-da-duh-dun, dun, dun dun, dun-da-duh-dun. I remember thinking: "How odd! They keep playing those silly twelve bars *over and over again*. What the hell are they doing?" Then it dawned on me that they might be waiting for me to come out. I swept out onstage with great flourish (but quite drunk) and promptly tripped over the electrical cables and fell flat on my face. A perfect Laurel and Hardy opening. Something you could never do again if you tried. After I'd picked myself up, I turned to the rather astonished band and said, "You all right, darlings?"

The Paradiso was a hashish bazaar, wasn't it? I *knew* they would understand. The audience was gratifyingly stunned by my grand entrance; they stood transfixed during the entire performance, dazed looks on their faces.

Back in the dressing room Ben was furious with me.

"Wot the fuck were ya doin', Marianne?" he shouted at me in his thick Solford accent. "Ya fell *over*."

"Oh, suppose I did, that could happen to anyone." (I was bluff-ing.)

"You were bloody crawling aboot the stage on your hands and knees!"

"Ben," I said, "you don't understand. It's all the-a-ter, isn't it? People paid good money to see that." To that he had *no* idea what to say, which I took as a sign that I had "won."

Ben wrote some songs, but he was a useless bass player. He was just about good enough for a punk band and that was it. A little better than Sid Vicious. On that level. I didn't want him in my band, and I didn't much want him playing on my records either. Not great for a love affair.

The tour was so bad I lost all interest in working, again. And *living* with Ben had now become a temporary hell as well. He was having an affair, he was always having affairs. I was miserable for months. After what seemed like an eternity, Barry rang me up out of the blue and said, "Let's get a band together and do some gigs." And we did. This time I got Steve York to play bass. Slowly, we were getting the right band together.

Ben occasionally did play on my albums and he wrote some great songs for me, but we never again toured together. He had his own ca-reer, in any case, and this was best for both of us. He was in a band called the Blood Poets. Ben sang and the other guy in the band, Drew Blood, also sang. That was about it. Drew was Polish and ended up marrying Angie Bowie.

Besides the Blood Poets, Ben was in the Vibrators. But every time Ben got a band together, something would happen where it would be fucked. He didn't get along with people. And he didn't understand the law of pop music, which is that you have to give away a lot to get any-thing. If you're not prepared to surrender almost everything, you won't get anything at all. He could never grasp this. He would demand all sorts of rights and conditions that would be out of the question. I don't worry about things like that at all. I never have.

Ben was always bringing people home, and one night he met Tim Hardin in a pub in  Chelsea and brought him back to the flat. Ben told him: "You got to fookin' write Marianne a song, Tim." To which he replied, "Can I crash here, man?" I didn't get on at all with Tim. We were both Capricorns. I wasn't even that crazy about his songs. Irritating as hell, but he had a knack for great hooks.

Tim was a bit over the top by this time. You know, "I'll have a triple Southern Comfort with pills, please." He finally came up with a song, but it wasn't, alas, intended for me. It was called "Unforgiven." Joe Cocker did it and so eventually did Eric Clapton. He was totally out of it twenty-four hours a day on the infamous Brompton mixture, a heroin and cocaine cocktail that you could get on prescription in those days. It kept him nicely scrambled. As interested in mood-changing substances as I was, after witnessing first Gregory Corso and now Tim on the stuff I was never tempted to touch it.

But where was *my* song, Tim? I nagged him. He had an idea. Two words, actually: "Brain Drain." This was the title and, for the moment, the entire song actually. Rather appropriate subject, given everyone's condition. Weeks went by and the song had not progressed at all. Finally Tim decided that he might be able to finish it "on a beach somewhere." So with great expectations Ben and Tim went off to Antigua together with John Porter, who had worked with Clapton on "Lay Down Sally" and (I add this in the interest of rock genealogy) ended up marrying Keith's old girlfriend, Linda Keith.

Tim brought along with him two huge pharmaceutical jars of the Brompton mixture, which he took through customs in Antigua. In the end he became too outrageous even for Ben, who idolized him. Ben left him in Antigua, disillusioned and frightened by the damage in this great writer. He couldn't concentrate for more than ten seconds, and needed a partner just to string the words together in the right order (a state Ben would find himself in ten years later).

Eventually we got together with the Grease Band, Tim Hardin's old group, and cut four tracks that ended up on a spurious album of mine called *Dreaming My Dreams*: "Wait for Me Down by the River," "That Was the Day (Coke Came to Nashville)," "I'll Be Your Baby Tonight" and "Honky-Tonk Angels." *Dreaming My Dreams*, except for these four tracks, was exactly the same as the *Faithless* album but issued eight years later as if it was a new release. Yet another seamy bit of NEMS monkey business.

Ben put me in touch with musicians again, with people who thought musically and played all the time. This was just what I needed.

My love affair with Ben was high romance and the intensity of this great love fraught with pain obviously affected people around us very profoundly. He was a gorgeous guy and dreadful women were always coming on to him! It was absolute torment. I'd never noticed this before. Obviously all these years I'd screened myself from it behind a narcissistic glass wall. I didn't notice any of this when I was with Mick. I did notice the affair with Anita but the rest of the stuff Mick did with other women went right by me. Probably because I couldn't have handled it.

Now for the first time in my life I felt horrible, searing jealousy, which reached a harrowing pitch during the making of *Broken English*. I was working on the album and Ben was off in L.A. having affairs. I was wild with jealous rage.

It was about this time that Denny Cordell got in touch with me. Denny was a well-regarded figure in the music business. He had started Shelter Records in the late sixties. He discovered J. J. Cale, Tom Petty and Leon Russell and produced Joe Cocker. He was an old friend of Chris Blackwell's (and of mine). Denny told me to go and see the poet Heathcote Williams (whom for some reason he always called Jasper).

"Marianne, Jasper's got this brilliant poem and he wants someone to make it into a rock song. It's *perfect* for you."

"Lovely. I'll give him a call."

"No. You'd better go round there. And pretty swiftly, too, Marianne — he's threatening to send it to Tina Turner or Mick Jagger."

"Hell's bells, how am I going to compete with *those* two?"

"It's not *for* Tina or Mick, it's for *you*, Marianne. Jasper doesn't know that yet. Go on, Marianne, go over there and straighten him out."

"Yes, sir!"

Heathcote read me his poem, which was called "Why'D Ya Do It?" and he had not spoken more than two lines before I knew this was going to be my *Frankenstein*. This was the very likeness of my anguish. Here at last was the text that would translate my hieroglyphic inner life into words.

I told Heathcote: "I would *die* to sing these lyrics, Heathcote!"

But he very politely reiterated what Denny had told me. "I'm terribly touched, darling, but *I* see Tina Turner."

"God! What am I to do?" I thought. "He's got an absolute *idée fixe* about Tina!" I realized a bit of theatrics was needed here to make my point and I fell about laughing uncontrollably.

"Look, Heathcote, Tina is *never* going to do this song. Hell will freeze over before Tina would do a song like this. Let me do it and I will *nail* it, darling, you *know* I will. You don't need a black singer to authenticate this; it *is* the real thing already."

Heathcote, in that English way, longed for the confirmation of his being through black soul. Like Mick, he felt only black things were valid. He wanted Tina because blacks were *authentic*. Or, failing that, he wanted Mick, an authentic black person impersonator. This, to my mind, was undermining your own blues, but that was sixties doctrine.

I had a hell of a time persuading him. It was like milking mice. I had to come up with some very good reasons. Long, convoluted, philosophical polemics, badgering and cajoling. He later regretted it, but Denny kept at him and he finally relented. Poor Heathcote didn't have a clue, he sold the publishing outright. He was a complete innocent.

The following morning, flushed with the knowledge that I had found my Rosetta stone, I made my way to the dingy little rehearsal space we used in Acton. With great zeal I read the lyrics to the band, enunciating each word.

Dead silence. You can't imagine the look of horror that came over these supposedly hip, liberated guys when I came to the line "Every time I see your dick I imagine her cunt in  my bed." Barry Reynolds, in his persona as Vernon the Victorian, practically fainted. They were all absolutely appalled and horrified. It was hilarious, they were actually prudish about it. Not Ben, of course. That was what was so wonderful about Ben. Being a Gypsy, he didn't have any preconceptions about proprieties. Ben lived so far outside society that he didn't see any of that. And he believed in me.

After the initial shock, we began trying to find a riff to propel the lyric. Oddly enough, it came from Hendrix. Joe Maverty, the lead guitarist, was obsessed with Hendrix. He could play all of Hendrix's stuff and as we were fooling around with words he began playing the riff from "All Along the Watchtower." It fit perfectly: "Why'd ya do it *dunh dunh*." On top of this Barry overlaid a reggae shuffle, which took it away from being a straight Hendrix riff and kept it from becoming too leaden.

But the most potent ingredient of all I got from Ben. "Why'D Ya Do It" wouldn't have meant anything to me if I hadn't been going through these very same emotions with Ben. Heartrending turmoil and seething jealousy. It's all about Ben. Mick liked that song, of course. And like almost everybody else I'd ever been involved with, he thought it was all about him.

The other song we worked on during this period was "Broken English." It was inspired by the German terrorist Ulrike Meinhoff. The Baader-Meinhoff Gang had just been arrested, and the phrase "say it in broken English" came from something that flashed on the TV screen, this mysterious subtitle: "broken English . . . spoken English. . . ." I don't know what it was in reference to, but I wrote it down in my notebook.

I identified with Ulrike Meinhoff. The same blocked emotions that turn some people into junkies turn others into terrorists. It's the same rage. "I won't have it! I won't stand for it! This is totally unacceptable!" A form of idealism that leads down different paths. The words of "Broken English" dictated the feel. A dark, threatening mood *dung dung dung dung.* Steve Winwood played great keyboards on this.

One of the reasons *Broken English* came off so well is that I worked with the band for two years before we cut it. We went to Acton every day to rehearse. It was hammered in gold. Every day we would start rehearsing at eleven o'clock. I realized we did our best work before we went to the pub, so I would try and cram all the best stuff in the morning.

We were now getting regular gigs at Dingwalls and the Music Machine, and we had gotten really good. There was a buzz going around London. "Why'D Ya Do It?" and "Broken English" were the highlight of our sets, which we opened with a put-on of me miming the words to "As Tears Go By" sung by Barry in a deep bass voice. We were playing at the Music Machine in Mornington Crescent when one night a producer called Mark Miller Mundy (who had worked with Steve

Winwood) came to see us and offered to put up the money to record two tracks, "Why'D Ya Do It" and "Broken English."

We were hot and we knew it. Right on the beam. The band was great and I loved them, but just before going in to the studio there was the obligatory loathsome, treacherous band scene. We were on tour in Ireland when they up and quit on me. They got through the tour until the very end and then they mutinied. They were upset because they weren't making any money and none of us had had much sleep and we were staying in Castletown, a great old country house on a huge estate outside of Dublin in much disrepair with leaky roofs and creaky stairs and no electricity (or room service). I love this sort of thing, but for the band it was a nightmare. We'd get back at four o'clock in the morning exhausted and there were no lights even to find where you were in that vast old house. Being stuck in the middle of nowhere in a drafty old mansion far from the things dear to their hearts — clubs, movies, chicks, hamburgers and record stores — was not the band's idea of a good time. They wanted to be in the Holiday Inn in Belfast. That's not even true. They wouldn't *go* to Belfast, the cowards. I had to get them there at gunpoint practically. Forced them on the bus telling them what a lily-livered lot they were.

To cheer things up a bit (as I thought), I suggested we all take mushrooms one night before the show. It was the worst gig — bar none — that I've ever played. The drummer couldn't keep the beat, Barry's guitar was leading him about like a dog on a leash, I couldn't for the life of me remember what song I was singing (and this was not the Avalon Ballroom).

Despite the raw conditions, I knew the incomparable experience of going on the road for six weeks before going into the studio. When the band walked out on me, the promoter refused to pay me unless I finished the tour. I called Ben and he came over and put a group of musicians together and we finished the bloody thing. I left trailing five-pound notes through Dublin airport.

There had been no band as such on the *Faithless* album. I'd used studio musicians. As good as they were, the album lacked coherence and heart and it made me realize that I wanted to do *Broken English* with my own band. At my first meeting with Miller Mundy he began reeling off a great long list of stars he wanted to line up for the album:

"What do you think, Marianne? We'll get Keith Richards in on guitar, blah-de-blah on drums, Stevie Winwood keyboards, Robbie and Sly on — "

I had to interrupt this deluded reverie before it set in:

"We will fucking *not!* We will use a real band, my band." After that he shut up about the superband business, but he was always trying to slip in a superstar whenever he could. He brought in a guitarist from Devo to do a pitiful lead guitar track. As awful as it was it did suggest something. What we needed was a truly demented guitar lurching through the track and Barry came in and laid it down in one take.

The only star I would allow on the album was Steve Winwood, and I wasn't entirely sure about *him*. I had the rough mixes of just me and the band and I was afraid when Steve came in he would over-sweeten it, overelectrify and oversynth it, so when he arrived at the session I proceeded to sit on his head. I wouldn't let Mundy say a thing!

After we cut the two tracks, Mundy took them to Chris Blackwell, who owned Island Records. Blackwell loved the tracks and said, "Let's take it the whole way." My God, we were on! We cut the rest of the album for very little money at Matrix, a dim, windowless studio. This was one of the reasons Blackwell loved *Broken English* so much. It was so cheap to make!

Mundy turned out to be useless as a producer as well as a flaming asshole. From the day we started recording at Matrix studios it was obvious he knew nothing about music. Much of the brilliance of *Broken English* that he took credit for actually came from Bob Potter, the engineer, who had worked with Joe Cocker and the Grease Band and knew what he was doing.

Writing with Barry was one of the most exhilarating things about making this album. It just *flowed*. Most of the time when you write songs with other people, you end up working independently. You write the lyrics and they take your lyrics home and work on them and then you take the music and rework the lyrics. But with Barry, the groove was instantaneous. I would show him some lyrics and he would say, "Yeah, I can do that," and pick up his guitar and play some chords. Sometimes he would come in with a finished song that had just popped into his head. "Guilt" is Barry's song. When I asked him where it came from, he said he had a cold and was taking large doses of cough medicine (with a lot of codeine in it, we assume). I knew about guilt, of course. I knew whereof it came.

Every song on the album was there for a reason. "What's the Hurry" is fairly obvious; it's about the fear you live with when you do drugs. "The Ballad of Lucy Jordan" is less self-evident. Lucy Jordan is me if my life had taken a different turn, if I'd become Mrs. Gene Pitney, for instance, and ended up in a big, empty house in Connecticut. It's a song of identification with women who are trapped in that life and the true private horror of the "good life," the one women are meant to aspire to.

I did a song of Ben's on *Broken English*. "Brain Drain," the one he'd written with Tim Hardin. When Tim died Ben just left Tim's name off the credits, which I always thought was really dreadful. It was Tim who put the incredible hook into "Brain Drain." "You're a brain drain. You go on and on like a blood stain." That bridge *makes* the song. The rest of the song would be completely pointless without it. But that was typical of Ben's small-time, hustling mentality. It comes from a lack of generosity. He had no environmental generosity whatsoever. What generosity he did have, I suppose he gave to me. But me being me, I just lap these things up without even noticing. I just take what's offered and move on. I don't think twice. I suppose my way of repaying him was to buy him expensive guitars and clothes. It didn't occur to me that he wanted anything else from me. Straight out of a country song, isn't it?

"Witches Song" is my version of sisterhood. It's my ode to the wild, pagan women I know and have always had around me. It even has a bit of my mother in it. Because if ever I knew a witch it was my mother. She came from a bewitched time and place where you could really believe that witches still lived and cast their spells in the Black Forest or the mountains of Carpathia. Eva had a very light loving side and its ominous twin, a very dark side indeed. The dark side came out especially virulently when I crossed her. When Nicholas was taken away it loomed quite balefully. I had brought bad fortune on her. I had entangled her in the life she had left behind after the war. The bohemian life with all its flaunting of morality, quasi-magical thinking and risk-taking. She had chosen a very straight life that all the goblins and demons of the creative life presumably stayed well clear of.

"Witches Song" is an instance of how long it takes things to cook for me. The first glimmer of it came to me on one of the trips with Mick down to Morocco in the Bentley. On the way we had stopped at the Prado in Madrid where they had an exhibition of Goya's Sabat paintings. Every one of them. I made Mick and Alan Dunn stay in Madrid for two days while I went round the exhibition and took mental notes on the twilight sensibility of these paintings.

I pull my songs from all sorts of places, they're everywhere. What fascinated me about "Working Class Hero" was the trauma of childhood. What happens to the artist as a child growing up, and the retaining of that child. The idea that you must learn to accept and embrace being an outsider because whatever you do you will never be accepted. (And that's the last thing you want!)

For me it's also a song of admiration for John Lennon, Mick and Keith, Iggy Pop, and David Bowie. For them as working class heroes. It's a nod to them. I'm saying "I see what you've done, I know what you've done, what you've had to overcome. It's wonderful. But I too am the same way; I too had the same experience."

In doing "Working Class Hero" I was trying to make my own life real (for the first time, actually), and stop living this dopey Angel Doll fantasy of Andrew Oldham's. With *Broken English* I felt that I had finally smashed it to pieces.

On June 8, 1979, Ben and I were married with assorted punk aristocracy in attendance (Johnny Rotten et al.). That November *Broken English* was released. With *Broken English* I at long last had my *Frankenstein*. Chris Blackwell commissioned the director Derek Jarman to make three videos to promote the album: "Broken English," "Lucy Jordan" and "Witches Song." They were way ahead of their time. Blackwell *loathed* them, of course. Since then they have come to be considered works of high video art!

*Broken English* dispelled the cobwebs and let me be an artist in my own right. It was the height of the punk era and *Broken English* was exactly on the pulse. With my trusty, murmurous band I was now ready to conquer the world.

# Dylan Redux

DYLAN rolled back into my life again in the summer of 1979, right after *Broken English* had come out. The album had apparently stirred his interest and he began making inquiries about me. Alas, yet again, I had just got married — this time I married Ben Brierly (to whom I'd made one of those farcical commitments). I get married, you know, when I don't know what else to do. It's one of my panic things. Everything is flying out of control and I go, "Aaaaghhh!"

Dylan had problems of his own. There'd been the divorce from Sara, the trashing of his film *Renaldo and Clara,* he'd been thrown out of his house in Malibu. He was overweight and down. At those moments the brief periods of glory in one's life always seem very alluring.

The meeting took place at my heroin dealer's flat in Kensington High Street. Diana was one of those great Chelsea witches and *the* queen drug dealer. When I first met Diana's roommate, Demelza, I recognized from the mystic tattoos on her face that she was in some way related to Valli, the witch who lived in a cave above Positano. I had fallen in love with Demelza and we'd been having an affair off and on for the past couple of years.

When Dylan came to England in 1978 he brought a new band with him and in this band was a fantastic conga player whom

Demelza, who played congas herself, desperately wanted to meet. So she called Dylan up at the Royal Garden Hotel where he was staying and told him she'd just got in from the States and that Mac Rebennack (Dr. John) had told her to look him up. None of this, of course, was true.

But a year later Dylan was back in England doing a series of concerts at Earl's Court and out of the blue he called Demelza up and asked if he might come over to her house for a visit. She was slightly bemused that he should want to come over to her poky flat for whatever reason. He had a few requests, which he then began to list quite methodically. Could she come to the hotel and pick him up? Could she take him somewhere that he needed to go? And, finally, did she know Marianne Faithfull?

And then Demelza called me. Another very strange conversation. Demelza was very mysterious, almost whispering into the phone: "Get over here, Marianne. Now."

"To what do I owe the honor?"

"Be serious, Marianne! Anyway, it's a, I don't know . . . *surprise?*"

"Well, I can't anyway, darling, Ben's here and I'm making scones." But nothing could put her off. She kept insisting. Finally, she resorted to telephonic hypnosis:

"Dope, coke, hash, all for you. Put your coat on, go out the door. Take a taxi, I'll pay for it. Just come alone." (Now that last part interested me.)

"Oh," I said without missing a beat, "it's *important?*" Now I was curious, and my curiosity got the better of me.

But one of the problems with this sort of adventure was that Ben was insanely jealous of me by then and I couldn't do anything without him. He would go completely mad if he knew I was sneaking out to a secret rendezvous.

Demelza went to pick Dylan up at his hotel. When she got there she found the lobby filed with fans who spilled out onto the front steps. She phoned the room. Dylan asked that she meet him at the lift. Down the lift came and out walks Dylan really hidden. Sunglasses, long coat, scarf, gloves, wrapped up like a mummy. Demelza and Dylan got in the car and drove off, fans clawing at the windows. He asked if she would drive him to Harley Street. They stopped at a doctor's office and Dylan went in on his mysterious errand. It was Dylan's day off and he hadn't started the concerts yet.

Where Demelza lived was at the side of a glitter boot boutique called Reflections. They sold spectacularly ugly things. Boots with plat-form heels and stars and moons on them. Bob stopped and stared for a long time at the window display.

"I'm gonna need some new clothes," he said and then they walked up the first flight of narrow stairs to the flat. They were dingy and close in and after he'd walked up the first flight he suddenly became appre-hensive.

"You know I *could* not know where I'm going," he said.

Demelza tried to reassure him. "You *could* not, but you do."

He wasn't quite convinced about this so he said, "I know that but I don't know where I am and you could just take me anywhere, now, couldn't you?"

They got all the way to the top and there in front of them was Demelza's massive all-but-impregnable steel-plated door. Diana and Demelza had been busted so many times it bristled with locks and bolts. Just to pull it open took a great effort. He must have thought he was almost certainly going to be kidnapped by now because it was a while before he would sit down.

Demelza asked him if he'd like a drink. He said no, but could he have some lemon tea. When Diana came in with a pot of Earl Grey tea, porcelain cups and silver spoons, he must have realized he wasn't going to be rolled into a carpet and taken away in a van and after that he relaxed.

I arrived half an hour later. As soon as I walked in the door and saw Dylan sitting there, I realized I'd been set up. You could have knocked me over with a top hat. My first reaction was one of acute shock. I went white. I was so stunned I almost turned around and walked out, but instead an automatic Anglo-Saxon attitude overcame me. I was Princess Margaret at a (slightly mad) garden party and I heard myself saying: "*Absolutely* ages since we've seen you in England. The family is well, I trust?"

But Bob was not going to be fobbed off with pleasantries. He took me by the arm and gazed into my eyes.

"Marianne! I've been waiting for a long, long time. So many years gone by and I never forgot that time when we first met."

"It was that time at the Savoy, wasn't it? Gosh, Bob, it *was* a long time ago, wasn't it?"

He had very vivid and romantic memories of meeting me all those years ago. He said he'd never forgotten me and always regretted the incident with the torn-up poem.

"I remember you as this little debutante figure that had come out of nowhere and after you left Penny kept saying, 'Where'd Marianne go?' And I said, 'Yeah, well, someday I'm gonna look her up.'"

He had a photo of me when I was seventeen and he'd kept it ever since and he took it out. It was a picture of me in front of a bus, probably from some tour, all creased and dog-eared.

We sat down on the floor in front of the fire and he took my hands in his and said: "I thought I'd never see you again."

I was an unexplored part of his past, a part that hadn't happened, about which anything could be imagined. Dylan adores women; they are the little goddesses of his songs, the Queen Janes and Johannas and Sad-eyed Ladies who change the weather in the rooms they walk through, and hold the keys to the past.

His chatting me up put me in sheer panic. I was trying not to pick up on this side of the conversation too much. The more infatuated he seemed the more nervous I became. He was in a very needy state. I did not honestly know how to respond. He stared at me with such intensity, I began to feel like prey. When I went into the kitchen, he got up and followed me there.

I idolized Dylan, but to be idolized *by* Dylan is a very different thing . . . an unnerving thing. Terrifying, really. As if the Minotaur had taken a liking to you. Although he *was* being very sweet.

When we sat down again he said: "It was a broken meeting."

"It was, Bob, it was bad luck really."

"I heard your record when it came out in the States. I went out and got a copy of it. It really amazed me. When I heard that song I remembered our meeting back then at the Savoy Hotel."

The broken meeting and *Broken English*. I bet you think this song is about you. But it was a bit odd after all those years of reading things into Dylan albums to have Dylan reading messages into mine.

That the subject of the album had come up was a tremendous relief. I now had something, thank God, to grasp on to. Diana had a copy of *Broken English* and I asked Dylan: "Would you like me to put it on?"

"I'd like to hear it again very much," he said. "There were a few things I wanted to ask you about."

"I could explain it to you while we're playing it," I said. I was being a bit tongue-in-cheek (what would there be really to explain?) but he was quite earnest about it.

"I wish you would."

Do you know what I did? I played him *Broken English* not once but several times. And as each track played I asked him if he knew what it meant. He was speechless. Just like I had been when he'd played me *Bringing It All Back Home*. I turned the tables, I just did it all back to him. It was almost unconscious, like a playback. And he knew it. I played him "Guilt," a self-explanatory song if there ever was one, and then said a little portentously, "Do you understand this?" I just sat there very grandly explicating my own songs. Out of nervousness I found myself talking about them nonstop. Dylan was forced to sit there as I played him *Broken English* and asked him carefully and pointedly and intensely after each song if he understood what it was about and did he get this bit and that bit. And he loved it!

About midway through this marathon I became overexcited from all this and I really needed something to numb me a bit so, being polite, I asked him if he might like to numb himself, too: "Would you like, uh, something for your head, man?"

We did want him to feel at home, or at least to be as high as we were. But he didn't want a thing. Demelza and I were up and down the stairs all night long taking stuff, getting high. Whatever Bob got from the doctor kept him going all evening. That sufficed him. He wouldn't touch a thing. Not a drop of alcohol, not a joint, not a cigarette. Just Earl Grey tea. And we offered him everything we had: wine, whiskey, hash and (a little more hesitantly) cocaine, all of which he turned down.

We didn't exactly offer him any smack because we didn't want to seem like the full-scale druggies we actually were. I would have, but Diana and Demelza wanted to keep up appearances. Dealers have higher standards than us mortals. Bob made no judgment about any of this.

Over and over we played the album. At the end I was almost in tears from having gone through this album that had been so cathartic and autobiographical for me so many times.

It was about eight in the evening when we started and went on straight through the night. It was such an extraordinary thing that I didn't know whether I was imagining it or if it was actually happening. I don't think any of us could believe it was really happening. It was so odd for him to be sitting there in this little doll's house and for me to find myself in this position again. It made me cry, he was so beautiful about it. An evening of respect in my otherwise squalid life.

But it became very intense. We were sitting in front of the fire holding hands, the world had stopped, no one else existed. When what was happening finally hit me, I became withdrawn. I was petrified. Diana came into the room and immediately sized up the situation. I was in a terrible state, blown out on the trail. I was beginning to hyperventilate, I was so panicked. Diana was brilliant. She took him upstairs to the bedroom and started doing all this clothes business, measuring him for the new clothes he'd been wanting. He didn't know what to get. Diana went out and bought all these clothes for him for the first night at Earl's Court. I just sat there by myself and cried.

About forty minutes later he came down again and I had by then got hold of myself. He plunged back into the conversation.

"Where did you go? What have you been doing with yourself?"

"Oh, well, this and that. I became a registered junkie and sort of disappeared really," I said in the tone of voice one uses to say, "These are all the things I've been doing since I last saw you, dearest."

"Well that would explain it," he said. "You seemed to have vanished from the face of the earth. No one seemed to know where you were."

"That's probably because I was living on a wall."

"You were living on a *wall?*"

"Yes, in St. Anne's Yard. It's in Soho."

"Oh, well, then, you were living on a wall." It obviously made no sense to him but he liked the sound of it. Things that rhyme mean the same thing.

He followed all this with a rueful sort of smile as if to say "If only I'd been there." And far from dismaying him I had ascended into that Dostoyevskian underworld of his mythology where all the true saints reside. Like Giacometti and Kerouac, he's obsessed with the holy underworld: hustlers and hookers, junkies, card-sharps.

He wanted to know how I'd got from my wall back into making records. Even to Dylan one doesn't just walk into a recording studio from living in a bomb site and start cutting a record.

And so I began to tell my tale:

"I met this guy and went to India, I lived in Madame Curie's basement for a while and then I had a hit in Ireland and formed a band and one day this poem came in the mail and when I read the words I knew it was a song I had to sing."

I was beginning to sound like one of those serpentine narratives of Dylan's: "Went to Italy inherited a million bucks. . . ."

At the very end of an evening that was very lovely, he said, "If ever you need me or if ever, if I only could, I'd write you that letter again." He said it like a line from one of his songs. At dawn we drove him back to his hotel. Perhaps in another lifetime I told myself. It will all work itself out one day. But it was bad luck, really, I must say, 'cause I adored Dylan. What can I say? When mortals in Greek mythology encounter the gods, they come away dazed and confused.

# The Lost Years

B ROKEN ENGLISH was gothic *and* high-tech, so I had a feeling it would do very well in Germany. Within six months it went platinum. We'd taken a lot of time and care to make it sound as clean as possible on good equipment. In 1979 the only places in Europe where people were rich enough to buy sound systems sophisticated enough to hear the subtext were Germany and Scandinavia. Didn't mean a thing in Britain, where they listen to Radio One on tranny little radios.

Then on to the States. It was my first venture to New York for years and years. I felt fantastic because I had arrived on the wings of a great album, but I was also scared to death. I was so incapacitated when I landed at Kennedy Airport that I couldn't fill in my immigration forms; Ben had to do them for me. And it had nothing to do with drugs, I swear. Even I knew you couldn't do a lot of drugs and tour and promote a record. For the first time in my life I was on the verge of being accepted for who I was, and it made me apprehensive. Also, unlike "As Tears Go By," I was conscious.

After years of poverty and struggle it was a magical trip for Ben and me. They were playing "Why'D Ya Do It" all over the New York radio stations and bleeping out words. Island put us up in the Berkshire Place Hotel. Anita came to see us. She was terribly pleased about my great success, and identified with it and shared in it.

Then came what was supposed to be my moment of triumph: guest performer on *Saturday Night Live!* Everything was fine until the night of the show, even the dress rehearsal went flawlessly (always a bad sign). I looked good, I felt wonderful. Then came an absolutely paralyzing attack of nerves, further exacerbated by Miller Mundy hissing poisonous little barbs in my ear like a demon:

"Tonight is *crucial*. The whole of Warner Brothers is here! People have flown in from the coast to see you. Don't blow this one, darling!"

I was still reeling from this barrage when I received a note from Mick wishing me well and asking if he could come backstage. God, no! The very thought that he was in the audience made me wobbly.

Maybe things were going too well, maybe old habits die hard. Because I suddenly decided I could use a little artificial energy to get me through, and asked one of the backup singers if she knew where I could get hold of some coke. Now this was absolutely the last person I should have asked. She had loathed me on sight, couldn't understand what I was doing there in the first place. She put me on to somebody and the little fucker sold me procaine. Procaine freezes your vocal cords. When I opened my mouth to sing, a strange strangled whisper came out. It was a moment of true horror.

Of course, there *are* those who claim it was one of the most fascinating bits of television ever aired. Its, uhm, *Living Theatre* quality. (The damn thing is rerun constantly!) I suppose it's human nature. People love to see the mad, hopeless junkie. Let's face it, I blew it spectacularly.

Despondent and angry I turned to the goddess, who at that moment happened to be Anita. She usually was in those days, albeit in her manifestation as Kali. Until that night I'd stayed away from smack. Now it didn't matter anymore.

Anyway, after a disaster like that, what else can you do but say: "I meant to do it! And I'll bloody well do it again if I wish!"

What endears me to Anita is that she just loves this stuff. In the dressing room at *Saturday Night Live!* she became positively operatic: "Yes! Yes, darling! What you must now do is go *all the way!* Forget about those fuckin' record-company eedyots with their fucking golf carts and their hot tubs! You are a punk diva and you must now go like Mohammed to the Mecca of punk."

"Well, yes, Anita darling, but . . ."

"No! No! Like you must go to the fucking Mudd Club, *tonight,* man, don't you see?"

"Please, Anita, coals to Newcastle! Mercy!"

"Don't think twice about it, baby. It'll be *outrageous,* man. I will be your angel from hell. At the moment you begin to sing 'Sister Morphine,' I will go into the ladies lavatory and shoot up."

Awful, but fun! Besides, I knew this would drive Miller Mundy round the twist for *good!* We got in a cab then and there and went down to the Mudd Club. I wobbled onstage and clung to one of the columns. At *Saturday Night Live!* I had been too freaked to hear what my voice sounded like. Now I could hear it. There was nothing wrong with it. It wasn't froggy or hoarse, it was just very faint. I spoke the lyrics in a whisper as if calling to my lost voice, summoning it up. In the reverential setting of the Mudd Club, it took on the quality of an incantation or so I thought. Not everybody appreciated it. After the first song Miller Mundy, who was at the sound board, spun out of the club in a fury like a splenetic rat. I sang a few more songs and then I came to "Sister Morphine." As the band played the first notes of the intro, I heard a loud Germanic voice shouting from somewhere behind the stage: "And I'm taking a fix right *now!*" It was like being in hell — the stage version!

After the show I went upstairs with Anita. We sat on a beat-up Victorian couch and watched videos of old Stones concerts on a big Sony monitor, posing as schoolgirls watching their favorite band.


*Broken English* changed me in the eyes of the beholder but it changed little in my day-to-day life. Ben and I returned to England and to our squat. It was a good two years before we saw any money from the album.

After *Broken English* a drastic shift took place in my relationship with Ben. In the very beginning we got along fine. And then within a couple of years everything changed. Things began to happen for me, which caused all kinds of tension between us. It was silly and immature, and Ben was even sillier and more immature about it than I was (if that's possible).

Relationships have a nasty habit of reversing themselves; whatever has been done to you in a previous involvement you'll do to the next person you're involved with, if you get half a chance. I treated Ben much the way Mick had treated me, and eventually Ben came to perceive me as an oppressor who had more money and more power and more control than he did, and he absolutely hated me for that.

I must have behaved absolutely ruthlessly toward Ben after the success of *Broken English*. Just because I happened to have the upper hand. I was still acting like a child, even though I'd been in the same situation myself.

I couldn't deal with the day-to-day stuff, in part because I was so fucking *high* all the time. It was just music all the time, and due to our drugged lethargy even that was drying up. We never went out and actually decided we needed a *liaison* with the outside world — someone fairly together who could deal with record companies and grocery stores.

And then one day a pretty girl named Kate Hyman showed up on my doorstep. She had heard *Broken English* and had come all the way from L.A. to sit at my feet. She claimed she would do anything. Could she work for me? I gave her a long list of books, all French writers, and pushed her out the door. "When you've read them all you can come back and work for me." *Madame Bovary, Cousin Bette, Le Rouge et le noir, Les Liaisons dangereuses.* I thought that was sufficiently preposterous.

But a week and a half later she was back and passed her test. Once we'd settled on her literary qualifications, we introduced her to our pharmacopeia, which by then consisted principally of smack and coke. Soon after she was hired by Island (ostensibly to look after me, but actually to spy on me). We did a few lines and had a good laugh over that one. In those days, Island gave me four hundred pounds a week. It was Kate's job to go and pick it up. Always on Fridays. By Saturday afternoon or Sunday morning at the latest it was all gone.

Just before I started on my next album, *Dangerous Acquaintances,* I got a new manager, Alan Seiffert. I suppose it was thought since he managed several of the most difficult women on the planet — Sarah Miles and Vanessa Redgrave among them — that he'd be the ideal agent for me. He was good at his job but in every other way quite awful. Just a draggy, English, middle-class, pop-music person. He was shocked at the way I was living (and with whom I was living). He got me an advance and a flat in Battersea. And at this point things began to get nasty with Ben.

Seiffert couldn't see the point of Ben at all. I guess *most* people I knew thought of Ben as a ligger, even a liability. He was constantly excluded. Everyone was saying things like, "Well, of course, for a start you have to get rid of *him*." Humiliating things went on all the time. Chris Blackwell's secretary would book me on the flight in business class and put Ben in economy! And I let them. Things for Ben just went down, down, down. There was no honorable way for him to deal with it. The only way out for Ben (as it had been for me) was to leave. But leaving, because of our druggy dependency, was a long way off.


Chris Blackwell had given us a ton of money as advance for my next album and we'd spent it all. Mostly on drugs and clothes. A *lot* on drugs. And there wasn't a note of music to show for it. We were sitting in our basement flat with not a thing down and we were meant to hand in a demo tape the following day. Kate was to take three new songs to Island or there would be no money.

We got hold of a bottle of whiskey from Roy, Keith Richards' minder. We went into the kitchen and set up the TEAC tape recorder and within a couple of hours had three songs down. Poorly recorded but tasty. Ah, desperation! "Intrigue" and "In The End" were the first two. For the last one I read Valmont's famous letter from *Les Liaisons dangereuses*, the one where he says, "If your heart is broken it is not my fault. Go, take another lover as I have taken one. . . ." We were very pleased with ourselves.

The next morning Kate delivered the tape to Blackwell and he handed her the much-coveted check. He was very good about that. He would always hand you the check first and then listen to the tape. But, later in the day when he had listened to the tracks enough to convince himself he really hated them, he called up.

"Just let me get a cigarette, darling. I'm dying to know what you think of them."

"Marianne, I'm sorry and all, but it's my duty to tell you . . ."

"Oh, darling. Do stop! You didn't like them just a teeny bit?"

"I can't stand them! I *hate* them!"

"Flattery will get you everywhere."

"They're so *down*, Marianne."

"Well, pumpkin, *Broken English* wasn't exactly a life-affirming album and you liked that."

"But it had a spark, it had energy and rage. This is just plain depressing."

I knew then what the problem was. What Blackwell wanted was what everybody wanted — another *Broken English*. *More* anger. We'll have, let's see, some rage, and lots of female ranting, please. It sold, and sold very well, so naturally they wanted more of the same. Just as the Beach Boys were summer and fun, I was to be the raging virago of pop. But I had moved on. I had done the rage-and-lust bit. I wanted to explore the emotions that interested me now: intrigue, betrayal, tenderness, claustrophobia.

Meanwhile, as a band, another emotion — listlessness — had us in its grasp. We had entered our own Sargasso Sea and we were drifting. Miller Mundy saw what was happening and felt, given our unfocused disposition, that if something drastic were not done soon it would all dissipate. His solution was to send us all off to the fucking *countryside* (damned inconvenient, given our advanced chemical dependencies). It was here that our new manager, Alan Seiffert, became quite useful. His main function was shuttling between London and Oxfordshire with drugs. We'd call him at three in the morning and say "Alan, dear . . . we need some herbal remedies, man. Oh, *could* you? You're a pet. When can you get here?" And bless his little heart, he'd get in his car and drive out with the essentials. Mainly coke and barbs. He had a safe in his office filled with sedatives and downers, which he was constantly popping himself (probably because of all the impossible women he had to handle).

Seiffert also had a minibar in his office, and Kate, as designated responsible person, was given the keys to the well-stocked liquor cabinet. We took out the vodka by the case and back at Chipping Norton we sat around drinking screwdrivers, reading Balzac and writing out lyrics fanatically as one does.

Before long everyone was going crackers in the country. Utter boredom set in. The band — with no girlfriends, no clubs, no neon — soon became lonely and morose. Ben was jealous and unhappy, and I was going out of my fucking mind.

To hell with the record, let's go visiting. I would swan off to see various friends, distant acquaintances and royal personages who lived in the vicinity — or in the British Isles generally. Didn't my friends Ben and Sarah Wordsworth say that Princess Margaret was going to stay with them at their house in Gloucestershire? I *had* to see her. I always loved Margaret. She was the naughty one. How far could it be? I took a taxi. It ended up costing me a hundred pounds one way. Well, that's what per diems are for, aren't they? It was a hell of a long way, but I felt drawn to her as if by royal fiat. I have romantic musings about an England that likely went out with the Tudors and the Plantagenets. Shakespeare's England, and mine!

When I arrived Margaret was dressed in a classic aristo country-weekend getup. Twinset and pearls. A little cashmere sweater with a cardigan over it and a tweed skirt. Very fifties, but that's what they do wear around Balmoral on grouse-shooting weekends. She must have seen from my reaction that I was a bit disappointed. I didn't expect to be greeted by ruffles, plackets and signet rings, but I did hope to see a Shakespearean princess of the realm. After she'd offered me a gin and tonic and sat me down in front of the fire she excused herself, went upstairs, changed, came down again in the royal person wearing an emerald green silk dress and decked out in all her emerald jewelry and earrings. Like a princess. I was enchanted.

She seemed quite nervous about meeting me. Expecting a perfect monster, I should think. She talked as if she had a bit of a plum in her mouth (as all the Royals do). Terribly grand but witty and a dab mischievous. We talked abut Nureyev and Shakespeare and she told harmless little stories involving "my sister, the Queen" and corgies and equerries, and the solecisms of foreign dignitaries. All in a slightly mocking, self-deprecating tone. She bit her nails, which cheered me right up.

Meanwhile not a lick worth preserving was being put on tape. The jams with Steve Winwood were extraordinary but when it came time to actually lay down tracks it all evaporated. Whether because of apathy, self-indulgence or Miller Mundy's inane directions ("Chaps, I want it to sound more like, uh . . . lemmings falling into the sea") no one seemed able to function properly.

And after driving the band to the brink of insanity, Miller Mundy proceeded to fall to pieces himself. Issuing muffled threats through the door, he locked himself in his room and refused to come out. Paranoid and shaky, he emerged days later and began to fire the band one by one, like a hijacker executing hostages. Every day he would walk into the studio and send someone else packing. Barry was the last to go; now we *had* no band. And then, with perfect symmetry, he fired me!

We packed it in at Chipping Norton and went back to London and finished it in the gloomy, windowless dungeon of a studio where we all felt at home.

*Dangerous Acquaintances* was the first album on which I wrote all the songs myself. Barry wrote most of the music. Ironically, the big mistake with that album was that we were in our own desultory way trying to make a commercial record. *Dangerous Acquaintances* came out about a year and a half after *Broken English*.

If *Broken English* had not made us rich (yet), it had brought a lot of unwanted interest from the cops. They're all cryptic record reviewers and guardians of the public morality, the police. I'm convinced that had it been a repentant or nicely-nicely little folk album they wouldn't have bothered us at all. But when they heard on *Broken English* naughty words that "loidies" don't use, they said to themselves, "She's up to her old tricks again. Better take a look in, lads. Where there's filfy language from a woman, there's bound to be uvver business going on, mark my words."

We were busted constantly at Danvers Street. At least once a month. That's an awful lot, especially if you're not dealing. Just smoking hash and chipping a bit.

They were convinced Ben and I were at the very least running a coke ring. When they dropped in on us and found nothing incriminating in our flat, they got into their heads that we must be keeping our stash in the flat above, which belonged to a dear old girl named Missy.

So they tore poor Missy's flat apart, too. Missy was from Knoxville, Tennessee, and had never taken a drug in her life. (Her poison was bourbon and branch water.)

It was a horrible experience, but not major. On one raid they found hash, on another they found traces of heroin and the last time they didn't find anything. Minute crumbs. *Microscopic* traces. 0.00014 milligram of heroin. I was a *user* after all. When I had drugs around, I used them up! But this tiny spec caused me endless aggravation. It has been a blot on my passport for years.

Whenever the police had to give their account of a bust in court, they never failed to mention their horror at the condition of our flat: "These individuals' premises was in a state of squalor that is beyond my powers of description, Your Honor. Disgustin' it was, they do nuffin' but take drugs and live in muck. Live like animals, they do."

The harassment came from the weird fantasy the police have always had about me that I must be at the center of all sorts of big dope deals and nefarious underworld schemes. They were looking for a pulp-fiction character, a hippie spider lady, *The Mastermind of the Chelsea Drug Set.* And that was meant to be me!

During this period I went to live in Wales. I stayed in a house owned by a lunatic bookdealer named Richard Booth in Haye-on-Wye near Cardiff. Crates of books were coming in, crates of books were going out. And as it happened, shortly after I arrived the police discovered that LSD was being manufactured in Wales. Just amazing. They put their noggins together — my presence in Wales, an LSD factory — and decided we were shipping out mountains of acid. I became the Acid Queen of Wales! After weeks of unpacking books about the astral plane, invoking the goddess and the continent of Mu, they gave up. It's so ingrained in them that I realized the only way I could put an end to this delusion was to leave England.

At one point we had a couple of days off. I went straight home and turned on the television. There were only two channels at the time. On one there was casualty lists from the Falklands and on the other the Pope playing Wembley. "I've got to get out of here," I thought, "before they get me."

To promote *Dangerous Acquaintances,* Alan Seiffert put together a U.S. tour and, to my utter amazement, it went quite well.

I came to New York and started living this strange life with Ben. We got a flat on East 18th Street between Second and Third. There was some culture shock at first, but I soon realized that in New York people understood what I was doing. It was a feeling I'd never had in England.

The thing with Ben staggered on. I didn't expect love from him. In the world of drug addiction, love is not one of the coins that you deal in. I did have a fantasy of comradeship, though. I got more into coke, and Ben, essentially, became my minder. When both people in a relationship get fucked up that's what happens. It becomes caretaking rather than love.

We had only been in New York a few months when the court cases for the Danvers Street busts came up. I had to go back to stand trial. It was just *like* being busted again all over. Ben flew back from New York and went to court with me every day. He was terrified I would stand up in court and say the drugs were his (something I would never do). I was found guilty of "hash and traces of heroin." The most they could fine me was a hundred quid. "Guilty. Pay one hundred pounds to the whatsit. Next!"

Back in NYC, we survived on coke and smack. I didn't mind because I was so selfish. I remember coming back to the apartment on East 18th Street one day and finding Ben curled up on the couch with these lines of pain on his face. You could just see it pouring out of him.

Nicholas, who was by now seventeen, came for the summer. A lovely holiday in New York with his mother. It was a nightmare for him. I met him at the airport in a limousine and as soon as he got in I offered him a line of coke in the backseat. He raised his eyebrows, looked down his nose and said, "Marianne, what are you thinking of? Of course not!" I was absolutely out of it all the time he was there. I just sat in front of the television all day watching PBS. In the evening I would manage to cook dinner, but only because Nicholas was there.

Things got worse and worse. It took a long time to stop. It was endlessly painful and mortifying and deadly. In New York the drugs got very, very intense; there was a period of almost paralytic inactivity. I'd done the tour, done the album and started work on a new album, *A Child's Adventure*. That's when Ben began working with Christina Monet. She was the wife of Michael Zilkha, the owner of Z Records, whose claim to fame was that he had discovered Madonna. Ben fucked

Christina and broke my heart. It was horrible, and humiliating. The thing with Christina had been going on unbeknownst to me for a year and a half before I found out about it. New York is a small village. Everyone knew about the affair except me. One day I walked in on them.

Christina was a singer and thought, probably because of what Ben told her, that he was my Svengali, and that he could do for her what he'd done for me. She even went so far as doing her own version of "Why'd Ya Do It."

I knew it was over with Ben, but I've always had a problem extricating myself from relationships. I never know how to let go in any remotely normal way. I simply get as high as possible.

The misery of being unable to live together and incapable of splitting up was terrible by then. He told me later that he'd hoped I would die, it would make things easier. A common feeling in these situations because you can mourn the death of the person you *once* loved.

I started to work very closely with Chris Blackwell on *A Child's Adventure*, which was produced by Barry and Wally Baderou. As I got closer to Chris I realized this would be a way of getting out of my contract with Mark Miller Mundy. Blackwell was beginning to, well, see the *point* of me. He could be very charming. He loved *Broken English*, though I'm not quite sure he really *got* it. I told myself the only thing that really gets you through is selling records. The Stones were allowed to do a lot of stuff that nobody understood simply because they'd sold mountains of records in the sixties. *That* they understand.

Finally I got a big fat check from Island. Ninety thousand pounds. My royalties from *Broken English*. There were a few dealers in New York screaming with delight at that, believe me. I blew an absolutely astoundingly huge amount of money in no time at all. Once again, I spent it all on clothes and narcotics.

And soon enough the demons started to show up. My self-hatred was getting quite malignant by this point. I developed delusions that I was infested by *things*. Cocaine psychosis. One afternoon I went into the bathroom and looked at myself in the mirror. In those days I spent half of my life in the bathroom. If people wanted to talk to me, they had to come into the bathroom because that's where I lived. The schizophrenic incident with Brian in the mirror was not for nothing!

So around this time I developed a recurring obsession that things were crawling under my skin. In the mirror I could see there were thousands of seething subcutaneous bugs about to burst through. This phobia became so bad that I felt I had to get them out by whatever means possible. I picked up a razor and I was going to cut a line down my face and peel my skin off. I made a tiny incision. Blood dribbled down my face and I screamed. At that moment, Jay, one of my gay friends, came in and saw what I was doing and stopped me.

"God, Marianne, what are you thinking of?"

He threw a jug of cold water over me. That snapped me out of it. I realized I was insane. I left for Jamaica the next day. I used to do that when I began to feel I had completely jumped the rails. To chill out. I had a premonition, too, that something very heavy was about to happen and I didn't want to stay around to find out what it was going to be. I went to Blackwell and told him, "I've got to get out of New York immediately," and he said, "Fine. There will be a ticket waiting for you at the airport." I got on the plane with my friend Dickey and went to Jamaica for what turned into six months. Got off dope, cleaned up, and met Sally O., my dearest friend. And while I was there the big jet-set drug bust came down.

Lord Jermyn, the Marquis of Bristol and a few other society types were involved. And Ben. Frin, who was at the center of the whole thing, was my dealer. I wasn't involved, thank God, but I might as well have been because whenever Ben came up in the newspaper accounts it was always "MARIANNE FAITHFULL'S HUSBAND NABBED IN JET-SET HEROIN RING." Some reporter got hold of the surveillance tapes and there were daily transcripts in the *New York Post*. There would be endless quotes of Ben ringing up saying, "Hi, Frin. Have you got anything? Got any more of that brown Chinese stuff, darling?"

When I got back from Jamaica I was taken down to Federal Plaza to be interviewed by the federal attorney. I knew nothing about Frin's deals, so I had nothing to conceal. I knew there were people flying in and out of India with heroin for Frin, but nothing else. Luckily I was single-mindedly at this time writing songs and doing dope. That's all I thought about.

Ben was deported. I stayed on, but it was a messy time. Facing another relationship smashed to dust and my ever-present need to destroy myself. I was alone in New York, a very tough place for me to be in those days.

I moved in with my friend Cynthia. To ward off the circling demons, I performed a little ceremony, putting an eagle's feather on the door. Despite the darkening atmosphere and the swirling craziness, no harm ever came to us. Well, there was one little episode. A crazed Mexican hacked down my bedroom door with an ax. I was bored, I'd got him high, he developed a passionate desire to ravish me, which I resisted. When the police arrived I signed autographs for them and noticed how young they were.

Immersed as I was in my life of indulgence and drugs I found time to do a bit of matchmaking. My press agent, Ellen Smith, came by Cynthia's one day to bring me an airline ticket. Frank Lauria, the writer of the Dr. Orient books, happened to be there. He knew Cynthia from Tangier. What a nice couple Ellen and Frank would make, methought.

I'm direct about these things. Rather the way a parent talks to her children.

"Isn't Frank intelligent," I kept saying over dinner. "Isn't he *interesting?*" and as I got into a taxi I said to Frank: "Speak Italian to Ellen!" I saw them walking together across Second Avenue, Frank speaking Italian, not knowing why. They've now been together ten years.

I saw a lot of "Baby Mink" de Ville and Johnny Byrne (who may forever be known as the man who sucked Fergie's toes) and then one evening Mick showed up at a party of Cynthia's with his friend Whitney Tower. He was very charming and funny and it was as if time had nearly collapsed. But I wasn't eighteen anymore, and he had become a most complicated trickster. He followed me with his eyes for a bit and then went off to another party.

*A Child's Adventure* was symptomatic of a profound physical and spiritual malaise. It's my most desperate record. The subtext of the whole album is a pervading sense of hopelessness, somewhat masked by the jaunty production, but it's there lying beneath the surface. One of my favorites on the album, which I wrote very high, is "Ashes in My Hand." I was so desperate I had reached a Zen plateau of negativity. All inhibitions and shame had vanished. It's the moment after everything comes to you. Your dreams come true, and turn to ashes in your hand.

I wrote all the lyrics but one on *A Child's Adventure*. "Falling from Grace" came out of the court cases connected to the busts in England. I got back to the States and began writing and that came out. I had the tune in my head. It was in a funny time signature, 6/4 time, and I had a bit of a job persuading Barry to do it that way. "Morning Comes" was something of a rip-off of an Emily Dickinson poem, written in Jamaica with Wally Baderou. Ben came in, put down some guitar, then left. By now I wanted him as little involved in my creative life as possible. "Running for Our Lives" is very typical of my state at the time, as if life were some endless escape. I was now running from everything. From Ben, from success, from myself. "Ireland" came about in the studio. We needed another song and Barry started with a riff.

I was trying to record what my life was like at that moment, my life in New York. "Times Square" is Barry's song, and I love its smokey melancholy. There's "She's Got a Problem," which Ben wrote with Caroline Blackwood. "In the end will it matter if you're gone? Would I see whiskey as a mother?" It was one of her poems, which she recast as a song for me. I adored doing it. Ben put it to music. That was the last thing I ever did with him. We parted ways after that. Thank God, or we would have killed each other.


After that it all goes by very fast. There's a five-year period of living in New York during which the self-hatred reached a fever pitch. I must have been a gibbering wreck, but I *felt* like I was doing this brilliant job of being a drug addict! Just keeping it together, doing all this great stuff. I don't understand how I managed to walk that tightrope for so long and stay productive. The real decline began when I returned to New York to finish *A Child's Adventure*. Whatever other people may say, I think until then it all went rather well. After that, my house of cards began to collapse.

I'd been doing drugs for quite a while, but not until I was living in New York did I have access to so *many* drugs. And to the drugs I particularly loved! But even then — until the very end — I held off shooting smack. Because smack I knew I couldn't handle. I never met anyone who could. You either stop or die.

When the album came out, I went to make a video of the single "Running for Our Lives." I had picked up this good-looking French boy in Paris called Jean-Pierre, and he came to New York to see me. I was doing a lot of coke. We went dancing one night at Danceteria. I had by that time been operating on my own and I behaved the way I would if I was on my own: dancing with people, laughing, flirting. Jean-Pierre became insanely jealous and had a fit when we got back to my apartment. He was quite young, from Corsica, with all these peasant notions about honor and "his woman." Then he turned on himself. He took a razor blade and cut his wrist. There was blood everywhere. I wasn't very sympathetic. I'd had it. I said in my coldest voice, "This just won't do at all!" Then I did something I'm profoundly ashamed of: I took ten dollars out of my purse and handed it to him and then wrote out on a piece of paper (because he didn't speak English): TAKE ME TO BELLEVUE. I gave it to him and said, "Give this to the cabdriver."

I'd do coke, write songs and when I couldn't think of anything else to do I'd go in the bathroom and pick my face. I did a lot of shopping. Perhaps because I don't remember a great deal of this period a number of stories have grown up about my outlandish behavior that I can hardly contradict. For instance, I'm supposed to have gone to Claus Von Bülow's house with Desmond and Penny Guinness and there become more blotto than I already was, gone into the bedroom, found Sonny Von Bülow's staggering shoe collection and begun trying them on one by one. I passed out and was found lying on the bed wearing pair number 57.

One night I got a box at the Met and took a couple of friends to the opera to see *Der Rosenkavalier* completely out of our heads on cocaine. It seemed like a good idea but it was ghastly. Nobody could sit still. When you're that high even going to the movies is a nightmare.

The boring version of me during this time is a totally 'luded out Marianne lurching from place to place with people pouring me into cabs. I, of course, thought I was mostly operating quite nicely on my own. I was mostly alone, very high, paying cabs with hundred-dollar bills, which I thought were tens, blacking out and wondering how I got home. To put a brake on the drugs I went to Jamaica and Martinique a lot. That was my way of not using drugs — getting clear and cleaning up a bit.

Money became horribly tight. I had to do something and in 1983 I did a long bus tour through Canada and the States. There was no money to buy clothes. I got around this by going to a thrift store and buying a secondhand tuxedo and passing myself off as the Marlene Dietrich of pop. The accommodations were not deluxe. It was a tiny bus and what with drum kits, amps, guitars and mike stands the quarters were cramped — it was a bit like living on a submarine. In Texas Cynthia joined the tour. And fucking hell if she didn't arrive with *ten* suitcases (and one very *large* person). She wouldn't hear of sleeping in a bunk and promptly commandeered my bedroom. It hadn't been easy, but I had finally found a friend more self-centered than myself.

The tour wound up in San Francisco. The day I arrived Yoko Ono checked into the same hotel. When I got back from the gig there was a box of chocolates and a note from Yoko saying: "Welcome, Marianne, to San Francisco! I'd love to see you. Perhaps we could have tea together. Would you call me. I'm in room such-and-such. Love, Yoko." A friendly note. *Too* friendly, I thought. Cynthia was jumping up and down:

"Yoko Ono! Oh my God, Marianne, Yoko wants to see us! Isn't that *great?*"

There was something about that note that made me think of Hansel and Gretel. We were on a health kick, on our way to a health spa, as it happened. Now, had she said, "I'll meet you at the bar" — there was an extraordinary redwood art deco bar in the hotel — that would have been different.

Since then, she came to see me at the Bottom Line and I must say my heart melted when she came backstage after the show and told me that John Lennon loved my version of "Working Class Hero." After that I became a huge fan of Yoko.

We rented a car and it was "Step on the gas!" There was no looking back. And, as we were driving on our way to the Sonoma Mission Inn we passed through a dismal patch of scrubland.

"God, Cynthia, what's happening? It's suddenly got very *dark* here," I said. "Where the hell are we?"

"Don't you know what this place is? Sugar, this is Altamont."

## Howard

WOKE up on Leroy Street starving. I was feeling strung out and exhausted, and there wasn't a single thing in the house except a few rolled-up dollar bills and a lot of dope.

I was living in New York with a musician named Hilly Michaels. What an awful time. For over a year I'd been doing too much of everything: cocaine, freebase, heroin. I must have been completely poisoned by then. Usually I managed to go away and clean up, but I had serious immigration problems. If I left the country I'd never get back in.

When I moved back to New York in the fall of 1985, I was well aware that in certain circles my name could be useful. Being "Marianne Faithfull" was a good thing, after all. I could use it to get drugs (good drugs, too). So I did just that. I ran up a lot of credit with a lot of people. I still owe several dealers in the city twenty grand — each. But there you go.

I saw quite a bit of Anita, who was pretty much in the same pickle I was. Very dope sick. She was living out on Long Island in a big house that used to belong to Bing Crosby, lying around watching TV "like a parasite, darling." Every few days she would rouse herself, get a driver and go into the city to score.

On the surface things didn't look that bad (especially compared to life on the wall). I had good clothes, a relationship, a nice place to live.

But for me everything seemed so . . . so *off*. Disconnected. When I'm with guys I can't talk to (and there have been a few of them) I spend my time reading. I'm in my beloved bubble.

One of the books I was reading was *Seth Speaks*. It was my first encounter with anything remotely occult since the sixties. After the episode with Brian and the I Ching I was horrified and terrified by anything supernatural. The idea in the *Seth* books that we make our own reality came as a revelation. It was a concept that was completely new to me. I had been living with the old European sense of compelling destiny, irrevocable fate.

Another thing this creature in *Seth* says is that we are always living parallel lives. Simultaneously. If you wake up totally exhausted it means you were busy somewhere else, and at Leroy Street I was waking up every morning completely drained, the pillow soaked, water pouring off my face. Admittedly, this had more to do with the huge quantities of alcohol I was drinking than my night work, but I took it as a sign nevertheless!

Little did I know I was about to crash through the abyss and come out the other side. You fall and fall and fall and fall. It just keeps getting worse, until you are in the lowest circle of hell and you know you are still going down and there are other circles underneath that. But eventually you fall through the lowest circle and then you fall into the light.

I'd been on this run for ages. Every day I woke up with such loathing, self-loathing and self-disgust. I hated my situation. I hated this man I was next to. I hated everything, but most of all I hated myself. I felt: "This is it now. I'll put an end to it. There's nothing else left. It's quite hopeless and I've had enough. I have to stop."

The funny thing is it never once occurred to me to stop using drugs. The classic agony of addiction. You can't stop and you can't go on. And that's exactly where I was. The pain of living without drugs was as bad as the pain of living with drugs. When you use drugs in such a willful way, you're transgressing some elemental code. You're destroying yourself, and body and soul recoils at it. That must be one of the reasons it's so appealing. It's so awfully dull to take care of yourself all the time, to do everything right. Unfortunately, on the other path there is only one conclusion, and that is death (by misadventure).


The boyfriend was asleep. I didn't like him at all, I didn't even *know* him, actually. I can't think of one thing I really liked about him. It had got to the point where I could only have sex if I took a handful of sleeping pills. That's where I'd ended up. It was the end of the road. I was a desperate, desperate junkie and he was just another form of Ben, really, a comrade in getting high. What always happened with these men was that I wound up taking care of them. Because they didn't know shit. They didn't make money. They didn't work. They didn't do anything. But of all the creeps I've lived with, Hilly was the worst. It was such a perverse situation. One of those grisly dependent relationships, all connected to drugs and sexual dependency. And he *looked* like Dracula.

Hilly, like Ben, saw me as being helpful to him in his career. Life's a hustle. About two years before I'd met him he'd made one big score, a record deal with a major label. He'd been given a huge advance, which he'd spent. Nothing had ever come of it, so he was in deep shit.

But how could *I* help him? I couldn't even get my *own* record together! It was going along dreadfully, but I was in too much of a fog to figure out how to extricate myself. It didn't occur to me at the time that I could just tell somebody I hated the record and wasn't going to do it and that would be that. Something was *very* wrong, and I didn't know what. I simply knew that it had to stop. I can't believe it now — it was only a record — but the only solution I could come up with at the time was to kill myself. I go through this every time I make a record. This time it was worse than usual. I was doing speedballs and I was freebasing. I was blaming everything as usual on my producer, Mike Thorne.

I've had a skewed view of producers ever since my first experience with Andrew. Andrew had been so insanely manipulative. A crazy notion evolved in me of what the producer was. A producer is a creature to fear; somebody who takes your gift and exploits it, or distorts it. Bloody hell, man, don't they always? This wasn't my producer, Mike Thorne, at all. He was very straight and even a bit like a machine, actually. My normal crisis on beginning a new record was mounting, but it was now compounded by drugs. So I fell back on my old standby: "If I can't stand it, I can always kill myself."

Once I'd made the big decision, I got out of bed and raved about the house, gathering up all the smack. It was incredibly strong compressed Chinese heroin. I put it all in a spoon, cooked it up and shot it. I knew the instant I did it that I was in deep trouble. It went straight to my heart. As soon as I realized I was dying, I no longer wanted to die. I suppose I must have experienced some natural instinct to preserve life. My solution was the addict's typical answer to everything: "Oh fuck, I've gone too far. I'd better get some coke!"

I was on my way to do just that but I didn't make it. I was lurching and staggering as I tried to cross the room. I fell to the ground and broke my jaw. I could feel my heartbeat beginning to stop. It was the Big Moment. Nothing like the pills in Australia. There, although I was in a coma, I was still somehow connected to myself. This time, I wasn't present at all.

I wasn't just out of the body, I was in a space that had nothing to do with the body at all. It was a very odd place to be, completely impersonal and at the same time very passionate and intense. Emotional without *being* an emotion. The life spark, perhaps. (Definitely not my usual state.)

My "normal" condition at the time was neurotic, unhappy and muddled. Here everything was incredibly clear, completely untainted by drugs or confusion. At that moment I asked myself a question that was startling in its clarity considering my prevailing murk: Do you really want to die in this strange place so far from the people who know you and love you and who you love? Is this how you want to end your life?

My answer was equally decisive: No I don't. A pure decision, something I had only moments before been utterly incapable of making. And having answered, I knew there was something further I had to say. I could feel the words "H-e-l-p m-e!" forming in my mind, and at that instant I came back. My heart was suddenly going *drumpdrumpdrump* again and I could feel a throbbing pain in my jaw. I could now hear the words "help me" ringing in my head. I knew I had to get to someone, anyone. I crawled upstairs to the boyfriend, who was passed out in what the papers usually label "a heroin-induced stupor." I shook him awake and said, "Help me." I was, by now, extremely experienced in this game. This time was just the most serious. I said, "Take me out-side. Walk me up and down until I come back." And I did. Then we went to the doctor to get my jaw set, and my heart examined. Then it was back to business as usual!

You'd think what had just occurred would've jolted me back to my senses, but not at all. It had shaken me up a bit. Even then I didn't stop. I just kept right on as if nothing had happened. As soon as I could walk again I went right back to West 58th Street to see my dealer. The addict psychology is a bit like a pancake. On one side you're better than anybody because you're higher. On the other side you're nothing.

The one thing that *did* dawn on me was that I had to leave Hilly. I came to this conclusion through my usual method of deduction — something was wrong, so it must be *him*. I called up Mike Thorne and said, "You've got to get me out of this place." I ran away, but all I did was move myself and my drugs into the Gramercy Park Hotel, leaving Hilly in Leroy Street, very upset, naturally.

My poor record producer! Here he was trying to make a record, and I hated it so much I had to kill myself to get out of it. It all goes back to my fucking ambivalence about everything. I know this is all I *can* do, I know it's what I *have* to do, but is it really what I want to do? It happens every time I begin a new record. There's a part of me that isn't sure and to make matters worse I'm terrified to talk about. After all, the people I work with would be horrified. They've just given me an advance! The record company, the album, the producer — it's all going ahead on the premise that I want to do it, that I believe in it. It would be like the pilot of a 747 saying in midflight, "I'm not really sure I'm into flying today." Horrendous.

The problem wasn't the record, obviously. Something in me was breaking down.

The album never came out. It did have one great song on it that I'd written with Hilly called "Park Avenue." Hilly was a good song-writer. I'll give him that. A very proficient, crafted sort of thing. It gives a very vivid picture of the state I was in. The lyrics were:

> *We were young, so in love*
> *Dreams of future, dreams of fame*
> *I just thought it was a game*

*Didn't even notice that you'd changed*
*Park Avenue, I'm missing you*
*It's where I want to be.*

It was a fantasy song about Mick. I was the childhood sweetheart of a guy who goes on to be the most powerful advertising executive on the planet. That was Mick. He leaves her behind and she's thinking about him on Park Avenue.

Soon after I'd moved into the Gramercy Park, Holly from Island Records dropped by. At Island they knew nothing about the state I was in. I must have got quite good at hiding it. All they knew was that I had broken my jaw. And so Holly (who is a very nice, bossy, healthy sort of girl) and I were talking about the much-dreaded forthcoming album, making lists of things and all that, and she begins busily poking about for a pen, opening desk drawers. And each drawer she opens is filled with drugs of one sort or another. There are works in one drawer, a tie in the other, coke in another, heroin in another. I might as well have written *help* in lipstick on the mirror.

Holly didn't say a word. She just said, "I have to go back to Island." I knew it was all over. I became very peaceful. I just sat in my room knowing it was all going to be taken care of. I knew Holly would call Chris Blackwell and tell him what she had seen, and they would do something about it, which they did. I saw a lot of Andrew Oldham while I was sitting there at the Gramercy waiting. My last days in hell talking things through.

I was admitted to the Hazelden Clinic in Minneapolis on November 18, 1985. It was a blast of reality I desperately needed. At Hazelden I knew at last that I had landed. It was like coming back through space.

Hazelden was hard-core detox. It was terribly dope sick and weak when I got there, and detoxing nearly killed me. They thought I was going to die. I knew exactly what to do, of course. I'd done it dozens of times. I asked for ten blankets, crawled under them and lay there for a week shaking and sweating until it passed.

I knew this was my last chance. I read all the books they left me, and I decided, "Okay, I'll do this stuff and I'll get better." I followed the program zealously. E for enthusiasm. Like my conversion to Catholicism it was a purely social decision. I was there six months and I took to it like a duck to water from the minute I got there.

It was exactly what I needed, a real spiritual charge. Of course, there *was* a bit of adjusting on both sides. When they asked me what my idea of a higher power was, I said, "The great god Pan." From the program I learned that although you have to help yourself, if you help *only* yourself it's useless. The reason you go through these things is so that you can help other people, too. And that is how you ultimately save yourself. I understand that now. I understood why I should have held the hand of that dying boy in Bexley Hospital. To really help another junkie, you have to be a junkie. You can't stand on a high place and lower your hand down to help the slimy addict. You can only help somebody by saying, "I know what you mean 'cause I've been there."

It wasn't until Hazelden some fifteen years later that I first realized that during the time I was with Mick I had no history of my own. As part of the program, everyone tells their story. I was at a loss what to say and so I called my press agent, Ellen Smith, and asked her to send down by post a copy of Spanish Tony's book, *Up and Down with the Rolling Stones.* I basically said to them, "You want my story? Read that." Because in those days I really didn't know I had a story of my own. I was just part of *their* story and I saw my own only through these books. As if it all happened to someone else.


It was at Hazelden that I first laid eyes on Howard Tose. He was one of the most damaged people I had ever met, and I liked him immediately because of that. He was in terrible shape. He had an uncontrollable twitch. He stuttered, he trembled, his eyes were unfocused. All those things connected with a cocaine psychosis. Damaged *beyond* belief, he was, and this was the person I liked best! I always tend to identify with whoever is the most hurt. He was very nice, Howard, and he was very sick. In addition to his multiple addictions, he was manic depressive and a schizophrenic. I understood none of this; the whole thing was like outer space to me. But I knew that he had used a lot of drugs, so I could obviously identify with that! He was quite mad and I rather liked that, too. It was all quite hopeless but, never mind, he was delightful and I fell in love with him.

What happened, I think, was classic: You take someone like me, who was dependent on every possible neurotic thing — heroin, coke, pills, alcohol, sex and money — and then withdraw everything from them, and they cleave to the first familiar thing. What I did was to fix on somebody, as I thought, just like me. He was obviously mentally very sick. I thought I was, too. I wasn't, as it turned out. I was just another confused fool trying to self-destruct. Not the same thing. The only thing we really had in common was we were both addicts. But otherwise he was not like me in the least. My problems were quite straightforward in comparison with Howie's. His addictions were the least of his problems.

I'm really a garden-variety drug addict. The first year I was in treatment I was dying to uncover a serious psychosis that I could pin it all on, but nothing like that ever showed up. My headlong descent had much more to do with a willful and heedless pursuit of hedonism. It sounds pretentious to say, but I profoundly believe I was passionately committed to a Dionysian way of life. Before this great experiment went haywire, it was all extremely exhilarating! By the time you feel yourself changing into someone else, it's already too late. With me it happened rather slowly. From the first instant I tried heroin I knew that I wanted to feel like this all the time. No pain.

Howie reminded me of John. He even looked a bit like John. He had prematurely gray hair and he was skinny. He had that oddly attractive quality of looking very young and very old at the same time. A young face with very gray, longish hair. And he was terminally cool. He had been a deejay and he made me wonderful tapes, compilations of songs that were little musical conversations with me. And being so isolated there and craving my own space — I was in a dormitory with all these other people — it was almost unbearable. And the only thing that I could connect to was the music.

Eventually I began to thrive at Hazelden while Howard became steadily more unhappy. After six weeks, when he could no longer tolerate it, he left — against *all* medical advice. I stayed and turned into the little sunbeam. I was my mother's ray of sunshine all over again.

Howard went to a halfway house in Minnesota and then to Boston. He would call me constantly, which was strictly forbidden. There was no physical contact between us, but it didn't matter. It was an obsession. I thought I was in love with him (of course the fact that I knew nothing *about* him helped). He just seemed like someone I *could* have loved if I'd been capable of loving someone.

After about two and a half months, the treatment began to get very tough. They were stripping me down. It was like open heart surgery with all the flesh peeled back. They were starting to probe to see where it *really* hurts. And bringing up things I didn't want to remember.

We had to do exercises called Sections. I loved "Preoccupation," in which you were asked to describe what you obsessed about: When will I get my next drink, my next fix? For another you had to write about a Day in the Life. Your typical day as an addict, your routine.

Then one day they presented me with a new Section, one that they hadn't tried on anyone else before. It was called Destructive Behavior. It was incredibly appropriate, so much so that I felt it had been made up expressly to torment me. It would have been good for me, but I balked. That was it for me.

I got on a plane and went to Boston. On the plane I had five brandies. My cockeyed idea in blowing my sobriety was that this way Howie and I would both start with the same amount of clean time. He'd gone to New York, relapsed and then come back to Boston and got clean again. Convoluted druggie logic. When I got off the plane I was drunk. Howard was in terrible shape, but I couldn't grasp this. He was a bit shaky, but I put it down to withdrawal. I thought, "He's just a bit wobbly, poor thing, but he'll get over it in no time, now that we're together." I expected him to be like me and I'm made of very stern stuff indeed. Not everybody is. I just didn't understand how absolutely desperate his condition was. I suppose I thought he just had to pull himself together, get a job, then everything would be fine. It was ludicrous, really.

For six weeks we lived together in a beautiful apartment on the thirty-sixth floor of a building that looked out over Boston Harbor. Practically the entire time Howie spent lying curled up on the bed in the fetal position, shaking. What *was* I thinking of? If I hadn't been so selfish and self-involved, it would certainly have occurred to me that he was in need of serious medical attention. He belonged in a hospital. He was critical; he needed care. It was a terribly dangerous situation but I didn't see any of that.

I just got right on with it as best I could. The day after I got off
the plane I was back going to meetings. I stayed clean and went to N.A.
meetings. I found a wonderful sponsor in my newfound friend Deb.
She was strong and beautiful and I knew that nothing would faze her,
including me. Very no-nonsense. Deb was my first contact with the
outside world, and I could tell that for some reason my asking her to be
my sponsor made Howie jealous.

After the meeting, everybody was milling around. Howie went up
to Deb and in a somewhat snide way whispered: "Think you can handle it?" Meaning: Do you think you can manage a real addict?

"Yeah, I can handle it," Deb said. "Can *you* handle it?" She meant:
Could he deal with real recovery?

While living with Howie, my jaw started to swell up. The pain
was excruciating. My jawbone was slowly rotting from the break and an
impacted wisdom tooth and various other maladies. But I honestly
believed that this was just the pain of living without drugs. I thought,
"Oh, this must be what straight people feel like all the time." I'd been
living clean and sober in Boston about a month, when it began to dawn
on me that the pain in my jaw did not come from withdrawal. Deb
didn't seem to be in this much pain and she was living without drugs.
And all the other people I saw at meetings didn't seem to be in excruciating pain either.

It became so bad I went to see an oral surgeon. Turned out that
when they removed my wisdom tooth at Hazelden they had chipped off
a piece of bone and the two bits of bone were rubbing against each
other. Because of my history they didn't want to operate, so they wired
my jaw shut. They put pins in my jaw and a handle on it so I looked like
a guitar. I could barely speak. Wonderful where drugs will take you.

I was very firm with Howard. Because I was recovering and had
no wish to do drugs, I assumed his condition was the result of his re-
lapse. I thought he was being an asshole, lying on the bed day after day
because he craved heroin. My fantasy was that we would get clean together and everything was going to be okay.

Our life went on according to my own willfully romantic picture
of it. He was a sweet guy, but he was very, very ill. The tulip incident
was fairly characteristic. It was spring, and one day I went out and I
bought some tulips and put them in a vase. The flowers hadn't yet

opened, so the petals were tightly furled. That evening we were sitting on the sofa and quite suddenly he froze and his face took on a look of horror.

I said, "Whatever's the matter?"

"The flowers . . . they're going to hurt me, I know they are."

I could see what he meant — they were a little spiky. I treated him just like a little boy. "Don't be so silly, darling, it's perfectly all right, they're just tulips. They'll open up, they'll be lovely, really they will."

And when they bloomed I remember pointing it out to him as you would to a child: "You see, you silly? They're fine." He seemed dubious.

Howie actually went out and got a job in a photographic lab. Everything I asked him to do, he did. Poor Howie. He just wanted to get high and do drugs. He had been to six or seven high-priced treatment facilities. He had cleaned up innumerable times and slid back. Treatment certainly loses its magic after the first half-dozen times. But it was all new to me. I was still at the point where all these sayings like "A day at a time" and "Live and let live" and "It gets better" sound incredibly wise. It's all very commonsense stuff, but if you've lived the way I had lived since I was nineteen, it was a revelation. To Howie they didn't come as quite such a bombshell. To him they were simplistic slogans rather than simple mantras. Just empty phrases he'd heard a thousand times before.

By this time I had been clean for a month and a half. I really wanted to get better and now saw it was possible, but I knew I wasn't going to be able to do it with Howard. I said to myself, "This'll be okay. But not with him. This isn't going to work. I'm gonna have to tell him."

We'd had a very nice dinner the night before with his sister Fran and we had a wonderful night together. Sexually, my relationship with Howie was incredible. It was the last great fuck I've had. One of the things that's so shocking was that that last night we had together was one of the most amazing experiences of my adult sex life. He poured his whole being into that night. I'd never had a night like that before or since.

The next morning when he got up I said to him, "Howard, love, I have to talk to you." We went into the sitting room. I gave him one of my straight talks. I don't know what I thought I was doing, talking to somebody in that condition the way I did.

He was sitting on the sofa naked and I was in my dressing gown, standing in the doorway. I lit a cigarette and sat down opposite him and started to tell him as kindly and calmly as I could what I was going to do. All through clenched teeth. It was just about a week after my jaw had been wired shut.

"I've thought a lot about us both and although I love you dearly, this isn't working at all. We both know it, darling. It simply isn't good for either of us. I think we should try living on our own for a while and then perhaps . . ."

He stopped me. "But what will you do?"

"Well, darling, this is what I've decided. I'm going to get a little house in Cambridge. I'm going to leave you now, you see, and you, my dear, you're going to have to go to hospital, you really are. You're lying on the bed and moaning for days on end. You've got a serious condition and I can't help you. Can't you see it's just not right? You can't finish anything, you can't function, you're not happy. You need to get some proper help, to go back into hospital. Your mother's coming tomorrow and that's what you will do."

He sat there. He was very beautiful. He sat there and listened without saying a thing. When I had finished he got up and this utterly incredible thing happened. His heart jumped out of his body. I couldn't believe what I'd seen. The muscle pushed out and made a big lump in his chest. It was astonishing. He saw it, too, and he was very frightened. It was as if his fear had materialized and congealed into a physical force.

He was very still and then he said: "The honeymoon's over, then?"

I laughed and said, 'Yes, I suppose it is." Then I looked at my watch and said: "Oh, well, Howard, it's eight o'clock, better get ready for work." He didn't say anything. He got up and went into the bathroom. I went into the kitchen to make a pot of tea. I turned on the radio and waited for the kettle to boil. I made the tea and sat in the kitchen smoking a cigarette, waiting for Howie to leave. But when after a long while I hadn't heard him going out the front door, I got up and started to look around the apartment. I thought he must be lying down somewhere. But I couldn't find him anywhere. I began to get very scared and my heart started to pound. I went round and round calling and calling him, "Howard, where are you? Howard!" looking in every room. Eventually I walked back into the bedroom and saw the open window. I went over to the window and stood on the ledge and looked down. It was a long way down, thirty-six stories. At the very bottom I saw what looked like a bunch of flowers, like the tops of hibiscus flowers lying at the entrance to the apartment building. They looked very beautiful, these beautiful red flowers, and then it slowly hit me what it was. It was Howie. I stood there for a long, long time and then I got down from the window and called the police, called his sister and called Deb, my sponsor.

Deb was initially quite hostile. I think she thought Howie and I had just substituted sex for drugs, that that's what was keeping us straight. She thought when I called her that day that Howie and I were playing childish lovers' games. He was hiding in the closet and we were going to end up laughing and falling on the bed and fucking. I finally convinced her it was not a game. Then I sat down and waited.

Deb came to get me. I packed my things and moved in with her. I went to the funeral. Went to see his mother. I stayed on in Boston for a year after that.

I knew I had a responsibility to his family. I had to help them as much as I could. And for a year I did. We all pretended everything was all right in the usual way one does. But it wasn't. It wasn't all right at all.

I had terrible dreams. They were all about having lost something very precious to me. He wasn't my husband or my child or my mother or my father or my brother. I don't know what he was. It was the first time in my life I'd given myself a chance to mourn — and I mourned for everybody. I began to run toward my fears and terrors instead of running away.

Brian's death had hit me very hard, but I hadn't felt directly responsible. I hadn't been quite so involved. And I hadn't been clean. With Howard it was very different. I remember one of the things I thought as I was waiting for the cops to come to Harbor Towers was, "Will they think I pushed him?" Although I knew I hadn't killed him, I wasn't entirely certain what my role *had* been. Howard must have been in much the same state as Brian had been at the end, but with Howard I had been there, watching it all happen day by day, not knowing what was going on at all.

How was it possible that we were living on the thirty-sixth floor? It was incredible, but I suppose it's quite natural for people to keep on believing that everything is all right even in the face of a hopeless situation. I obviously did. I was in complete denial about what was going on. After Deb came to pick me up, I never went back to Harbor Towers. I just couldn't face it. She went up to empty out the fridge and there was all this proper food that I'd been cooking; roast chicken and soup. There was Howie going through cocaine psychosis and God knows what other hells and I was cooking pea soup and setting the table. Telling myself that this is what normal life is. Real food in the refrigerator. Regular meals. That's what you learn in the program. You get up in the morning and you brush your teeth and you make your bed. I still do that. I still say my prayers when I can.

There's a persistent illusion that love will heal all wounds, but it just isn't so. Love is transcendent, but it can't mend everything. I felt as if I had lost my child. I felt I had been given something precious to look after and lost it.

For the longest time I felt that it was over for me. I felt afterward as if I must have pushed him. I had hallucinations. I would see waves of blood everywhere.

I asked Dr. Bergman, my psychiatrist at MacLean Hospital, "What's going on? Am I mad?" He told me I was going through a series of delayed reactions. Experiencing all these things for the first time. In the past when something disturbing happened, I'd just get higher.

Dr. Bergman told me to read Freud's essay "Mourning and Melancholia." I recognized Howie in it very clearly and I recognized myself: "We have never been able to explain what interplay of forces can carry such a purpose [suicide] through to execution. . . ."

And Freud answers that unanswerable question — how can the ego agree to its own destruction? — in this way: "The ego can kill itself only if it can treat itself as an object — if it is able to direct against itself the hostility which it harbors towards others."

In severe melancholia, pain and anger become so intense that you eventually split yourself into two entities. You disconnect from the hated, humiliated part of yourself. You say to it: "You're obviously sick and you're going to do something dreadful, so now I am going to separate from you and become autonomous." You decide to dispose of it, to kill it off. You imagine you will be able to watch as it jumps out of the window, and rid yourself of it forever. This is such insanity and you go so mad that you believe that there will be a *physical* part of you that won't be killed. A part of you, you think, will be left behind to watch the Bad You fall to its destruction, to observe your own death and gloat and say: "Ha! ha! ha! See, I got you! Fool!" But halfway down you realize that you have made a terrible mistake. There is no other half. There's no one left to gloat. The joke is on you, but you're not laughing anymore.

In the split second between your vengeful act and extinction you always regret it. I know because I did when I took the sleeping pills in Australia. You have a moment of truth where you see your gesture for what it is. Which is a very petty thing. It's a hostile act. And it's insane because you're trying to get back at things through an act of such ultimate revenge that it involves your own annihilation. At just that instant you hit the ground and it's all over.

At Howie's funeral, it struck me that I had never thought about the havoc suicide wreaks on the lives of those around you. I had no idea of the pain people go through when somebody commits suicide. I had never even *thought* about it. And I'd tried the same thing myself. Twice.

Howie's death wrenched life into focus for me. Up till then I had seen life as a game. If I made the right moves and put the pieces in the right place, why then I'd *be* all right. With Howie's death I suddenly knew it wasn't a game at all. There's no rehearsal. This is it.

After it happened I asked myself if there was any sign that this was going to happen. And, of course, there was. One of the strangest things he did was sit down and tell me all the things he wished he hadn't done to his family. All the little unkindnesses, especially to his mother. And after he was dead I tried to tell his mother what he'd said.

I had to stop obsessing, to stop blaming myself, and when I did it was as if I had come back from hell. Somebody with amnesia who had forgotten how to do the most basic stuff. A lot of things were completely foreign to me. I couldn't work the washing machine. Didn't know how to balance my checkbook. (Still don't.)

After Howie's death I moved into a little house in Boston (on the ground floor this time) and Eva came to stay with me. It was about the best time we ever had together. Deb was around, of course, and so was my friend

Howard. Another Howard. Howard Tose was dead, and I was looking for someone else named Howard. This one was an incredibly bright William Burroughs worshipper. A hapless junkie, now in the program.

I was in what is lovingly known as early recovery, and Deb and Howard felt that I shouldn't be the one to go to the liquor store for me mum's bottle. She drank half a bottle a day and every two days someone had to go out and get another bottle. So dear old Howard was elected to go out and get it. He's one of those alcoholics who's quite capable of living with a full bar and not drinking. So every two days he would nip out to get Eva's bottle. And he'd decided, since Eva was now living in America, that she had to have bourbon. The *vin du pays*. People in A.A. obsess about this stuff endlessly. Should it be scotch or Irish, blended or single malt? They would sit about discussing it and occasionally Eva would pipe up and say, "I zink you should let me decide vat I like."

And they would say, "Oh no, no, Eva, you don't know the kind of whiskey you can get here. We'll get you something very special, don't worry, we're old hands at this."

"But how can you know it, you're not even *dwinking* it."

Eva wasn't exactly delirious about my recovery. She was happy I was over the worst of my addiction, but she couldn't help saying: "Marianne, you really are much too sober." Eva felt that I was getting a little *too* straight; she found me dull. Funny, I'd always aspired to an uneventful life, but I never thought I'd achieve it. Anyway, I got very serious and dour — a bit like my father. Just what Eva was looking for in a companion! Lucky for her, I couldn't change overnight into a professor of Renaissance studies (although I still might).

I was as zealous as any convert to a new religion, poring over the old Alcoholics Anonymous Big Book as lovingly as any monk. One of my favorite passages is Step Two, which is about the savages. That's very much what being an addict and an alcoholic is all about. You go back to a completely savage state.

But once out of that feral stage one is not, alas, automatically cast into a state of grace; just being clean does not transform *everything*. Indeed, it is precisely the "everything" of life that is pretty much the same. The same shit happens without drugs and alcohol — the same troubles with money, the same fears (actually, more fears).

*    *    *

One of the consequences of my willful behavior while with Howie was that, due to the surgery on my jaw, I could speak only through clenched teeth. I had a handle sticking out of my face with two bolts and a bar on the outside. And it was like this that I went to see Bob Dylan, who was playing in Boston with Tom Petty and the Heartbreakers. It was only when I saw the way he was staring at me that I realized how strange I must look. I was too elated about my recovery (and seeing him) to let a little prosthetic appendage get in my way.

"Well, well," he said. "What's happened to you?"

"Oh, Bob, what's happened to me is *incredible!*"

"I bet."

"I got *clean,*" I said, launching into my recovery story. "I was doing a lot of heroin as you may recall and la, la, la. And then I went into treatment at Hazelden. And then I came to Boston. And . . . and I fell in love with this guy. And he jumped out of a thirty-sixth-floor window. And now I'm fine. I'm going to meetings every day. And I'm about to begin a new album. Isn't it wonderful?"

He just acted as if I was lying. All I got from Bob was "What? You? Nah!"

His reaction was fairly typical of the rock contingent. They liked me better on heroin. I was much more subdued and manageable. It's very common with rock stars. They surround themselves with beautiful and often brilliant women whom they also find extremely threatening. One way out is for the women to get into drugs. That makes them compliant and easier to be with.

Somehow I don't think Bob was too pleased to hear my glad tidings. I was too sure of myself to play the willing victim. I certainly wasn't contrite. I think we're always expected to say how wrong we've been. But I don't feel I've done anything wrong. I'm not guilty of anything. People assume I must feel unending regret. Where do they *get* this idea? (My songs, probably.) You must feel very badly, they say. No, not really. I feel guilt about not looking after Nicholas, but apart from that, precious little shame.

When I called Keith and told him my good news — how I'd stopped drinking and wasn't doing drugs anymore — he was sympathetic but a little, well, worried. He paused for a beat and then said: "Ah, Marianne! But what about the Holy Grail?"

# Loose Ends

And all shall be well
and all manner of things
shall be well.
JULIAN OF NORWICH

HAD wonderfully allegorical dreams in my first year of recovery. It was during a time when I was very buoyant, a sensation of things happening and breakthroughs. Not that the dreams were all positive. They weren't.

Once I dreamt I was walking through vast Baroque rooms, the rooms of palaces, down endless staircases, through great colonnades of spiraling pillars. Very charged, mnemonic spaces, like the menacingly monumental spaces in Piranesi engravings. As I passed through them I realized that I was going backward through my life; the balconies and loggias were crowded with people and scenes from my past.

It was the palace of memory I read about in Frances Yates's books. These cavernous rooms were all about despair and Paradise Lost. People who were once my friends turned away. Bitter scenes from my own *Inferno*. As the dream ended, the palace opened onto a Roman amphitheater where I was tied — to eight white horses and dragged through the arena to my death. But death in dreams, as we know, does not bring peace.

Shortly after this I had a disturbing dream about Mick, a real corker, right in the middle of the hottest day of summer. I was way out in the country and I just lay down on the ground and dozed off — the whole thing was right out of *Picnic at Hanging Rock* — and I had this stupendous dream.

In the dream I was a very grand old lady . . . well loved, respected, greatly honored. I was reading in my beautiful four-poster bed surrounded by my Dalmatians when suddenly a hooded messenger burst into my room with the news that Mick Jagger was dead. And as he spoke, the walls of my house began to crumble and fall. Walls fell down, but in their place other things appeared. Where there had been a wall, suddenly there appeared a great staircase; where there had been a doorway, there appeared a great dolmen arch. The ceiling became the sky, the walls became trees, the floor became grass — and everything transparent through everything else. It was as if the house had turned itself inside out.

When I awoke I could hear flies buzzing around my head. I had no idea where or even *who* I was, although I'd probably only been asleep for ten minutes. I shielded my eyes from the sun, and brooded on the messenger's news. I began to get nervous. The next day I dragged myself to Boston and went to see Dr. Bergman, who was always excited when I came in with a new dream.

"Does this mean I want Mick Jagger to die?" I asked, just to hear him say no. Which is exactly what he said, at least four times.

"Oh, no. No, no, no, Marianne." (So comforting!) "It means that we're really *getting* somewhere, it means that the foundation upon which your house was built was faulty. Now the ground has shifted and you see new vistas." Great, I thought. Time to make a record.


On my three previous albums I'd written most of the songs myself, but I knew that at this point I was in too much pain to write. Summer was a time of intense suffering. I saw blood everywhere. Then in the fall I began to get over it, which is what always happens to me. Something to do with going back to school in the fall. When September comes, I think: "Right! Back to school, back to a normal routine (whatever *that* is)."

I wanted to take the classic jazz and blues love songs of loss and yearning, and filter them through the devastation I was feeling about Howie's death. A sort of exorcism. I talked to whoever would listen. I talked to Hal Willner and I talked to Tom Waits. I had developed a phone friendship with Tom, who is also on Island Records.

Tom's concept was quite different from mine. His idea was to do an album around the theme "the whore's revenge." He wanted to do the album in New Orleans. It was going to be called *Storeyville,* after the old red-light district in New Orleans. There I would be, in Tom's view of it, bawling out raunchy songs in a pair of fishnet stockings and a garter belt. It's always curious the way people see me, which is always in a much more sexual light than I see myself. Much as I'd love to believe that sexpot image of me, I don't really see myself as an unrepentant hooker belting out blues from the bordello.

A project like this requires weeks and weeks of sitting around listening to old records and tapes, and the person you usually end up working with is the one who has the time. Tom wanted to do it, but he was busy having a life: getting married, having children, making records. What came out of our conversation was the album's title song, "Strange Weather," written by Tom with his wife, Kathleen.

Hal Willner had the time and the patience to come up to Boston and sit with me and listen to piles of records, which is how I came to do *Strange Weather* with him. He has an absolutely staggering collection of old records. The other nice thing about working with Hal was that unlike anybody else I've ever worked with his approach was: "Why don't we find out what *Marianne* wants to do?"

I'd done a track on Hal's Kurt Weill album, *Lost in the Stars,* before I went into treatment, and I knew the moment I met Hal that this was going to be one of the greatest friends of my life. One of those friendships where no rules apply.

Meanwhile, Mike Thorne — my poor producer who had been working with me on the album I started before I took the overdose — wanted to finish *that* record. But I'd gone past that sensibility a long, long time before. I didn't know what to do, and out of the blue I got a call from Chris Blackwell. He was quite nervous because he thought I, too, wanted to finish that album. He thought I was going to resist.

Very hesitantly he began. "Look, Marianne, about the album you were working on with Mike Thorne before you went into Hazelden . . ."

"Yeeees?"

"Well, dear, I really don't think it's such a good idea."

"You *don't?*"

"No. What I really think you should be doing is working on that record with Hal Willner."

Pulling myself together, I said, "Well, maybe. Can we do *anything we like?*"

And Chris, very relieved himself, said, "Sure, go right ahead. You've got my blessing."

It all happened very quickly. Howie jumped in April. In September, Hal and I began putting *Strange Weather* together and in October we recorded it. *Strange Weather* is dedicated to Howie. It's a song cycle similar to the messages Howie used to make for me in Hazelden. The song "Strange Weather" that Tom wrote for the album contains all sorts of allusions to Howie. "I believe that brandy's mine," is the brandy I drank on the plane from Hazelden to join Howie in Boston. That line came out of my phone marathons with Tom, during which I recounted to him the whole sorry story of Howie and me in cinematic detail.

Hal was more than happy to make an album of cover songs — he never really liked the songs I wrote anyway. And in the process of singing other people's material I stumbled across the fact that I'm not a bad interpretive singer, something I would never have found out if I hadn't made *Strange Weather.*

The idea was to find songs I *would* have written if I could have. I wanted to do Dylan's "I'll Keep It with Mine" and "Penthouse Serenade." Hal wanted me to do Billie Holiday and Dinah Washington songs. We did a Doc Pomus/Mac Rebennack song. We ended up covering an awful lot more songs than we needed. We just went mad. We tried loads of things that didn't work out at all. We did a Robert Johnson, a Bessie Smith. All the things you've ever dreamed of doing if you're a singer, I did 'em all. There's a whole other *Strange Weather* in the vaults at Island Records. Chris wanted a beautiful tragic album of melancholy ballads, and that's what he got.

Whenever I speak to a friend who's in a situation of heartbreak and despair, I tell them: "If you think *you're* in bad shape, go and listen to *Strange Weather.*" When it came out, one of the reviews said, "From Marianne Faithfull, music to slit your wrists by." I took it as a compliment!

One of the things I do when I'm working is to conjure up scenes from my life. All the songs on *Strange Weather* are about people and places I knew. "Penthouse Serenade," for instance, I first heard in a little hut in the Himalayas where we had tea. Oliver was playing it when I got there. I had the slightly demented thought that if I put it on my album I might end up in a penthouse with a lovely man. Oh, well.

Eva died in May of 1990. She was eighty. In the last five years of her life my mother had been the sweetest, most radiant person (an incarnation that was rare for her). I was on tour in Australia when John called to tell me. It's a long flight, and on the plane back to England I reread *The White Goddess* in honor of my mother, who was for me a form of the Goddess, the infinite, shapeshifting spirit that for the Celtic bards imbues life.

> *I have been in many shapes*
> *Before I attained my harmonic form*
> *I have been a drop in the air*
> *I have been a shining star*
>
> *I was in the Ark*
> *With Noah and Alpha*
>
> *I am a wave of the sea*
> *I am a tear of the sun*
> *I am fair among flowers*
> *I am a salmon in a pool*
> *I am a hill of poetry*
> *I am a god who forms fire for a head*

When I got back to England I went to see my mother and she looked beautiful in the coffin. Not like a human being at all anymore. Like a bog lady. A woman that had been drawn up out of the bog. Her face looked almost carved.

I went home and I said to my sister-in-law, Jane: "We will dress her." The next day we went into the garden and picked rosemary and white May blossom — armfuls of it — and we took it to the funeral home and we covered her in flowers. We gave her a crown of white May and rosemary all around her face, and white May blossoms on her heart, crossed with rosemary and a bunch of flowers in her hands. A true pagan ceremony to send her off.

My mother's true religion was Art. People used to ask me, "What did your mother think of 'Why'D Ya Do It'?" My mother, of course, thought it was absolutely great: "Darling, *at last* you're getting some of your *real things* out!" she would tell me. She knew that art was art and it was judged by different rules. She was European, she was an aristocrat, she had none of that British prudery. She knew the true aristocracy was that of art. All art is a tribute to the Goddess.

When I went back to see my father after Eva had died I was walking through a grove of yew trees at Brazier's Park and everything reminded me of my mother. The moon, the wind rustling, the leaves of the yew, the yew itself, one of the Five Magical Trees of Ireland. But particularly the moon, the mirror of the Goddess. My mother was clearly a goddess figure for me. God "the Father" has never done it for me. The Virgin Mary doesn't do it for me. The patriarchal religions don't do it for me. I always begin my prayers with "Our Mother . . ." I had to find a real god or goddess of my own understanding, one that I could believe in. My own pantheon. The Great Goddess and the Great God Pan. I dedicate every drink I have to the Great God Pan. I ask for protection. And for me, my mother was the first manifestation of the Great Goddess.

Shortly after Eva's death I was cast as Pirate Jenny in *The Threepenny Opera*. That's where I met Frank McGuinness. Frank did a new translation of the Brecht play. Directed by Patrick Mason, now the artistic director of the Abbey, and produced by Michael Colgin of the Gate Theatre. I cried all the way through rehearsals. I'd come home and see my mother's face everywhere. In the stars and the water and the trees and the moon.

On opening night Jerry Hall and Mick sent me a beautiful bouquet of flowers, a beautiful bunch of white lilies, the flowers I have always loved, and with them a note saying, "Break a leg!"

The reviews were fantastic. Overnight I became respectable. Journalists to whom all these years I'd been a series of caricatures all of a sudden came to the conclusion that there was a point to this person. It was fun, I must admit.

Still . . . although one can come to terms with one's past, one can never really kiss it good-bye. Every now and again a past like mine is bound to rear its ugly head!

Before I went into treatment I had contributed, against my better judgment, to an awful, muckracking book about the Stones. The author, A. E. Hotchner, had written a well-received book about Hemingway and I assumed that he was going to give the Stones something of the same treatment (hah!). He lured Anita and me into his sleazy venture on the strength of his literary credentials, but Hotchner had no feeling for the period whatsoever (and even less sympathy for the people involved). His book, *Blown Away,* turned out to be a tricked-up piece of trash, treating every maudlin and sensational tabloid headline as gospel.

He taped Anita and me at a very vulnerable point in our lives. We were both still using. We were confused, and angry about our pasts. And (dare I say it?) he got me drunk! Sorry, but it's true. I would get high and just ramble. And out came the story about Mick's beating me up in Genoa. Mick was furious. The way Hotchner wrote it up made it sound as if Mick was a habitual wife-beater, which he isn't, at all. I've known a few and Mick ain't one.

I got word of Mick's displeasure while I was on tour. I sent Mick a very curt fax saying, "Dear Mick. Did that interview *ages* ago. For a hundred bucks. Was very out of it. Slimy journalist got me high. Please forgive. Much love, Marianne."

The reason Mick was so upset was because the story had gotten into the *Daily Mail* and his parents found out. A week after the book came out, I was due to attend a Stones concert at Wembley with Chris Blackwell. Chris, always observant of the protocols, called Mick to see if it was all right to bring the disgraced Marianne.

"Yea, waaal, awright, but it's really uncool for my parents," Chris reported to me. When I arrived at the party backstage (Chris was pretending not to know me) Mick was appropriately frosty while managing to maintain his irrepressibly sociable demeanor. An act only Mick can handle. But as usual, he got my back up. Now I was determined not to appear the least repentant.

Eva and Joe Jagger, Mick's parents, were there. His mum is so sweet, but she's a nightmare for Mick. She was moaning about how bossy Mick is:

"It's a crime the way he bosses me about all the time, really it is. He tells me when to drink a glass of water, and he tells me to go and pee, and tells me when to — it's just awful."

Joe was trying to shut her up, but nothing could shut Eva up, believe me. I was listening to all this, quite delighted and charmed.

And I said to Eva, "Oh well, yeah, that's how he is. And let's face it, we're never going to change him. He's always had the potential for being a serious control freak."

And then Mick said, "Oh, come on, Mum! That will be enough of that," trying to shut her up, but in the process managing to confirm what we were saying.

"Do you see what I'm dealing with, Marianne?"

Mick turned to me for a bit of moral support. "But I'm sure Nicholas bosses you about, doesn't he, Marianne?" It was a little olive branch from Mick and I should have been a little kinder and taken it. I wish I had had a bit of compassion, but I couldn't help myself and I said:

"What, Nicholas boss me around? Certainly not!" (He doesn't, actually.) "He wouldn't *dream* of telling me what to do. And I wouldn't dream of doing that to him. We just don't have us that sort of relationship."

And then Jerry Hall walked up with a bit of jet-set gossip about Tina Chow. Jerry is me translated through Texas. Everything is naturally *bigger*. More hair, taller, bigger jewels, a more flamboyant personality. And *grateful*. (Whereas I am nothing if not ungrateful!)

But all was not so gallant with Mick. Later in the year, the terrible business about Yew Tree cottage came up. Yew Tree was the sixteenth-century thatched cottage Mick bought for my mother to live in in 1967. Eva lived there for twenty-odd years and it was always the home I came back to, and for Nicholas it was a magic place. When my mother died, there was some question as to what would happen to it.

It had to be discussed. There was one call from Mick. It was incredibly hard to arrange. Anita set it up. I went to her flat only to find her phone was out of order so I had to go down to the empty flat below to wait for the famous call to come through.

When the subject of the cottage came up, I said: "Take it back. I don't want it. I never liked it. Do what you wish with it."

He was so charming and I was so proud. Pride is something Keith would understand, but it's not a quality Mick understands at all. To Mick, a proud woman is a contradiction in terms. They don't exist. Women to Mick are all fawning creatures who just want as much of his money as they can lay their hands on.

Unlike almost all his other relationships with women, ours was never about money. No money changed hands and never will. So, I felt I had honorably dealt with the Yew Tree situation and that was the end of it. But what do I find, having so proudly and gracefully declined the cottage, but that my only son, Nicholas, wants it. Wants it very much. He's terribly attached to Yew Tree, and naïvely believes Mick will give it to him when he hears he wants it. Ha!

So I decide to double back and eat crow. Go to see Jerry Hall and beg and scream. We couldn't get any response from Mick at all. It was horrible, especially for Nicholas, who couldn't understand why nobody was calling us back. It was as if we didn't count, and, of course, we don't.

The unfortunate outcome of my going back was that Mick finally managed to place me in that despised realm where Other Women (who are only after me for my money) dwell. And we didn't even get the cottage!

I wrote a song about this incident called "Flaming September." Filled with lines like "Don't bother to tell me. Don't bother to call me." In my imperious fantasy I'm telling Mick not to call me — when he never intended to. Trying to strike a deal with the dealer. I gave you everything, and now I just want this *one* thing. That's me, still trying to get a happy ending.

I stupidly thought it would be a godsend to Mick to end it with such style. How easily Keith could have done it.


One of the advantages of a decadent past is that you get to meet other Famous Jaded People. My two favorite decadent monsters of the last decade are Madonna and Robert Mitchum.

I was in Los Angeles and a friend of mine, the photographer Stephen Meisel, called me up and wanted to get together. He said,

"Meet me at the Four Seasons at seven o'clock." It was six thirty at the time, so I put myself together as best I could and went to meet him. He was with this beautiful boy. And he stared at me and said, "Well we're going to see Madonna." I was absolutely dumbfounded. And very scared. But he reassured me, "There, there, Marianne, it'll be all right. She'll *adore* you."

And so off we went to Madonna's house, which was absolutely wonderful, of course. A gym in her bathroom. Huge. And a very impressive collection of paintings. Everything she did was strange. She was wearing lingerie. And I thought, "Dear God!" But the funniest thing was her kitchen. There was a magazine rack like the ones you see in a dentist's office. But all the magazines on it had her picture on them! Wow! *That's* entertainment.

We all went to the theater to see Rupert Everett in a really dull play, Noel Coward's *Vortex*. After the theater, we went to a club where Madonna could dance. It was a gay club where everyone knew her and nobody was going to gasp when she walked in. And where it would all be very cool. And it was. Nobody even raised an eyebrow.

I felt a bit like the elder statesman. I could see that she regarded me with a certain amount of remote respect. At some point she asked me to dance. I nearly died. She dances incredibly. Proper steps as if she's onstage. I felt very odd. To me it was just like something out of Molière. But of course Stephen Meisel loved it. So I thought, "Oh, well, if it pleases him I'll do it."

Unfortunately, at this point I was starving. I had expected that we'd at some point, well, *eat*. I ended up very hungry and got quite grumpy. It was all getting a bit much for me. For one thing, it was past my bedtime! But there was nothing I could do. Until *she* left, *we* couldn't leave. Being with Madonna is a bit like being with royalty, you know. Actually, cocktails with Princess Margaret was a little bit more relaxed. It *was* fun though, especially looking back on it. Anyway, all my friends' kids were terribly impressed.

In 1993, Bruce Webber asked me to be in his documentary about Robert Mitchum. He'd made a wonderful film about Chet Baker called *Let's Get Lost* and he wanted to do something along the same lines with

Mitchum. But there's a world of difference between these two guys. Chet Baker was emotional and introspective — a classic bebop jazz musician. Mitchum plays his cards very close to his chest.

I don't know what business I had being in the movie, period. The ostensible reason was put to me in the hard-boiled lingo Bruce had borrowed from the *film noire* movies Mitchum starred in during the forties and fifties.

"There's only three things that get Bob excited anymore: a vodka martini, a Lucky Strike and a beautiful woman."

But I suspect the real reason I was there was to help Bruce pull the personal stuff out of Mitchum, which I never could have done even if I'd wanted to. Hell would freeze over before Bob Mitchum was going to bare his soul. He's from the old school. He *is* the old school at this point in time. And in the classic era of Hollywood, men didn't spill their guts to fan magazines, or any one else for that matter. There's a telling moment when Bruce asks Mitchum what went through his mind when he was arrested for smoking pot. Bob brushes it aside.

"Who gives a fuck what I felt like."

I remember pulling myself together for this dinner at the Château Marmont. I looked at myself in the mirror and said: "Well, well, you actually look like a cross between a limousine driver and a slut. I think this must be the right outfit!" Short black skirt, high heels, décolleté blouse.

Mitchum had a few vodka martinis. Utterly charming. Very tall and slim and graceful. Great stories of old Hollywood. Bruce said the most bizarre thing about Mitchum later on. He said: "Didn't you think it was a bit like working with Marilyn Monroe?"

I said, "Whatever do you mean?"

"I mean he's one of the last great sex symbols."

And he was very sexy — but cool. And then there was a moment of complete abandonment as we were coming out of the restaurant. In the middle of Hollywood Boulevard Mitchum took me in his arms, leant me back in a real 1940s clinch and gave me a classic movie kiss. I was so stunned I almost forgot to kiss back. Whenever I find myself in these potentially romantic situations, I never know what to do. If I'd been watching it on TV, I would have loved it. I did quite enjoy it anyway, mostly because I don't feel all that bad about saying no.

Maybe that's one of the reasons I've got so cool in my old age, and sort of reserved. I don't know *what* it would take to get me into bed now. And it's not Catholicism, really — it's just too much trouble. The dangers are too great, and the traps are too numerous. Nor am I up for the Mick and Jerry story either: find a partner, settle down and have kids, be respectable, have a normal life. But this is much harder for women to do than for men. If I were a man, I could probably find a woman who would put up with me! Of course, if I was gay . . .

In the last decade I've had the dubious honor of being officially denounced as a witch by the Vatican Press. The article cited Mick Jagger, Anita Pallenberg and myself. Mick as a warlock, and Anita and I as his coven of witches. When I showed it to Anita she shrugged it off as the complete absurdity it is, but then Anita has always been much less bothered by other people's opinions. Still, we wondered why this was happening all these years later. The unmanageable woman has been seen as a very dangerous quantity from the dawn of time, or at least since patriarchal religion clamped down on us.

I've also had the disconcerting experience of reading my own life story and wondering who the hell they were talking about. I'm sure that when he began writing my biography, Mark Hodkinson was counting on my keeling over at any moment. He has said in the British press that any day now he expects to hear that I've overdosed in some street corner lavatory. Well, dream on!

The publishers of this scaly biography just waited and waited to put it out. They thought if they waited till I was in my mid-forties, I would be sure to die. *Then* they would have a great little package! A nice, neat ending for their book. And you feel it in the book, how disappointing it is. There's a great hole there.

I'd already been married twice and should have known better than to leap into another one so suddenly, but, like I said, I never learn.

I met Giorgio della Terza at a Narcotics Anonymous meeting. He was good-looking and intelligent and urbane and he made me laugh. He was a writer and quoted Dante to me, which I've always found irresistible. He also had a wonderful family, something I've always been a sucker for. His father is a professor at Harvard and the foremost Dante scholar in the world. That impressed the pants off *my* father.

Essentially I married someone who made me crazy. I must have done it in a fit of mad idealism. I would never have got into such a pickle if I had been in what is laughably called my right mind. But I have to remind myself of what the Big Book so wisely says: One never does get more than one can deal with.

Giorgio had a very skewed image of me. He thought of me, until he'd almost lost me, in terms of blond hair and big tits. Most of the time I was with Giorgio I spent on tour, which he hated. And life for him at the Shell Cottage was house arrest. He was a junk-food addict who loved the bright lights, and here he was stuck in the middle of nowhere behind a twelve-foot famine wall, for Christ's sake! Eventually he began to fool around. One day I came upon a letter from the girl-friend written in an incredibly drippy and illiterate style. That was it! There was one final black comedy scene involving this girlfriend. I had unwittingly asked her, not realizing she was Giorgio's girlfriend, to help me get my looks together. She took me to a stylist who promptly cut off all my hair and dyed it gray!


In the last couple of years I've started working in movies again. I like doing films because while you're working on a film there's this com-forting illusion of being part of a family. And there's nothing like losing yourself in a part.

I play a ghost in Sara Driver's *When Pigs Fly*, and in *Moondance* I play a mother — an anthropologist who goes off and leaves her chil-dren to lead her own life, and then in the nick of time comes back and turns into a seeress character, the one who knows the answer and is very wise. One step above ghost.

*Moondance* was shot on Garech Browne's estate, Lugala, one of the most beautiful places on the face of the earth. The house is an eigh-teenth-century pasteboard castle, rebuilt in the thirties, and encircled by mist-swathed hills. Moss-covered boulders and great ancient trees tum-ble down an antediluvian landscape to a beautiful lake.

Van Morrison is doing the sound track for *Moondance* on which I sing

"Madame George," with Van producing. Done in the blink of an eye. Flew in to Dublin, took a two-hour nap and went into Ring's End to put down me vocal. There was Van with Phil Coutter with his patch over one eye. Phil discovered the Bay City Rollers and wrote "Puppet on a String." He was the pianist on the session. Two takes for the vocal. There's not much messing about or agonizing over tracks with Van.

He's like my mentor, really, Van. I tell him about my personal problems and he gives me advice. It's like having a hotline to God. Better than God, because he's *here*.

Whenever I give someone a hug, my tits get in the way. It's always a bit much for Van. He whispers in my ear — he's got a very comical Belfast accent — "Couldna we gait to know each other a bit bettah?" I give him a killer look.

Van the Man is one of my dearest friends and very funny.

"You know, Van," I told him when I got back this last time, "I think Jamaica is really like Ireland in a way."

"With *wan* big difference."

"What's tht?"

"*We* don't fuck."

Drink, religion, music, wildness — you can have anything you want, but no sex. I'm not alone in feeling I have to leave home for a bit of fun.

But I love Ireland. I moved there five years ago. My mother was ill and she wanted me to be closer to her. I didn't want to come back to the U.K. It was either Paris or Ireland, and in Ireland my friends have sustained me through a very fragile period of my life. Ireland is sanctuary. I don't feel I have to watch myself all the time in Ireland. I sometimes put my foot in it and say stupid things, but I don't feel that bothered about being me. They're very forgiving.

For years I had dreams involving architecture. I often dreamt about being in octagonal, hexagonal, strangely shaped rooms. When I first walked into the Shell Cottage — where I live today — my mind was blown. I saw a five-walled living room built just so Queen Victoria could stop and have a cup of tea on her trip to Ireland. It's commemorated outside in colored pebbles and hearts. She came to Ireland for one day smack in the middle of the potato famine. There's a very high famine wall that surrounds Carton Demesne, the estate on which the Shell Cottage is built.

The other part of the Shell Cottage is an eighteenth-century folly, a beautiful room entirely decorated with shells and moss and a miniature pagoda and a Chinese village at one end. There are two other wonderful follies on the estate, a ruined tower and an Egyptian obelisk. I look out the windows of my pentagonal room on to a weir and artificial lake designed by the eighteenth-century landscape architect Capability Brown. Heaven.

I have always wanted to make an album that would re-create the movie that plays continually in my head. Scenes from my life in cinematic sequences, the sound track washing over the listener, inducing a dreamlike state. Interior dialogues with hallucinatory intimacy!

Streams of consciousness. Even something as apparently political as "Broken English" — about the Baader-Meinhoff gang — is actually sung to myself. The part of me that's on one side of the question is singing to my devil's advocate. ("Why'D Ya Do It" is also two people, a dialogue. Most people don't get that.)

I'd been banging on for years about making the sound track to my mental movie when my friend Kevin Patrick suggested Angelo Badalamenti. He had worked with David Lynch on *Blue Velvet* and *Twin Peaks*. I decided he was obviously the one and I pursued him relentlessly, as if I were tracking an elusive animal through the wilds of New Jersey.

But almost as soon as I began working with Angelo I came up against a serious predicament. From his collaborations with David Lynch he had developed a style of working based on the way David Lynch works. Fragments. Angelo kept saying: "Fragments, fragments, fragments! We need more fragments!" Who did he think I was, Heraclitus?

One of the real joys of writing for me is shaping and refining the material. You get the rough stuff down and then you take out a word here, add a phrase there, push it and pull it until it begins to take form.

After weeks of polishing and fiddling with my scribbles I would send Angelo what I considered beautifully finished lyrics and back would come enigmatic messages scrawled across the bottom of the page: "No, no! Not *fragmented* enough." What did it mean? Shoring up fragments against my ruin, indeed! *Life* is fragmented, not art.

Last year I became Granny Faithfull. Nicholas fell in love with Carole Jahme, an actress, and they had a beautiful little boy, Oscar (named after our favorite writer, Oscar Wilde). Oscar looks just like me and therefore is the best thing ever. Nicholas, having studied planetary science at Harvard, has now gone into film! The beat goes on.

I run into Keith a lot at airports lately. He's no longer the Byronic lad I once knew. More a Shakespearean character, a combination of Prince Hal and Falstaff. It's always very reassuring to see him. I feel, when I'm with him, as if we are the last remaining compatriots of a long-vanished kingdom who have not entirely renounced the old ways (although we do differ on the interpretation of the alchemical creed). I may be the revamped, recovered, rehabilitated Marianne, but I'm still as flummoxed as ever about things, and Keith is always ready to give me quick crash courses on how to cope. He's very good at this.

Apropos of yet another casualty in our ranks, Keith volunteers: "It's always so baffling when somebody commits suicide. Not you, in Australia, of course, yours was a perfectly *valid* reason." Thanks, Bud.

The subject of drugs inevitably comes up.

"What we really need is the next great chemical truth," says Keith enthusiastically. "I'm still waiting for the pharmaceutical companies to come up with the fucking *breakthrough* molecule of all time. Most of the stuff they cook up just fucks with your head."

It *is* in the great alchemical tradition, this quest for the ultimate potion, but I have gone beyond the point where I think drugs are the Holy Grail.

Drugs are like a mask. When I finally got clean, I was horrified to find I had built up such an effective front I couldn't get it off. It was as if the mask had been glued on to me and had stuck. It had to be peeled off layer by layer. I was afraid I was going to be trapped inside it for life.

While the Stones were cutting their new album in Ireland last summer, I shanghaied Keith into producing my track on the Irish AIDS benefit CD. I do a version of "Ghost Dance" by Patti Smith and Lenny Kaye, and I'll do two other songs with Sinéad O'Connor and Bjork, formerly of the Sugar Cubes. Keith is a great producer. He can coax a rabbit out of a cocked hat.

One should never lose the opportunity to mention the seven deadly sins and, as it happens, they've become something of a second career. For the past few years I've been performing Kurt Weill's *Seven Deadly Sins*. Perfect for me, not simply because I've committed them all, but because the music corresponds so perfectly to my own moodiness, and conjures up my mother and the world she was part of.

Three years ago I was made a Professor by Allen Ginsberg. The certificate says: MARIANNE FAITHFULL, PROFESSOR OF PO- ETICS, JACK KEROUAC SCHOOL OF DISEMBODIED POETS. It was a real ceremony in which he dubbed me, saying, "Arise. You are now educated. 'Cause I say so."

I'm off next month to sing "Ruby Tuesday" for a Chris Kimsey tribute album. *Interesting People Sing the Rolling Stones* type of thing, I assume. The circle just turns and turns. . . . Somewhere behind us is the hand of the great master himself, Mr. Richards, juggling this as he does everything and always has done.


Have I forgotten anything? I've always thought that the proper way to end one's life story is with a bit of practical advice. Something that sums up one's long and hard-won experience. How to pack a suitcase, how to butter a biscuit without breaking it. I loved Marlene Dietrich's autobiography, which really has nothing in it except how to sew lavender bags, lay a drawer and brush a dog.

Let's see. . . . How about my chicken with lemon and garlic?

Okay, here goes: chicken, butter, garlic, fresh tarragon — has to be fresh — snipped with a scissors. Salt and pepper the chicken liberally inside and out. Put half a lemon inside the chicken along with a nob of butter and the fresh tarragon. On the outside you put the garlic, juice of a lemon and butter. Baste continually. And the thing about mashed potatoes is not to forget that pinch of nutmeg.

# Acknowledgments

Would each of you conjure up a tiny, sparkling halo around your names? That's just how I see you, my darlings; I couldn't have done it without you.

Demalza Val Baker, John Bauldie, John and Isabella Boorman, Delia Boyle, Ben Brierly, Garech Browne, Tony Calder, Art Collins, Denny Cordell, Coco Dalton, Susan Dewsnap, John Dunbar, Glynn Faithfull, Cynthia Fitzgerald, Lynn Francek Urian, Christopher Gibbs, Allen Ginsberg, Desmond and Penny Guinness, Kate Hyman, Iris Keitel, Allen Klein, Steve Mass, Mike Mattil, Pamela Mayall, Frank McGuinness, Miles, Andee Nathanson, Roderick O'Connor, Chris O'Dell, Andrew Oldham, Anita Pallenberg, D. A. Pennebaker, Michael Pietsch, Barry Reynolds, Richard Sassin, Tony Secunda, Ellen Smith, Antonia Stampfel, Deborah Theodore, Wendy Truscott and Hal Willner

# INDEX